better to burn out

better to burn out

the cult of death in rock 'n' roll

by Dave Thompson

THUNDER'S MOUTH PRESS • NEW YORK

Published by
Thunder's Mouth Press
841 Broadway, Fourth Floor
New York, NY 10003

First edition

Library of Congress Cataloging-in-Publication Data

Thompson, Dave.
        Better to burn out : the cult of death in rock'n'roll / by Dave Thompson.
            p.   cm.
        ISBN 1-56025-190-5
        1. Rock musicians—Death.   2. Rock music—History and criticism.
    I. Title.
    ML394.T56 1999
    781.66'092'2—dc21
        [B]   98-28635
                                                                                   CIP
                                                                                    MN

Photo research by Natalie Goldstein

Manufactured in the United States of America

contents

contents

dedication

TONY SECUNDA, one of the undisputed legends of British rock management, died suddenly at his San Francisco home on February 10, 1994. He was fifty-four.

Raised in the English seaside town of Margate, Secunda was among the founding fathers of the British music industry as it emerged from the shadow of the late 1950s.

A merchant seaman, he first heard rock'n'roll in America, passing through the Panama Canal with rebel radio filtering through the ether. He jumped ship in Seattle, worked briefly in the local logging industry, then made his way back to England, where he started hustling shows. He staged the first rock'n'roll concerts half of southern England ever saw, initially alone, but also in a loose partnership with the entrepreneurial giant of the age, manager Larry Parnes.

In 1960, now working alongside manager Guy Robinson, Secunda was a key element in the team which launched Johnny Kidd and the Pirates to fame. A quarter century on, he still enthused, "The Pirates were the first authentic British rock'n'roll band," whose 1960 number one, "Shaking All Over," was "the first authentic British rock'n'roll record." And while history insists that the Pirates never repeated that monumental triumph, Secunda always argued otherwise.

"The Pirates were a live experience. In concert, you'd never seen anything like them, and that was where their appeal lay." That same intuitive grasp of outrageous showmanship would itself become a hallmark of Secunda's own career, as he rose to steer act after act to those same heights of success.

In 1964, Secunda discovered a Birmingham R&B band called the Moody Blues, paired them with an untried twenty-one-year-old producer named Denny Cordell, and watched as the team's first-ever session together produced a worldwide hit, "Go Now." A little more than a year later, Secunda was managing the Move and preparing them, too, for global stardom.

A stunning strategist and a brilliant publicist, Secunda refused to allow the Move to record until they developed a killer live reputation—something he ensured by choreographing every step of their stage act, from the autodestructive encores which reduced the stage to rubble, to the arrival of the riot squad at the end of every major show.

The Move became one of the first groups signed to Straight Ahead, the pioneering production company Secunda and Cordell formed in 1966. Over the next two years, Straight Ahead scored hits with Procol Harum, Joe Cocker, and Tyrannosaurus (T.) Rex. But the Move remained its biggest attraction.

The Move peaked with "Flowers in the Rain," the first record ever played on Britain's Radio One, and the subject of Secunda's most outrageous promotion yet, a postcard intimating that Prime Minister Harold Wilson was having an affair with his secretary. Wilson sued, and won; Secunda and the Move parted company shortly after.

Nineteen-seventy saw Secunda and Rolling Stones producer Jimmy Miller become partners in the Monaco-based pirate radio station, Geronimo. They also masterminded Balls, a short-lived rock group which paired the Move's Trevor Burton with the Moody Blues' Denny Laine, and whose legacy survives in the lascivious mouth logo the Stones adapted from Balls' own.

Following Balls' breakup, and Laine's recruitment into Paul McCartney's Wings, Secunda was offered the post of that group's manager. He turned it down, but not before McCartney immortalized him in "Band on the Run." The song's Sailor Sam character combined Secunda's maritime career with an alias provided by another of his clients, Marc Bolan, who recruited Secunda to renegotiate his record deal in 1971. Secunda won him his own record label instead, and Bolan thanked him by writing his next number one hit, "Telegram Sam," for and about his mercurial business manager.

Breaking with Bolan in 1972, Secunda turned his hand to record production, handling John Cale's epochal recording of "Heartbreak Hotel," and also overseeing sessions by one of Bolan's former colleagues, Steve Peregrine Took. Meanwhile, as manager of the folk-rock band Steeleye Span, Secunda proved he had lost none of his flair for publicity. In Australia, he dreamed up the "Win a night with a band member" competition which almost got Steeleye run out of the country; in London, he ended a concert by showering the audience with pound notes—the night's entire earnings.

From one musical extreme to another, Secunda turned his attention next to metal pioneers Motörhead, setting them on the road to their early-1980s dominance. But he was tiring of rock'n'roll, and in 1979, he left Britain for America. His final act was to record the demos which landed Chrissie Hynde and the Pretenders their first record deal.

In the mid-1980s, after several years spent traveling, Secunda and his second wife, Frankie, settled in San Francisco, and moved into publishing. Secunda had tried the waters before, a decade earlier, when he launched journalist George Tremlett on the now-legendary series of rock biographies that became many British teens' first taste of pop literature.

Representing a stable of authors, myself among them, Secunda would be responsible for the publication of biographies of the Grateful Dead, the Red Hot Chili Peppers, Depeche Mode, Kurt Cobain, and Marianne Faithfull's *Faithfull* autobiography, as well as books on topics as far afield as cookery, ecology, and the Kennedy assassination. At the time of his death, he was coordinating the launch of his own publishing house, coincidentally, in tandem with this book's U.S. publishers, Thunder's Mouth.

But it wasn't to be. With shattering but perhaps characteristic irony, Secunda's death from heart failure came just days before he was scheduled to fly to Ireland, to be at the side of his old partner, Denny Cordell, himself dying of cancer. "Denny can't die," Secunda swore the previous afternoon. "That wasn't part of the deal."

Unfortunately, he hadn't read the small print properly; he went instead, to clear the way for Cordell to follow. It was what he'd always done in life, throughout their Straight Ahead partnership; it made sense he would continue to do the same thing in death.

It is to Tony Secunda, then, that this book is dedicated, for all of the above and much, much more.

preface

A MUSICIAN FRIEND recently went shopping for a pair of 13.5-inch drainpipe trousers. Not 14-inch, not 13-inch: 13.5. He never found any. Store after store assured him that such a thing did not exist, until finally he caved in, and had them made to measure.

This book had a similar genesis. For over twenty-five years, since Charisma Books published the first-ever "casualty report on rock-'n'roll," a compendium of essays titled *No-One Waved Goodbye*, a veritable bookcase of similar tomes has arisen, all dutifully detailing the familiar lives (but strangely, less-well-detailed deaths) of the Grim Reaper's Greatest Hits.

The routine is predictable. Each updates its predecessor's index as another icon bites the dust: Presley, Vicious, Lennon, Mercury, Cobain, Hutchence; each recounts the curtailed career, as though every tale was being told for the first time. But few go further, to detail the foot soldiers who line up behind the undisputed leaders. And fewer still acknowledge that they matter just as much. That is the void which this book—the 13.5-inch drainpipe of death, as it were—is intended to fill.

Across twenty chapters, more than seventy untimely, unexpected, and just plain unfortunate deaths are discussed, some in passing, some in depth, and some in almost painful detail. A few, the front-page passings everyone recollects, will of course be familiar. But greater attention is given to the names which fill the rest of the newspaper, the Metro section, and the small-print obituaries, the lives maybe only a handful of hardcore devotees can truly say they remember, but which have impacted on the modern music scene nevertheless.

For every John Lennon, for example, there was a Stuart Sutcliffe, whose life was the subject of the *Backbeat* movie. For every Janis Joplin, there was a Dwayne Goettel, a founding father of industrial music. For every Elvis Presley, there was an Alma Cogan, the subject of a Whitbread Prize–winning novel. And for every American pioneer, there was a British one, which is why Wally Whyton gets more space than Bill Haley—and Tracy Pew, an Australian, gets more than either of them.

So, not all the names will be familiar, and not every song mentioned will strike a chord. But if careers can be measured by the influence they exert, every artist profiled here is worth their weight in gold.

Necrographies—books documenting the deaths, as opposed to the lives of their subjects—have never been very well represented on the musical shelf. True, such topics as "Who killed Kurt Cobain?" will always find a ripe market, while Elvis Presley's afterlife is a publishing industry in its own right, with John Lennon close behind. Move away from conspiracies and spiritualism, however, and barely a handful of titles remain, with even fewer standing alone as books which truly do avoid the most obvious trap—preparing for the death with a lengthy look at the life.

Yet the lives of musicians are readily available for scrutiny. With every passing year, rock encyclopedias grow more detailed; CD booklets grow more elaborate, the Internet becomes more exhaustive. Magazines such as *Goldmine* in the U.S., and *Mojo* in Britain, regularly present vast career biographies of artists past and present. In literary terms, the dead are everywhere. But beyond the last couple of sentences, and a valedictory sentiment, few of these delve into the death itself—even though death is the single most important event in any artist's life, not only for its physical finality, but also for the abrupt halt it brings to the artistry itself.

At the time of his death, Brian Jones was a wasted recluse, rattling around the mausoleum emptiness of Winnie-the-Pooh's old house, in search of one more high to better the last one. Jim Morrison was a drunk, washing away his talent in the twilight alehouse of his Parisian retirement. Buddy Holly was a falling star, Michael Hutchence was reduced to the comeback circuit; and Jimi Hendrix, according to the string of posthumous releases which attempt to re-create the album he was working on at the time of his death, was preparing to relaunch his faltering career with a collection of old jams and outtakes.

Today, all five burn as brightly as they ever did in life, their failings forgotten, their triumphs enlarged, and their lives and reputations enhanced by an avalanche of what-might-have-beens which it is fruitless to try and respond to . . . as fruitless, perhaps, as it is to attempt making sense of any of the myriad deaths which have rocked rock over the last forty years. Perhaps that explains why, in the literature of the genre, it is the lives and the accomplishments which take center stage, because those are the events which can be documented and analyzed. Alongside them, the deaths remain simple sad codas—codas which, nevertheless, are collected together here.

Senseless ODs, drunken driving accidents, pointless plane crashes, tragic fires, sheer stupidity. Claude François was one of France's biggest-ever pop stars, but even the idol of millions sometimes must stand naked. It was just unfortunate that François was in the bathtub at the time, and changing a lightbulb without having first switched off the electricity.

Some deaths are linked by flukes of geography—the sequence of passings which bookended the antipodean rock invasion of the early 1980s, for example, and the string of deaths which haunted Seattle's hour of grunge-flavored glory a little over a decade later. That the city was simultaneously immersed in a heroin culture that provoked even the attention of European news crews and magazines, of course, adds a certain piquancy to that scenario, but it is also dangerously illusive. Drugs kill, but so do shotguns and stranglers.

Other deaths fall together with the same symmetry as the Rock Family Trees executed by British music historian Pete Frame: On March 5, country star Patsy Cline and her band were killed in a plane crash while flying home from Kansas where, ironically, they had attended the funeral of a disc-jockey friend. Two days later, singer Jack Anglin perished in a car crash, on his way to attend Cline's funeral.

More are conjoined by simple bad timing: KISS drummer Eric Carr passed away the day before Freddie Mercury did; Swell Maps founder Epic Soundtracks (born Kevin Paul Godfrey) was upstaged by Michael Hutchence; and news of Austrian rocker Falco's death in a road accident was pushed aside when Beach Boy Carl Wilson succumbed to cancer.

And others still can be linked through often eerie chains of coincidence, by prophecies of doom, or premonitions of chilling certainty. The night before he was killed in a helicopter crash, guitar legend Stevie Ray Vaughan dreamed of attending his own funeral; the night before setting off on his last ever tour, Buddy Holly dreamed of a plane crash. Lynyrd Skynyrd's Ronnie Van Zant was convinced he would not live to be thirty; producer Joe Meek swore he would never see forty. Eddie Cochran's final single was called "Three Steps to Heaven"; Freddie Mercury's was "The Show Must Go On."

But all this really proves is that everyone dies eventually, and some simply go more ominously than others. Chuck Willis might well have savored the irony of dying within days of releasing a record called "What Am I Living For," but wouldn't it have been even better if he could have stuck around longer, and maybe found out?

Discussing the death of English singer-songwriter Nick Drake, Peter Holsapple of the dB's remarked, "Nobody commits suicide as a career move." But still, Colonel Tom Parker was speaking the truth when he admitted Elvis Presley was worth more to him dead than he had been alive, and Gene Vincent died still convinced that Eddie Cochran was murdered so that his manager might reap the memorial fortune.

It was these coincidences, and many more, that provided the impetus for this book, albeit a deceptively dead-ended one. For, once having detected the coincidence, where can it lead? Beyond a rough historical chronology, therefore, there is no real pattern to the arrangement of the deaths in these pages. Neither is there any attempt to debate or investigate their causes and effects. Any patterns which emerge are for the reader alone to analyze; any lessons are for history to absorb. But every name included here has at least one thing in common. They all have left an indelible mark on the face of the music we listen to today. This book will help you find it.

acknowledgments

WHEREVER POSSIBLE, I have attempted to let the dead, and those who knew them, speak for themselves. In some instances, where biography creeps into a story, it is to place a new spin on an old saga; in others, it is to illuminate avenues which other histories have left unexplored.

For that illumination, I would like to thank everybody who so kindly offered their time, their energy, and their own research materials to me. The bibliography will acknowledge the specifics, but fellow writers and researchers John Aizlewood, Mark Arscott, Rob Cherry, Carol Clerk, John Michael Cox Jr., Kevin Crace, John Donovan, Mick Farren, Ben Fisher, Bill Glahn, Jo-Ann Greene, Amy Hanson, Sabrina Kaleta, Dave McNorie, Fred Mills, Oedipus, Mark Paytress, Brian Perera, Julian St. Paul, and Paul Trynka in particular should be singled out for extra special attention.

The heart of this book is drawn from well over a decade's worth of personal interviews and conversations. Again, where elements of these interviews have been previously published, the specifics are detailed elsewhere.

acknowledgments

Thanks here, however, are due to Gaye Advert, Martin Atkins, Boz Boorer, Angie Bowie, John Cale, Nick Cave, Jayne County, Tony DeFries, Peter Frampton, Dana Gillespie, Graham Gouldman, Bob Grace, Dave Grohl, Pam Hardyment, Peter Hook, Jack Irons, Brian James, Alain Johannes, Amy Jonas, cEvin Key, Ivan and Lynette Kral, Krist Novoselic, Nivek Ogre, Andrew Oldham, Iggy Pop, Lou Reed, Cliff Richard, Mick Rossi, Dave Ruffy, Sabrina Satana, Bobby Schayer, Vince Seggs, Brett Smiley, TV Smith, Alvin Stardust, James Stevenson, Thomas Thorn, John Towe, Maureen Tucker, Nik Turner, Twink, Mike Vernon, Tony Visconti, and Bill Wyman. I'd also like to remember times spent with those people who ended up finding their own way into this book: Stiv Bators, Kurt Cobain, Michael Dempsey, Gary Holton, Ronnie Lane, Shane Lassen, Steve Marriott, Nico, Mick Ronson, Tony Secunda, Wally Whyton, and Rozz Williams.

Finally, special thanks to everybody who helped make this such a great book to write: my agent, Sherrill Chidiac; my publisher, Neil Ortenburg; Anchorite Man, Bateerz, Scary, Scratchy and Baby Bats, Blind Pew, Drum Tobacco, Back Ears (whose ears are on backwards), Barb East, Ella, the Gremlins who live in the furnace, K-Mart (not the store), Geoff Monmouth, Nutkin, Orifice, Snarleyyow, Spiny Norman, Sprocket, and the late Dame Gaiety Tomcat.

IN MARCH 1958, backstage at one of five triumphant London concerts Buddy Holly would be playing on his first British tour, the bespectacled Texan rock'n'roller found out when he was going to die.

As such things go, it was not a particularly Shakespearean moment. There was no blind soothsayer conjuring dire riddles around the ides of March, no wizened sisters on some blasted heath, scrying the future through entrails and fluid. Just a slightly portly, and very nervous, recording engineer who introduced himself as Joe Meek, then mumbled something about a Tarot-card reading; something about bad dreams; something about Buddy dying on February 3.

Which February 3? Meek wasn't sure. The cards gave him a date, but they didn't bother with a year. That was the trouble with spirit messages, they were often infuriatingly vague. But Meek wasn't taking any chances. Immediately after he received the message, a couple of months before, Meek had contacted both Holly's music publishers and his record label, trying to get a warning

Wreckage of the plane that had carried Buddy Holly
(Archive Photos)

**Buddy Holly and
the Crickets**

(Showtime Archives, Toronto)

through. But they'd just laughed him off, and were probably laughing even harder when the dread day came and went.

But it wasn't a laughing matter, and had Holly cared to listen, the whole story would have come tumbling out: how Meek, the singer Jimmy Miller, and an Arab friend named Faud, were relaxing with the cards after a recording session, holding hands around the table while Miller shuffled and turned the deck, and Faud sat waiting with pen in hand.

No one could explain what happened next. But suddenly Miller was gripped with such a sensation of fear that his fingernails pierced the flesh of Meek's left hand. And at that same moment, at the far end of the psychic chain, Faud dashed off three phrases: *February 3, Buddy Holly,* and *Dies.* Again, if Holly had listened, Meek could have told him all that. But Buddy simply smiled and thanked him; promised that he would be careful when that date rolled around again, then got on with the rest of his life. Close to another year would pass before anybody gave the warning a second thought, and by then it was far too late.

In the early hours of February 3, 1959, the light aircraft carrying Buddy Holly, "La Bamba" hitmaker Ritchie Valens, and the Big Bopper, J. P. Richardson, to their next scheduled engagement, slammed into a field outside Clear Lake, Iowa. When the wreckage was discovered shortly after daybreak, the local newspaper reported it was not even recognizable as a plane.

Along a skid path the length of four city blocks, the *Clear Lake Mirror Reporter* continued, "small bits of the plane and its contents were strewn." One body, pilot Roger Peterson, lay broken and entangled in the wreckage. Two more—Valens[1] and Richardson—were discovered about twelve feet from the plane. A fourth, Holly, was lying about forty feet away. All had perished upon impact.

News of the disaster hit the world of rock'n'roll hard, all the more so since the victims were so young—and youth was what rock'n'roll was all about. For the first time in entertainment history, a style had grown up which never would grow up; which was larger than life, and therefore epitomized life. It was thirty, forty, fifty years before most of rock's progenitors would even need to start thinking about their own deaths, and, at an age when a year seems a veritable lifetime, that meant rock'n'roll was immortality itself.

Now reality came screaming in, shattering the teenage dream, trailing cops and reporters and coroners and mourners. The gory physical details of the state of Buddy's remains were splashed across the headlines—his shattered, scooped-out skull, the tear in his scrotum and the hole in his chest, and the crimson stains in the mud-scarred snow which fresh snowfall could only absorb, not disguise.

In London, Joe Meek felt physically sick. He heard about the crash that evening, and as he sat and tried to absorb the news, one thought alone sprang to his lips. "Why didn't he listen to me?" Meek asked; and then, "Why didn't I try harder to warn him?"

Deep into the night, Meek and a few friends stayed awake, playing Holly's records. The following morning he bought every newspaper he could lay his hands on, and scoured the reports for details. He did not understand why he had been singled out for forewarning of the disaster. But he knew that he needed to follow it through.

Already fascinated by spiritualism, Meek began attending and conducting more séances than ever, desperate to make contact with Holly once again. He would succeed, as well, and beyond his wildest dreams. Not only was Holly's spirit among those with whom he now regularly communed, the dead musician also became a silent partner in his, Meek's, own songwriting.

But there was a dark side to the bargain, the knowledge that, like Holly, Meek was doomed never to live out his allotted biblical span. He told friends he would die before he reached forty—a milestone that in 1959 lay just a decade away. If any single reason can be found for the relentless drive which characterized Meek's subsequent work, this belief stands above all others. If he didn't do it then, he never would get the chance again.

Joe Meek would indeed die before he reached forty. On February 3, 1967, North London police were called to an apartment above the A. H. Shenton leather-goods store at 307 Holloway Road, to investigate reports of gunshots.

It was a far-from-routine occurrence. Even in the hands of Britain's criminal fraternity, guns were a rarity. Their use in domestic situations—for surely that was what this particular incident amounted to—was all but unknown. So was the sight awaiting the constables upon their arrival.

There were two victims. The first, Violet Shenton, was the wife of the downstairs store owner. Shot in the back at close range with a 12-gauge shotgun, she was still alive when the police arrived, dying in the ambulance as it raced toward the nearby Royal Northern Hospital.

The second casualty, a man in his late thirties, apparently had then turned the same weapon upon himself. A witness to at least part of the drama, the dead man's secretary, Patrick Pink, would describe the corpse's head as looking like a burnt candle; the headlines of that evening's newspapers completed the grisly tale: "'TOP OF THE POPS' COMPOSER AND WIFE SHOT DEAD." And only that composer's closest friends understood the significance of the date.

The first few years after Holly's death were good to Meek, a benevolence which he credited almost exclusively to the Texan's influence. By mid-1959, Meek was manager of the prestigious Lansdowne studio complex, recording some of the biggest names of the age in one of the greatest studios in the world. Yet within a year, he had built its equal in his own apartment, a sprawling warren of junk-piled cupboards which even he referred to as "the bathroom." But it was what he did in "the bathroom" that mattered.

It was there he produced his first signature recording, actor John Leyton's remake of the teen death epic "Tell Laura I Love Her"[2]; there he recorded his first major hit, Leyton's gothic spinechiller "Johnny, Remember Me." And it was there that he created "Telstar," the first single by a British group (the Tornadoes) ever to top the American charts, and still the best-selling rock instrumental of all time. Most important of all, it was there in "the bathroom" that he recorded his personal ode to his idol and mentor, "Tribute to Buddy Holly," in 1961.

The passing of time had not lessened Meek's fascination with Holly. If anything, it only increased it, and when he first signed a young singer named Mike Bourne, the producer readily acknowledged it was the performer's vocal resemblance to Holly which attracted him.

Inspired by the same punning reverence that had already caused him to publish his own songs through Ivy Music (as in "The Holly and the . . . "), obsessed with omens even when he had to engineer them himself, Meek renamed his young protégé Mike Berry. And days later, Meek's partner Geoff Goddard turned up with the song that would fit the young man like a glove.

Goddard wrote "Tribute to Buddy Holly" after the dead singer appeared to him in a dream. Like Meek, Goddard was both a convinced spiritualist and an aspiring medium, and in the fervent atmosphere of Meek's Holloway Road studio, his story was utterly believable. So was the message they received from Buddy himself, a few nights later when they staged their next séance and played a tape of the song to the singer. The tumbler responded, "See you in the charts."

Meek pulled out all the stops to win the support of Holly's living representatives.

A preview of "Tribute to Buddy Holly" was arranged for members of the singer's Appreciation Society; Norman Petty, Holly's producer, was contacted for an endorsement; and Mike Berry himself received a letter of thanks from Holly's parents. Indeed, Meek took the whole affair so seriously, that long after Mike Berry's chart run was over, when Goddard came up with a second Holly song, "My Friend Buddy," Meek changed the title (to "Bobby") to avoid offending supporters in the Holly camp.

"Tribute to Buddy Holly," like "Johnny, Remember Me" before it, and "Telstar" six months later, established Meek's fame, for all eternity confirming him among the most influential producers in rock'n'roll, up there with contemporaries Phil Spector and George Martin as a spearhead of the revolution that reshaped the infant rock'n'roll industry.

Roy Thomas Baker, an engineer at Decca who later would go on to massive success as Queen's producer, worked with Meek on a handful of occasions, and recalled, "Joe was attempting to do the wall-of-sound thing, but instead of using echo and things like that, he was using compressors." It worked just as well, as Meek knew it would, and he was so proud of his accomplishments that when he was contacted by Phil Spector, whose own wall-of-sound techniques were generally reckoned to be pretty good, Meek accused the American of stealing his ideas, then slammed the phone down so hard it broke.

Meek surrounded himself with equipment, but nothing he could not customize and improve on. Ceaselessly seeking out new sounds and expressions, he saw potential in everything he could lay his hands on, from a comb and paper to a fork banging on the wall; from knives vibrating on a Formica tabletop, to blowing bubbles in a glass with a drinking straw.

He recorded the sound of a toilet flushing, then played it backward. He threw things down the stairs and taped the crashing. He rattled things, shook them, hit them, anything to provoke an unusual effect. One of his favorite tricks was to short-out an electrical circuit, and capture the resulting *phhhzzz*. Another was to leave the tape recorders running when he went to bed at night, then play back the tapes in the morning, for the sound of the house settling down. If his hyperactive imagination discerned anything else on the tapes, then that, too, was simply the price he must pay for his gifts.

The apartment was haunted, Meek was convinced of that. Mysterious footsteps echoed through the passageways at night, marched up and down the stairs, disturbed objects he left on his desk. It was only as time passed, and Meek's profes-

**Joe Meek in his bedroom
studio in 1963**
(Hulton Gertly-Liaison)

sional star fell into decline, that the identity of this nocturnal visitor began to per-
plex him more and more.

The turning point in Meek's fortunes came in October 1964. That summer he
scored his fourth British chart-topper with the Honeycombs beat classic "Have I the
Right"; now he had the right to regard the future as brightly as he could wish. That
mood of optimism lasted all summer long, right up until he read about the death
of David Box.

∎ ∎ ∎

Harold David Box was still at school when he was invited into the studio by the Buddyless Crickets, to handle lead vocals on their version of "Peggy Sue Got Married." Six years later, he was still enjoying a Hollyesque career, cruising local Texan charts with the effervescent "Summer Girl."

On October 23, traveling with a local pickup band and with drummer Bill Daniels, a qualified pilot, in the cockpit, Box hired a Cessna Skyhawk 172 to fly to a gig in Harris County. He was due in Nashville to record his next single the following day, so immediately after the show, the entourage headed back to their homebase in Houston.

They never made it. Shortly after takeoff, the plane nosedived into the ground. The entire group—Box, Daniels, and guitarist Buddy Groves included—were aboard; all were killed in the crash. A few days later, Box's parents met with Buddy Holly's, and learned what the future held for them. "People will tell you the pain eventually goes away," the elder Mr. Holly told Box's shattered family. "I can tell you now, it never does."

It was the series of inexplicable coincidences that hit Meek the hardest. Almost precisely two years earlier, on October 25, 1962, Ronnie Smith, who replaced Holly for the remainder of the ill-fated 1959 tour, hanged himself in the bathroom of the state hospital to which he'd been committed for drug abuse. Two years before that, on January 8, 1960, Holly's former backing group, the Crickets, accompanied Eddie Cochran on what would prove to be his last-ever recording session.

Now another Cricket was gone, and in almost identical circumstances to Holly: like Buddy, Box was just twenty-two; like Buddy, he hailed from Lubbock, Texas, like Buddy, he perished in a plane crash following a concert.[3]

There was also the matter of the baleful curse which suddenly appeared to be riding on the back of Peggy Sue. Buddy wrote about her, Smith and Box sang about her, and Meek had recorded her. It was Berry's version of "Peggy Sue Got Married" that prompted Meek to sign him in the first place; it was his version of "Peggy Sue" that helped win over the Buddy Holly fan club on the night they previewed "Tribute." A reasoned mind may have suggested that if anybody was going to fall foul of the curse, Berry was a far more likely victim than Meek. But Meek was beyond reason now, and his assurance grew. He would be the next to go.

Meek had always sought guidance and solace from spiritualism. Now he turned to it for confirmation of his worst fears. Forewarned, he believed, he could be fore-armed.

But how could he defend himself against failure? The hits had dried up—by early 1966, Meek had not even sniffed the chart in more than six months; had not enjoyed a major smash since "Have I the Right."

His landlords, Albert and Violet Shenton, announced that they were selling the building, store and all, and gave him notice to quit the warren of apartments which were his home and workplace. The Board of Trade, suspecting irregularities in Meek's accounts, was harassing him. His personal bank account was overdrawn; bills were piling up, and the little money which he did have was being split with increasing frailty between his most pressing creditors and an equally voracious drug habit—amphetamines to keep him up, barbiturates to bring him down.

He became a familiar sight around the fortune tellers who then teemed around London's Soho district, determined to unravel his own increasingly foggy future. He spent hours with a sting of mediums. He took up ghost hunting, recording everything that struck him as unusual, then hightailing it around to the headquarters of the Society for Psychical Research, where every unexplained sound was presented as proof of a spectral presence. At home, his Tarot and Ouija were seldom out of sight, and his private library began to swell with books he believed might further aid his search for solutions.

He turned toward the darker side of the occult. He started with Dennis Wheatley, the infinitely gifted author of a series of black-magic novels through the 1950s and 1960s. He absorbed the scientific studies of Colin Wilson, the modern-day professor whose research was finally raising the the occult from bunk status. And from there, it was just a short step toward magician and Satanist Aleister Crowley, the self-styled Great Beast, and the final repository of all things Unholy.

Entertaining charlatans as readily as genuine practitioners, and quite aware of that fact as well, Meek plunged into the heart of the Satanic underground, as desperate as he was naive. But if just one person could tell him what he wanted to hear, he would know in his soul whether or not it was true.

He built his contacts slowly. He befriended Graham Bond, one of the fathers of British R&B, fascinated by the popular conviction that the burly organist was one of Crowley's illegitimate sons.[4]

The Tornadoes' guitarist, Ritchie Blackmore, possessed an interest in the occult which he gladly shared with Meek. So did Blackmore's pretty German wife, Margaret, and while Ritchie was away on tour, she would frequently stop by to visit Meek, to discuss their beliefs long into the night.

With his newfound associates, Meek became a frequent visitor to nearby Highgate

Woods, where he lived out the rituals he once had only read about. There, one night he encountered the High Priest of British witches, David Farrant. There, too, it was said, Meek and various unnamed accomplices did indeed succeed in raising Crowley's spirit; a visitation he then became convinced accounted for the muffled footsteps and sounds of moving furniture that haunted his apartment with renewed nocturnal vigor. One thing, however, could not be doubted. Whatever forces Meek had invoked, they were not doing him much good . . . and things only got worse.

Back in November 1963, Meek was arrested in a men's public lavatory near his home, and charged with "persistently importuning for an immoral purpose." In his own mind, then, he was already a marked man, one whom the authorities—in league with the record-industry mavens who resented his success—would not hesitate in bringing down, the moment they were given the chance. So far, he had been able to keep one step ahead of them, but in early 1967, the dance came to an end.

On January 16, a tractor driver working in a field in the tiny Suffolk village of Tattingstone spotted a pair of suitcases lying beside a hedgerow. Curious, he clambered down and opened one. It contained approximately half a human corpse; the remainder, logically, was contained within the other.

The victim was one Bernard Oliver, a seventeen-year-old warehouseman from the North London suburb of Muswell Hill, who had been reported missing a few days before. He was a known homosexual, and according to the media (which delightedly dubbed the slaying "the Suitcase Murder") Scotland Yard intended contacting both the dead boy's acquaintances and all known homosexual offenders. Meek, who once briefly enjoyed a sexual liaison with the unfortunate Oliver, fell neatly into both categories.

Days earlier, Meek had been happily planning a vacation in Cairo. Now, terrified out of his wits, he withdrew completely into a world of frightened paranoia. He became convinced the police were tapping his phone, even bugging his apartment—fears, incredibly, that were born out by the discovery of several listening devices in the apartment. It was never ascertained whether they were planted by the authorities, by jealous rivals, or even by the East End gangsters who Meek claimed once had tried to extort the Tornadoes out of him. So he suspected everybody, including his landlady, Violet Shenton; Meek was several months behind in the rent at the time, and fiercely resented her plans to sell his home from beneath him. He would not put it past her, or her husband, to be spying on him in the hope of finding some incriminating means of evicting him even sooner. Whoever was responsible, the consequences were inevitable. Meek stopped talking out loud. Instead, he wrote notes, surreptitiously handing them around to his visitors, then retrieving them after they were read.

On the evening of February 2, 1967, Margaret Blackmore decided to pay Meek one of her visits. It was, of course, the eve of the day Meek held most Holy, the anniversary of Buddy Holly's death. Blackmore knew that, and was sure Meek could probably do with some company. But when she knocked on the door, she barely recognized the man who answered it. White faced, bulging eyes, clad in black from head to foot, she later said Meek "looked like a devil."

But it was his actions which puzzled her more. Constantly, but abstractedly, Meek was writing on pieces of paper, then ripping them to shreds, and murmuring repeatedly, "There's somebody who'd try to steal it."

"Steal the paper?" Blackmore asked.

"No, steal it from my mind," Meek replied.

Blackmore said later that she could only think of one person who would, or could, do that: Aleister Crowley; a suspicion Meek confirmed as the evening wore on. "I'm not by myself," he told her. "There's somebody around me, somebody in the air." And then, "There's somebody inside me. I can't get him out." The last thing Meek told her before ushering her out of the flat was, "Margaret, you are so much like Lady Harris." At first, Blackmore didn't know what he was talking about; it was only later that she realized Lady Harris was Crowley's girlfriend.

The following morning, February 3, Meek seemed calmer, more at ease. He had been recording with Patrick Pink, his live-in office assistant, and when the young man awoke, it was to find Meek already working on their tape. But the smell of smoke hung in the air, and all through breakfast, Meek was burning things, scraps of paper, letters, documents. Pink knew better than to ask him what they were.

Following the meal, Meek returned upstairs to his studio, but fifteen minutes later, he came back down, to hand Pink a note. It read, simply, "I'm going now. Good-bye."

Ten minutes after that, a visitor turned up at the studio, a high-school graduate Meek was employing to stack tapes for him. Although Pink knew what Meek's response would be, he nevertheless went upstairs to announce the youngster. Meek told him to fuck off. Then, as Pink started back down the stairs, Meek appeared at the top of the landing, and called down to him. "Get Mrs. Shenton up here."

And Pink, not knowing why Meek could possibly want to talk to his landlady this early in the day, hurried downstairs to get her.

IN AUGUST 1963, bidding to launch his latest protégé, Heinz Burt, Joe Meek seized upon the still-thriving cult which surrounded Eddie Cochran, in a bid to prove that lightning could—and would—strike twice.

Cochran had been gone for three years, but the impact of his death was still fresh in many minds. Just months before, a previously unissued recording of "My Way" gave Cochran his sixth posthumous British hit, while the late rocker's material was a standard inclusion in live sets all across the country. And just as "Tribute to Buddy Holly" saw Mike Berry launched as a superstar-in-waiting, Meek was convinced that a similar tribute to Cochran would send Burt soaring equally far. Weeks later, "Just Like Eddie" was slamming straight into the Top Ten, and while Burt would never climb so high again, Cochran remained immortal.

Eddie Cochran was everything Buddy Holly wasn't. Where Holly hiccuped, Cochran roared; where Holly strummed, Cochran riffed; and if Holly was the boy next door, Cochran was the thug from the other side of the tracks.

Born in Oklahoma, raised in Minnesota, but bred in Los Angeles, which he always considered home, Cochran burst onto the scene in 1956, aboard *The Girl Can't Help It*, the celluloid rock'n'roll riot (starring Jayne Mansfield) that electrified America. He got his start in hillbilly music, touring with the unrelated Hank Cochran in a moderately successful country act called the Cochran Brothers. But then he saw Elvis and he never looked back.

"Twenty Flight Rock," Cochran's sole starring turn in *The Girl Can't Help It*, landed him a record deal; the way he looked and the way he held himself took care of everything else. To the boys, he was a role model, to the girls, a tough to tame, and to anybody over the age of thirty he was every worst nightmare come appallingly true. "Summertime Blues" hit the Top Ten in the summer of 1958, and for anybody who was too young to vote, who couldn't use the car, who didn't work late . . . it wasn't a simple pop song, it was an invitation to rebellion. It *was* rebellion.

"Man, Cochran was it," rock impresario Tony Secunda enthused. Secunda was still a seaman when he first heard the singer, during a visit to the Americas, and by the time Cochran was ready to make his British debut, Secunda already had the guest bedroom prepared—figuratively, if nothing else.

"He slept on my couch. Years later, my old lady tried to get me to throw it out— 'It's horrible, it's full of cigarette burns.' Fuck you! They were Eddie's cigarette burns. He'd fall asleep smoking, the butts would burn through the sofa. Anyone else who ever stayed—'Be careful on the sofa!' 'Why? It's already full of burn holes.' 'Yeah, but they were Eddie's.'"

Cochran arrived in the U.K. in January 1960. His fame was drifting in America; his last couple of singles were out-and-out stiffs, the few before that barely scraped the grade. Cochran himself knew "C'mon Everybody" was a great song, as great as "Something' Else," but it was now eighteen months since "Summertime Blues," and even those songs hadn't given him a follow-up hit.

Britain, on the other hand, was ripe for the picking. While America drifted into old age and retirement, and ballads came back with bobby socks and letterman sweaters, Britain was still waiting for something to happen. Homegrown rockers Cliff Richard and Billy Fury,[1] Johnny Kidd and Terry Dene, all curling their lips in best Elvis style—they were fine, and they did a good job. But the kids wanted something exotic as well, someone who didn't buy their shirts from the same stores as them, who didn't curl up to the same TV as them, who didn't walk like them and talk like them. Cochran fit the bill.

The first time he appeared on British television, on producer Jack Good's *Boy*

Meets Girls, Cochran tore the place apart, and Good promptly rebooked him for another three shows. Cochran's ten-week British tour never saw an empty seat, and long before it was over, he was invited back for more. "Eddie Cochran was pure rock," swore journalist Nik Cohn, one of a million impressionable teens who caught him on television. "Other people were other kinds of rock, country or high-school, hard, soft, good or bad or indifferent. Eddie Cochran was just rock. Nothing else."

Again, it was not difficult to pinpoint Cochran's appeal. Clichéd allusions to his "smoldering good looks" and "rough, rocker appeal" barely began to describe a twenty-one-year-old whose every gesture seem designed to out–Elvis Presley, upstage James Dean, and leave every last hopeful on the British rock'n'roll scene gasping at the gate. Certainly his native companions on that ten-week British tour—Billy Fury, Joe Brown, and Johnny Gentle—didn't know what hit them, and, with fellow American Gene Vincent cleaning up the spots Cochran missed, all three admitted that they weren't even along for the ride.

Like Cochran, Vincent was rebellion personified. Crippled in a motorcycle accident during his days in the U.S. Navy, when a woman ran a red light and plowed into his side, he wrote what became his signature hit, "Be-Bop-a-Lula," while recuperating in Portsmouth Navy Hospital. A couple of years later, it would become the first record young Paul McCartney ever bought.

Released from the hospital and the service, dragging his damaged left leg behind him, Vincent landed both a record deal and, alongside Cochran, an appearance in *The Girl Can't Help It*. The pair met again when they were booked to headline the weeklong Rock-and-Roll Jubilee of Stars, in Philadelphia. And from then on, they were all but inseparable.

It was Jack Good, again, who made Vincent—who choreographed a quiet, well-dressed American singer's transformation into a demon dripping in black leather, and told him to play up his natural limp; who had him twisting his body beneath a single white spotlight, barely moving, never smiling, just sweating and smoking and oozing through his outfit.

Good couldn't have molded anything if it hadn't been there to begin with, but by the time Vincent first set foot on a British stage, the mutation was complete. Cochran was every cocky teenager's dream come true; Vincent was every outcast's idol. Together on the same concert bill, they reached out to every rock'n'roll fan in the land.

Cochran topped the bill, of course. Nik Cohn again: "[Cochran] was the first major American rocker to do a full, unaborted [British] tour, and his impact was

Gene Vincent (Pictorial Press Ltd.)

tremendous. . . . He was a mover and writer and voice. He played his own thing on guitar . . . he sang songs that weren't just crap. All of that was new. So Billy Fury saw him and woke up. Or the Beatles saw him, or the Stones or the Who or the Move. He was the starting point from which British pop really began to get better."

The British tour ended on April 16, 1960. Cochran would fly back to Los Angeles for a couple of weeks, then he'd be back, to continue annexing the country. He'd been homesick all tour, calling his mother every day, just to say hi and make plans for his return. If he cut out of London as quickly as he could, he'd be back in L.A. in time for Easter, and that's where they left it the last time he called; with the whole family preparing to welcome the conquering hero.

   The last show was in Bristol, out in the west on the border of Wales; Cochran would be heading back to London immediately afterward, to catch an early-morning flight. He hired a car and driver for the three-hour journey. Piling in with him were his girlfriend and co-writer, Sharon Sheeley; roadie Patrick Thompkins; and costar Gene Vincent—a full load, a dark night, and a chauffeur, George Martin (no

you can phone the ambulance now, mama

Eddie Cochran with Sharon Sheely
(Showtime Archives, Toronto)

relation to the Beatles producer of the same name), who wasn't completely familiar with the route. After the show, Martin drove out of Bristol, through Bath, into Chippenham, then made a wrong turn, and suddenly the car was speeding back through Rowden Hill, back toward Bristol.

Sheeley and Cochran were singing along with the radio, Vincent was sleeping, and Martin stepped on the brake as the car emerged from a railroad tunnel, coming up for a bend in the road. Then the whole world turned upside down. The last thing Sheeley remembered was seeing Vincent asleep on one side of her, and Cochran on the other, leaning over to protect her as the car lurched out of control and careened into a concrete lamppost.

Sheeley awoke to find herself lying on a grass traffic median dazed, bleeding, and completely paralyzed. She didn't know it at the time, but her neck was broken. White things were fluttering around her: sheet music blew out from the car and was caught in the light breeze. Somebody—it turned out to be Martin—was standing, then pacing, head in hands, a few feet away, and, in the half-light from a nearby streetlamp, she could see someone crawling toward her. It was Vincent.

"How's Eddie?"

Vincent paused. "He's okay. Just a bit shaken up. But he's okay."

Sheeley instinctively knew he was lying.

Cochran was flat on his back on the edge of the verge. A few feet away, not even scratched, his Gretsch guitar lay in the road. First on the scene, a neighboring farmer, Dick Jennings, laid his coat under the singer's head, but he knew it was already too late. Blood oozed from Cochran's nose, ears, and eyes, and, when the farmer raised the singer's head, his mouth fell open and blood drained from there as well.

Another local arrived, and laid his old army greatcoat over Cochran. His wife placed hers over the now-sobbing Sheeley. Thompkins appeared—he had already called for an ambulance—and Vincent obviously was going to be fine. He'd bumped his head, and the lump hurt like hell. But he was smoking a cigarette and cursing his lungs out, and everybody just let him get on with it. It was only later that he discovered he was suffering from a broken shoulder, and also a fresh break in his crippled left leg.

The first ambulance arrived minutes before midnight, just as the preset timer on the small town's streetlights clicked off for the night. The medics worked by flashlight.

Sheeley and Cochran were taken away in the ambulance; Vincent, Thompkins, and Martin left with the police. Sheeley was slipping in and out of consciousness now, but one memory has always remained with her. At one point in the journey to the hospital, she awoke to find Cochran's hand clenched tightly around hers. She thought he'd regained consciousness, and that gave her hope, right up until the end. It was only later that the ambulance attendant told her what really happened. "[He] did it. He knew we were in love, so he locked our hands together in case we came to."

Singer Johnny Gentle, traveling back from Bristol in his own car, was next on the scene, although he would be back home in London, on the phone with his manager, before he realized what he'd seen.

"Sometime after midnight, I was driving around Chippenham looking for petrol. In those days there weren't any all-night garages. We found a local [policeman], and he said we were in luck because there had just been an accident and there was a [tow] truck around the corner that we might be able to get some [gas from]. We drove round just as the ambulance was pulling away.

"Sure enough, there was this awful wreck of a car, and the [tow] truck driver said we could siphon off the petrol from the wreck. So that's what we did. We siphoned the petrol off, and drove home. It wasn't till the next day when my manager rang up and told me what had happened, that I realized whose car it had been."

In fact, very few people seemed to know what was going on. Cochran remained critically injured throughout the night and late into the following afternoon, but the first his family heard about the accident, as they gathered together at his mother's house to await him, was when the news came over the radio, just about the time Cochran's plane should have touched down. A short time later, they received a telephone call telling them Cochran had passed away, just after four P.M.

Like Holly's death, little more than twelve months before, Cochran's passing was as staggering as it was senseless; like Holly, too, the first single released following his death could not have been titled with more poignancy. "Three Steps to Heaven" was one of the last songs Cochran ever recorded, during a session with Holly's old backing musicians, the Crickets, shortly before he flew to England. His U.K. label, Liberty, had already scheduled it for mid-April release.

And while America ignored its tragic loss, Britain brimmed with regret. "Three Steps to Heaven" would spend two weeks at number one that summer, and would precipitate a Cochran cult which kept him on the British chart for much of the next three years, and in British hearts even longer than that.

In 1963, Heinz Burt delivered the heartfelt "Just Like Eddie"; in 1968, a rock-

you can phone the ambulance now, mama

'n'roll revival in Britain saw "Summertime Blues" return to the charts. The Who kept the same song in their live set for years, and, almost two decades after Cochran's death, in 1979, ex-Sex Pistol Sid Vicious demonstrated that even punks possessed a sense of history when he revived both "Something Else" and "C'mon Everybody" for inclusion in the movie *The Great Rock'n'Roll Swindle*.

The Rolling Stones resurrected "Twenty Flight Rock" during their 1981 tour, and in 1988, Sharon Sheeley's recollection of the first time she met Cochran, at a party in L.A., inspired a commercial for Levi's jeans, while "C'mon Everybody" jump-started every memory. Reissued once again, the song hit the British Top Twenty that spring, but it wasn't just nostalgia. Cochran's songs may have been almost three decades old, but they still made sense: a voice loud and proud in the ears of British youth, an invitation to come out and play, and party and strut, and tell the whole adult world where to stick its rules and regulations.

But if British rock never wanted to escape the shadow of the dead rock'n'roller, Gene Vincent was never allowed to. Wherever he went, Cochran's memory pursued him; whenever he talked, his ghost was still there. Journalist Mick Farren remembered, "I talked to him in 1969 [and] he was drunkenly obsessive on the subject. By that time, he'd totally convinced himself that Eddie's death was the product of a sinister conspiracy by his then manager, Don Arden."[2] Farren recalled Vincent repeating over and over, "Eddie was alive when we got him into the ambulance."

Vincent's logic was painfully, if paranoically, simple: Arden, having witnessed the commercial aftermath of Buddy Holly's death—having seen, too, the tidal wave of grief that accompanied actor James Dean's passing four years before that—had realized that Cochran was worth much more dead than alive. Of course, the logic is flawed, but Vincent wasn't searching for logic. He was looking for answers, nine long, painful, and often sordid years after his best friend was taken away from him.

Drunk when he wasn't pilled, stoned when he wasn't tanked, Vincent's decline through those years was obvious to all. America completely disowned him. The IRS tore him to shreds, and what they didn't take, former wives and business associates divided between themselves. Television all but blackballed him after one too many drunken performances. Even the crushed leg which did so much to make his reputation in the first place, providing him with a fighting stance and an image-laden shuffle, had finally turned against him. Osteomyelitis, an infectious inflammatory disease of the bone, set in, and amputation seemed the only cure.

Vincent fled to Europe, to a sanctuary he knew (or at least, believed) was

Cochran's alone, but which had always treated him well. By 1965, though, even he couldn't stand the diminishing returns of a career on skid row. He spent eighteen months back in California, but was never allowed to fit in. The Love and Peace Generation had no time for an old rocker like him. The news that English rocker (and sometime Vincent clone) Johnny Kidd was considering recording an entire album's worth of Vincent covers, revived Vincent's spirits temporarily—the two gigged together in the early 1960s, and Kidd never was shy about admitting his stylistic debt. But the album never happened. Kidd was killed in a car crash in October 1966, returning home from a gig,[3] igniting echoes which brought all Vincent's horrors flooding back.

Still, there was nothing left for Vincent in America, so he returned to Europe, where he at least found the financing to record a new album with producer Kim Fowley. Then it was back to L.A., where he would finally be presented with his very last chance of salvation.

Gene Vincent's friendship with Doors vocalist Jim Morrison[4] was the kind of relationship novels are made of, a twilight noir zone where one broken rocker's Hemingway slurs up to the other's shattered Dylan Thomas, and they drink each other under the table. Morrison was still firing on all cylinders then, hanging out at the Shamrock Inn on Santa Monica Boulevard, just enjoying being famous, with his own disintegration far, far off in a still-unscripted future.

It was Morrison who bartered, begged, and finally blasted Vincent onto the bill of the Toronto Rock'n'Roll Revival Festival, on September 6, 1969. Alongside traditional rockers like Chuck Berry and Jerry Lee Lewis, and with behind-the-scenes negotiations for John Lennon's Plastic Ono Band, the Doors were already booked to appear at the festival; the idea now was for them to join Vincent onstage as well, and give everyone a treat.

It didn't happen like that, but Toronto was a triumph nonetheless. Scheduling problems saw Vincent pushed onstage before the Doors even arrived at the venue, so he took the stage with a barely rehearsed, and certainly unsuspecting Alice Cooper Band[5] behind him . . . and he still blew everybody away.

By the end of the set, after a scorching "Be-Bop-a-Lula," half the crowd was in rapture, half was stunned into silence, and Lennon himself was onstage, embracing his idol in tears. Years later, recording his *Rock'n'Roll* album, Lennon would do his damnedest to recapture that precise moment, with his own magnificent cover of Vincent's signature classic. It was great, one of the best things on the entire album—and it still didn't come close to what Vincent did that evening.

The Toronto Festival should have relaunched Vincent as a superstar. Rock'n'roll was making a comeback then, riding its own iconic Harley within a phalanx of hard-rocking Angels and crashing through the barricades of Flower Power and acid-drenched whimsy. Sha Na Na[6] infiltrated Woodstock; the Stones were back playing Berry; the Who were rocking Cochran in their live show; and Lennon's entire set in Toronto revolved around "Blue Suede Shoes." Straightened out, standing tall, Vincent could have bounced back for all time. Instead he returned to the gutter.

He was thirty-six, but he looked sixty-three. In Europe, he barely completed a ramshackle tour which left even hard-core devotees watching in disdainful disbelief. Still, he kept trying. In London, through February 1971, he scooped up a pick-up band called the Houseshakers and recorded two desultory sessions for the BBC. On another occasion, he went into the studio with the young David Bowie, himself still awaiting the jumpsuited jump-start his own career needed, and filling in time by playing producer. Bowie had tried designing his own star, but Arnold Corns never caught on; he'd tried inventing another, with a young boy named Micky,[7] and a song about his car, "Rupert the Riley." That hadn't worked, either. Now Bowie wanted to try his luck with a bona fide legend. They tried a couple of numbers. In 1986, trying to remember back that far, and admitting he really couldn't, Bowie's guitarist Mick Ronson thought "Hang On to Yourself" was one of the songs, "simply because David tried the song with everyone, because he knew it was a hit." Either way, the session broke down in confusion and alcohol, and Vincent floated away again.

He was back at the BBC on October 1. Disc jockey John Peel, whose Dandelion label released the album Vincent recorded with Fowley, met him there briefly. "He was very polite. I didn't realize quite to what extent he was in a mess."

Vincent flew back to L.A. a few days later, straight into another nest of vipers. His wife Jackie had left him, taking the car, the kids, most of their possessions, and all of his money. He reacted like he always did, by going out and getting hammered. He drank for three days, hard liquor slamming nonstop straight down his throat, a binge that killed so much of his pain that he didn't even realize that his already ulcerated stomach lining was finally giving way. All he knew, was that when he tried to stand up, he was barely able to walk.

With his lifeblood literally draining away into his gut, Vincent made his way to his mother's suburban home in Saugus, then collapsed to his knees, throwing up blood. His last words before he lapsed into unconsciousness were, "Mama, you can phone the ambulance now." An hour later, he was dead.

Vincent's last-ever recordings, that final session for the BBC, was broadcast on

November 8, 1971, but beyond host Johnny Walker's opening comments about its historic import, few listeners paid it much mind. Just another sad old rocker playing out his sad old tunes, and for the most part, that's what it was: with only slightly more enthusiasm than Vincent himself appeared to be mustering, his latest pick-up band cranked out five songs, obligatory revisions of "Be-Bop-a-Lula" and "Say Mama," and a couple of other graying rock'n'roll staples. Then they went into their closing number, and suddenly something clicked, as though they knew they were meant to try and say something, only Vincent hadn't told them quite what it was. But for anyone who heard it, Jim Reeves' funereal swan song, "Distant Drums," would never sound the same again.

Though today he is the object of just as much interest as Cochran, at the time, Vincent's death barely drew comment. He had not perished in a trap of senseless wreckage; he had not burned hard and bright, then been extinguished overnight. He simply wasted away, a chemical consumptive whose time passed before he did. By 1971 a new decade, a new generation, had grown up, for whom Vincent was simply another name in the history books, no more relevant to what was "happening" now than Julius Caesar or President Woodrow Wilson.

In the age of T. Rex in Britain and James Taylor in the States, Vincent fell so far from either pole that even his barnstorming appearance at Toronto just two years before, seemed a million miles away. The days when he was widely regarded among the most authentic rock'n'rollers ever to walk a stage, were far behind him: when a young Mick Farren "moved heaven and earth to get tickets to see him"; and Ian Dury was so moved that a generation later, he'd write "Sweet Gene Vincent" about his fallen idol.

It is only now, with time and perspective, that an entire career can be telescoped until good rubs shoulders with evil, and a decade-long decline becomes a few bad years at the end. Time, like the good PR man it so often is, erased every one of Gene Vincent's failings . . . and all it cost him was his life.

they just couldn't resist her
with her pocket transistor

JOHNNY THEAKSTONE IS the forgotten man of early British rock'n'roll. Many others vie for the title, but none of them even comes close. Dead before his seventeenth birthday, in 1961 he was unknown, and therefore publicly unmourned. Theakstone nevertheless would live on when his group, Shane Fenton and the Fentones, persuaded roadie Bernard Jewry to slip into the lead singer's role to help them through a crisis; and then Theakstone died again, when Fenton's own star slipped into obscurity, and Jewry reinvented himself as glam-rock idol Alvin Stardust.

"Johnny was a great guy, and always seemed to be full of life," Jewry recalled. "The sort of guy who had a joke for every occasion, and was always laughing." It was Theakstone who formed the teenaged Johnny Theakstone and the Tremoloes, a Mansfield-based combo specializing in dead-on Everly Brothers covers; it was Theakstone, too, who resolved to go for gold by convincing his bandmates to record an audition tape for the BBC in late 1960.

The BBC was constantly on the lookout for new acts to guest on the top-rated *Saturday Club* radio show, and though the chances of being accepted were staggeringly slim, Theakstone was convinced his Tremoloes were equipped with everything it took to succeed—except for a name. Adopting "Shane" from the writing credits of a recent Gene Vincent single, and "Fenton" from a garage they'd passed on the way home from a gig, Shane Fenton and the Fentones dropped their precious tape in the mail, and waited. They were still awaiting a reply when Theakstone died.

As a child, Theakstone had suffered a prolonged bout of rheumatic fever, an illness which so weakened his heart, Jewry mourned, "that he never should have been doing the sort of things he was doing with the group. He was going out to work during the day, and then in the evening he'd go off to do a gig and sometimes not return home again until four in the morning. But no one ever stopped him because that was the life he loved."

The first sign anything was wrong came when Jewry dropped by Theakstone's house one evening, to pick him up for a show. "I found him sitting on the settee in the lounge, with blankets wrapped all around him, very ill and too weak to stand." Jewry stood in for him onstage that evening, and when Theakstone was admitted to the hospital, the roadie continued to deputize. "And then one day there was a knock at the door and it was Cliff Hardy, who was the local musicians' union branch secretary: 'Johnny died last night.'"

The effect on the group was shattering. "We thought the best thing to do would be to fold it up, out of respect for Johnny's mum. And then—about a month after Johnny's death—a letter arrived from the BBC, saying they liked the tape we sent them, and were now offering us a studio test.

"Johnny's mum came round to see us and said she'd been turning it over in her mind, and didn't want us to give up now, just as the BBC had shown interest. 'I'd like you to carry on. It was Johnny's life. He would have wanted you to do that.' So we got the group together again, and then she came to see us again and said, 'Would you be offended if I asked you to use Johnny's name?'" Jewry agreed.

Reborn, Shane Fenton and the Fentones sailed through the audition, early in 1961, and the following month, they appeared on *Saturday Club*. Before the end of the day, the show's musical director Tommy Sanderson, became the Fentones' manager; by the end of the week, he had landed them a deal with EMI. Over the next twelve months, Shane Fenton and the Fentones notched up four successive British hits.

By the end of 1962, however, it was all over. The group splintered; Jewry himself, tied by circumstance into a dead man's shoes, graduated to the cabaret circuit, and he, too, might have been forgotten—*was* forgotten, in fact, until a sharp-eyed BBC disc jockey walked up to newly launched glam-rock superstar Alvin Stardust to ask him, "Didn't you used to be Shane Fenton?"

Yes, he was. But he wasn't the first one.

The musical landscape over which Eddie Cochran and Gene Vincent exploded so dramatically, and into which Johnny Theakstone and his Fentones plunged themselves, was one of almost unrelenting flux. Britain's first homegrown rock'n'rollers notwithstanding, the music scene was still dominated on the one hand by the last gasp of "skiffle," the proto–folk-rock hybrid led by ernest young men playing washboards and semiacoustic guitars, and on the other by an even earlier wave of wholesome "family entertainers."

Future (and now former) Rolling Stone Bill Wyman spoke for an entire generation when he reflected, "Pop music was sung by very ordinary, horrible people in evening clothes, that copied American hits. You had Guy Mitchell. You had David Whitfield and Lita Roza and Dickie Valentine, doing all these songs like 'Green Door,' 'How Much Is that Doggy in the Window,' all the Doris Day songs, all the Connie Francis songs, they were all covered by these quite ordinary, middle-aged people. There was no scene."

But there were still stars, and among all the detritus, a handful of names still ring with a clarity that defies the dreadfulness recalled by Wyman. Indeed, throughout the first years of the 1960s, and following the Beatles' 1963 breakthrough, skiffle king Wally Whyton remained as integral a part of the "growing-up experience" as he ever was in the 1950s, after he abandoned a conventional recording career to become Britain's first rock'n'roll children's-television presenter.

Whyton first emerged on the skiffle scene at the helm of the Vipers, one of the multitude of performers discovered and nurtured by producer George Martin in the years before he found the Fab Four. Ostensibly, they had little to do with rock'n'roll. Talking about the Vipers' early days, in 1986 Whyton admitted, "If I was aware [of Bill Haley and Elvis Presley], it was something that didn't appeal to me. Even now, I can't take Presley. [And] I always thought Bill Haley looked like a bundle of shit tied up. I didn't really go for his music. I suppose I was pretty much a musical snob."

But though the Vipers themselves may not have "rocked," their records certainly did, unconsciously absorbing—and then redistributing—rock'n'roll as though it were going out of fashion, and creating a fusion whose rudiments remain integral to even the most modern "Britpop" band.

Hank Marvin, Jet Harris, and Tony Meehan were all, briefly, members of the Vipers. Reunited in 1958 as Cliff Richard's backing group, the Shadows, and applying the hiss of the Vipers to the snarl of sundry Presley standards, this same trio would redesign British music, taking the Vipers' unconscious vision to the next level. Within five years, the Beatles would take it even further, until there was no looking back.

The Vipers broke up in 1959, shortly after the release of their tenth and final single, a cover of Eddie Cochran's "Summertime Blues." According to legend, Whyton fulfilled the band's last few shows alone, with Wee Willie Harris's backing group furiously busking behind him. Asked by curious journalists where the remainder of the "real" Vipers were, Whyton claimed they'd been involved in a car accident; in fact, they had run away to the Canary Islands, to escape various voracious creditors.

Whyton moved into session work briefly, recording with Peter Sellars and Joe Meek among others, but by early 1960 he was best known as the guitar player on the early-evening children's television show, *Musical Box*, the first step in a career which would take him through the next six years.

Small Time, co-hosted by the dog and cat puppets Fred Barker and Pussy Cat Willum, followed; and later, the twice-weekly *Five O'clock Club* (with the owlish Ollie Beak replacing Willum). Another show, devised by Whyton in 1964, later evolved into one of the longest-running puppet shows in British television—a variety show fronted by an irascible, eponymous fox named Basil Brush.

Throughout these shows, Whyton rarely played anything more adventurous than nursery rhymes, but to a preschool audience, his rocking renditions of "London Bridge Is Falling Down" and "Froggy Went A-Courting" were still a memorable initiation into the world of sixties pop; for an American audience, the nearest equivalent would be a young Bob Dylan playing "Puff the Magic Dragon." And if that sounds unlikely, then it only intensifies Whyton's impact.

Whyton could have remained in television forever, but, ever restless, by the late 1960s he was working Britain's nascent country-and-western circuit, a process which peaked in 1973, when he toured with Tex Ritter, and the following year, when he made it to the Grand Ol 'Opry.

"I was crapping—'God Almighty,'" he recalled. "Just thinking about the Opry stage and all the people who'd played on it, and however many thousand people were there. And when I got there, Tex said, 'I'm sorry, but there have been so many from abroad that they won't let anybody else sing.' And I was so relieved, I said, 'great!'"

they just couldn't resist her with her pocket transistor

Back in Britain, Whyton became the host of BBC Radio's long-running *Country Club*, among other shows, but early in the 1990s, he was diagnosed with lung cancer. He worked and battled on, and at least lived to see the Vipers receive the CD boxed-set treatment (from Germany's Bear Family label) in 1996. But less than six months later, on January 22, 1997, the sixty-seven-year-old finally succumbed to his illness.

Whyton's reinvention of himself, as an entertainer rather than a performer, became a common move as the British scene evolved through the early 1960s.

Not everybody succeeded in making the transition. With an attempted acting career in ashes behind him, Michael Holliday took his own life on October 29, 1963, just three years after scoring his second U.K. number one hit single, "Starry Eyed."

Mike Berry, Joe Meek's living tribute to Buddy Holly, moved into acting, and became a star anew through TV's *Are You Being Served?* Balladeer Paul Raven became glam star Gary Glitter; singer Adam Faith became movie star Adam Faith. Some names moved into variety, others followed Whyton into broadcasting, and some retained their sparkle by simply carrying on as though nothing whatsoever had happened.

By the standards of the time, Alma Cogan was a revelation. Running up twenty hit singles between 1952 and 1961, she possessed a natural flamboyance which dazzled a nation still recovering from the oppressive austerity of the war years. As a child, Cogan dreamed of becoming a dress designer; as a star, she put those dreams into maniacal practice, creating the outlandish flounce-and-frill-bedecked bouffant skirts that became as much a trademark as her voice. When she performed. "Twenty Tiny Fingers," a song about the birth of twins, her flamboyant dress had twin dolls sewn into one pocket.

A natural on television, radio, and print; a star in the first stage production of Lionel Bart's *Oliver*; a tireless interviewee; and the darling of every freelance photographer in the land—by the time Cogan scored her first number one, 1955's "Dreamboat," she was unquestionably the best-loved British entertainer of the decade. And nothing—not the onset of rock'n'roll, nor her own growing interest in jazz—could dislodge her.

In 1957, Cogan was invited to New York to appear on the *Ed Sullivan Show*, and she took America by storm. She was immediately asked back to headline the Persian Room at the Plaza Hotel, and had she persevered with her U.S. ambitions, she certainly would have conquered the country.

Instead, she barely looked back as the possibilities of worldwide jet travel took her on what amounted to a four-year tour of the planet. Between 1958 and 1962, Cogan visited most of Europe, Africa, Australia, Israel—even Japan, where her 1962 single, "He Just Couldn't Resist Her with Her Pocket Transistor," proved to be one of the biggest hits of her career. And later, though her record sales dipped, her celebrity never lapsed.

She was a regular around swinging London's most prestigious nightclubs, and the parties she threw were legendary. The guest list for one, celebrating her thirty-second birthday on May 19, 1964, included all four Beatles, their manager Brian Epstein, producer George Martin, American rockers Chuck Berry and Carl Perkins,[1] comic playwright Noel Coward, and the head of EMI, Sir Joseph Lockwood.

That same year, she was seen "stepping out" with Epstein himself, and if you didn't know the quietly homosexual Epstein like his friends knew him, what more natural arrangement could there be? The Beatles were the biggest pop sensation ever, but Cogan had been just as big and, two years Epstein's senior, she had almost sixteen summers of totally self-managed success behind her. Pair her experience with Epstein's enthusiasm, and however they pooled their talents, the results could only be spectacular.

Of course, it was not to be, but Cogan remained a key figure in the Beatles' circle of friends. Paul McCartney played drums on her 1964 recording, "I Knew Right Away"; she was a guest on TV's *Ready, Steady, Go!* the week the Beatles appeared as guest hosts; and when McCartney wrote "Yesterday," he previewed it on Cogan's piano. He was worried, he later confessed, that he might have subconsciously stolen the melody from somebody else's work, "so I took it round to Alma . . . because she was a bit of a song buff. And she said, 'I don't know what it is, but it's beautiful.'"

Offstage, too, both McCartney and John Lennon adored her, gleefully teasing her with their own childhood memories of her earliest hits. Lennon was just thirteen, and McCartney eleven, when the twenty-one-year-old Cogan scored her first hit single, "Bell Bottom Blues," in 1954, and such was her omnipresence that they couldn't have avoided her records even if they'd wanted to. "We never interacted musically. She was a little too old for our generation—not much probably, but it seemed like an eternity," McCartney later explained. But in 1986, on the twentieth anniversary of Cogan's death, McCartney would contribute liner notes to a new compilation of her best work.

In 1965, rumors of her "romance" with Epstein having been joined by further reports of an affair with John Lennon—he called her "Sarah Sequin," and the pair were often seen out together—Cogan met the man she would in fact settle down with, Brian Morris, the owner of the ultra-hip Ad Lib club.

Yet what should have been the happiest time of her life was marred by tragedy; first when the Ad Lib burned down one night in 1965, then when Cogan fell sick with the illness which would ultimately kill her. Rushed to the hospital with severe stomach pains, she was informed that she was suffering from mild appendicitis. In fact, she had been stricken with inoperable stomach cancer.

At her family's insistence, the condition was kept from her, to save her further distress. Unperturbed, then, Cogan resumed her career. She completed work on her forthcoming *Alma* album; she recorded a lovable tribute to *Man from U.N.C.L.E.* star David McCallum; and in September 1966 she set out on a Swedish tour.

Her stomach still was bothering her, but the show must go on. Not until the final night of the tour did Cogan let on how much pain she was suffering; not until the show ended did she allow herself the luxury of collapsing in agony. She was rushed home on the first available flight, and admitted to the hospital. But there was nothing more to be done. She died shortly after, on October 26, 1966.

Cogan's final album, *Alma*, was released the following spring, a magnificent record which saw her finally embracing modern pop styles, while remaining completely true to her own trademark style. At the time, more than one reviewer remarked that the album itself was so vibrant that it was impossible to believe that its maker was gone; and, in the mind of novelist Gordon Burn, a quarter century later, she might *not* have been.

Burn's 1991 Whitbread Award-winning novel *Alma Cogan*, tells the story, in "Cogan's own words," of her life both before and after she "kissed off" her previous existence, a tangled tale which catapults the now middle-aged diva into the mid-1980s, and (among other things) an encounter with an obsessive fan/collector. For him, Cogan's "return" was no more remarkable than spotting Elvis at the burger bar or Jim Morrison at the car wash, and it is this quiet acquiescence that remains at the heart not only of the novel, but of all such posthumous tributes. For how can anyone remain truly dead when their life is kept alive through the medium of their art—or indeed, when that art itself becomes "alive"?

On August 16, 1997, Elvis Presley performed his first live concert in over two decades. Accompanied by both his original Sun Studios backing group and the later Taking Care of Business Band, a thirty-voice gospel choir, and the sixty-piece Memphis Symphony Orchestra, Presley took over Memphis's Mid-South Coliseum and hammered through a live set which combined every great performance between 1968 and 1973; reprised every great stage costume he wore through those same crucial years; and he didn't look a day older than the last time he played the city. Which really wasn't bad for a man who'd been dead twenty years.

Three giant video screens suspended above the stage relayed the action. Beneath them, the performers cavorted, looking like the same busy ants you see at any stadium concert. Close to a hundred musicians were stuffed onto the stage, and two of the screens ensured that almost every one of them had his moment of visibility. But most eyes in the room, those of the 8,300-plus fans who paid between $50 and $80 apiece for tickets, were fixed on the central screen, and the image of Presley most of them couldn't believe they were seeing.

Everything was exactly as it always had been. While the theme from *2001: A Space Odyssey*, Strauss's "Also Sprach Zarathustra," boomed out over the PA, a long black limo flanked by police motorcyclists slowly pulled across the auditorium; onstage, band and orchestra broke into "See See Rider," while the limo disappeared behind the curtains.

The riff grew louder, the crowd noise rose, the screens flashed into life. Presley was running up the backstage stairs, resplendent in the white rhinestoned jumpsuit which was his early-1970s trademark, and then bursting onstage, "Thank you very much." The audience exploded.

Elvis in Concert was the climax to 1997's International Elvis Presley Tribute Week, Elvis Presley Enterprises' "official" contribution to the twentieth anniversary of the singer's death; the climax, too, to several years of secret planning by producer Todd Morgan, and months of rehearsal for the musicians.

Working only with the vocal tracks from a variety of filmed Presley concerts, the team re-created one seamless performance, working around Presley's singing, and working in his ad-libs as well. When "Steamroller Blues" moved toward its guitar solo, and the celluloid Presley ordered James Burton to "Play it" . . . the guitarist stepped forward and played. As Presley introduced the musicians, each took his bow. "I saw Elvis thirty-four times," one concertgoer told reporter Geoff Barker, "but this is the best goddamn show ever."

But it was also, as poet and National Public Radio commentator Andrei Codrescu remarked, a fitting climax to "the most surreal week in American history," a week which saw over 75,000 people—pilgrims—descend upon Memphis from all over the world, to pay homage to the King: a man, polls declare, who is the third-most-recognized icon in the world, behind Mickey Mouse and Jesus Christ; a man who would soon be making his return to the silver screen as well, as the cameras rolled on his latest movie, director Scott Lane's *Everything's George*. Truly reality had taken a well-deserved vacation, and Virtual Reality came back in its place.

And death, the cold, hard, unyielding finality of eternal oblivion, could never be the same again.

they just couldn't resist her with her pocket transistor

that was a hoax, right?”

(CHRIS FARLEY INTERVIEWING PAUL McCARTNEY)

THE BEATLES CHANGED THE WORLD, and history makes it all sound so simple. From the Liverpool skiffle of the protoamateur Quarrymen, to the tighter rock shuffle of Long John and the Moondogs; from a fleeting tangle with fame by association when they tried out as Billy Fury's backing band, to the baptism of fire in the cesspits of Hamburg; and through the haze of a reality which has all but turned into mythology, names fall into place in the burgeoning tapestry:

Klaus Voorman, the bass-playing artist who was still on the scene almost forty years later, designing the covers for the Beatles' *Anthology* series; Astrid Kircherr, the photographer who first mowed their moptops; Tony Sheridan, the beatmaster supreme who scooped up the ragtag boys to back him on a few singles . . .

Then there's the ones who passed by along the way: Raymond Jones, the legendary, and certainly fictional, youth who first alerted manager Brian Epstein to the Beatles' very existence; original drummer Pete Best, the sacrificial lamb at the altar of producer

George Martin's perfectionism; and finally, Stuart Sutcliffe, the Beatle who left them behind.

An art-school friend of John Lennon's, Sutcliffe joined the group in January 1960, selling a painting and buying a bass, and though he couldn't play it, the others were impressed. He was in.

Lennon, Paul McCartney, and George Harrison were still Johnny and the Moondogs when the bassist arrived, but they were already thinking of changing their name. Sutcliffe provided the answer, the Beatles, taking his cue from one of the motorcycle gangs in Marlon Brando's movie *The Wild One*. The "Beatals," as in "beat alls," was Lennon's twisted forerunner, but finally they settled on a more conventional spelling.

Forever hustling, constantly playing, in July, Sutcliffe and Lennon got their first taste of fame, when they and sundry scruffy friends posed for a photographer from the *People* tabloid, to illustrate a story about the so-called Beatnik Horror.

Early Beatles, l. to r.: Pete Best, George Harrison, John Lennon, Paul McCartney, and Stu Sutcliffe (Archive Photos/LDE)

The following month, the Beatles took off for a seventeen-day residency at the Indra Club in Hamburg, Germany, the only group out of the half dozen promotor Allan Williams asked, who were shiftless and unemployed enough to be able to do it. Only the band's regular drummer, Tommy Moore couldn't make it; Pete Best, whose mother ran the Casbah Coffee Club in Liverpool, stepped in, and on August 17, 1960, the Beatles played their first show in Germany. By the end of November, with a stint at the Kaiserkeller behind them as well, they'd played another 112 all-night live sets, which tightened their trousers and screwed down their chords.

They cut their first record. Wally Eymond, guitarist with Rory Storm and the Hurricanes,[1] was recording a version of George Gershwin's "Summertime," pulling in the Beatles to back him, but swapping their drummer, Best, for his own, who was better. It would be months before anybody gave a second thought to the fact that for the first time, the quartet that would conquer the universe, John, Paul, George, and Richard "Ringo Starr" Starkey, played together in the same room. Sutcliffe's presence would merely add poignancy to the event.

Four Beatles returned to Liverpool at the beginning of December; Sutcliffe remained behind in Hamburg to spend Christmas with photographer Astrid Kircherr. Wealthy and wise, Kircherr lived with her mother on the Eimsbuttelerstrasse, one of Hamburg's most exclusive neighborhoods, and one that baffled the Beatles the first time they visited. "We'd only seen the Reeperbahn," McCartney marveled. "We didn't realize Hamburg was so posh."

Neither did they realize how irresistible Sutcliffe had become. "[He] was entering the good-looking period," McCartney explained. Teenaged pimples and greasy hair vanished overnight, replaced by a clear complexion and a keen Kircherr cut. "He wore his James Dean glasses, a nice pair of Ray-Bans, and he looked groovy with his tight jeans and his big bass. Stu became a complete dude."

He and Kircherr had been dating almost since they met. "When I saw Stuart for the first time, I thought, 'Oh my God!'" Kircherr recalled thirty-five years later. "It sounds so overromantic, like in books from Barbara Cartland. [But] he was so charming and so sexy. He knew exactly what was going on. He felt exactly the same, if you might call it, love at first sight, or attraction. It sounds so unreal, but it was right, it was like that. We fell in love."

The post-Hamburg Beatles astonished everyone who caught them, especially anyone who'd seen them beforehand. Sutcliffe returned early in the new year, and over the next three months, the Beatles took the Liverpool scene by the scruff of the neck and shook it till it dropped. From rank outsiders six months before, the Beatles were now the best band in sight, and with another Hamburg stint looming, they were only going to get better.

While his bandmates fell back into the Hamburg routine, popping pills and picking up fräuleins, Sutcliffe fell straight back into Kircherr's arms, and ever more under her sway. Though her English was barely any better than his German, the two seemed to understand one another intuitively; it was only cynics, Paul McCartney among them, who insisted that this "understanding" simply meant that Sutcliffe did whatever Kircherr told him to.

Sutcliffe, however, seemed content to do her bidding: seldom socializing with the band; moving out of their lodgings and into the Kircherr family's spare room; missing rehearsals . . . even fighting McCartney onstage one night, after the guitarist made a rude remark about Kircherr. When the Beatles' residency at the Hamburg's Top Ten Club finally came to an end in July, Sutcliffe announced he would not be returning to Liverpool. He had been invited to study under the Scottish-born (if not-named) artist Eduardo Paolozzi, and returned to his painting with a vengeance.

"Stuart's first love was painting," Kircherr said. As far as bass playing goes, "he didn't give a shit. He just played his note and he was sure that John adored him because of the way he looked. He only did it as a joke because John talked him into it."

Sutcliffe and Kircherr formally announced their engagement in November 1961, then traveled to Liverpool to break the news to Sutcliffe's family. The visit was a disaster. Kircherr and Millie, Sutcliffe's mother, got on so poorly that the couple eventually went to stay with friends for the remainder of their stay. And Millie's natural maternal concerns for her son's well-being were only exacerbated by his appearance.

Sutcliffe looked dreadful, and when Millie pressed him on the subject, it transpired that he was feeling pretty lousy as well. For eight or nine months now, he'd been suffering from sense-shattering headaches—later, some of his friends would date them back to a violent run-in the Beatles had had with a bunch of local thugs, shortly before they left for Hamburg. But others have blamed Lennon, for whacking the bassist on the head during a personal fight. Either way, the headaches were getting worse, and a string of doctors' visits hadn't done anything to relieve them. Rather, they seemed to be gaining in both intensity and regularity.

Sometimes Sutcliffe felt as though his head was about to explode; at others, it was impossible to tell where one attack ended and the next began. The only relief came when he blacked out, something else that was happening more and more. His entire world, it seemed, revolved around that dull, thudding pain.

If the doctors couldn't end it, Sutcliffe himself would. One night, Astrid Kircherr and her mother were just in time to stop him from hurling himself out of a window, three stories above the ground. Another night, Astrid was horrified to discover the true meaning of the phrase "blinding headache" as the pain literally, if mercifully briefly, wiped out Sutcliffe's vision.

Kircherr knew that "he was ill, and had these severe headaches. But when you're that young, death is so far away from you. You don't think about it. If somebody says, 'I've got this terrible headache,' well, it's a shame and I felt so sorry for him. I went to the doctors with him and everywhere. But it never crossed my mind that I would lose him."

Sutcliffe's letters to Lennon told nothing of his problems, the pain that now kept him in bed for most of each day. Instead, he chattered about his art, his new life in Hamburg, and his future with Kircherr. Lennon responded with news of the Beatles' steady progress, the occasional setbacks they'd learned to ignore (Decca Records was the latest label to reject them, in January 1962[2]), and their imminent return to Hamburg. In his last letter back to Lennon, Sutcliffe promised that he and Kircherr would be at the airport on April 11 to meet them.

On the night of April 9, Sutcliffe went to bed as usual, but awakened at some point, and got up. Then he collapsed to the floor. He was still lying there the following morning, when Kircherr herself arose and crossed the hall to his room.

An ambulance was summoned, and together Kircherr and the attendant carried the unconscious artist down three flights of stairs. He died, felled by a massive blood clot in his brain, before they reached the hospital. Astrid alone greeted the Beatles at the airport the next afternoon.

Although he was no longer a member of the group, and certainly played little part in their subsequent success, Sutcliffe's memory never strayed far from the Beatles' own. His presence was never oppressive. Even though several subsequent biographers would make the effort, he never, for example, became the Brian Jones figure the Rolling Stones' consciousness—and consciences—have been forced to contend with for so many years.

But neither has his influence shared the benign, neopaternal aspects history has granted to Brian Epstein. Epstein's suicide, from an overdose on August 27, 1967, was simply the last act of a tragedy which had been nearing its conclusion for years now, ever since the Beatles finished doing everything he imagined they could do. Ambition is rarely an end to itself, but when you run out of dreams, you run out of life.

"remember when all those people said you were dead? that was a hoax, right?"

Rather, Sutcliffe became a talisman of sorts, a spectral watchdog both guarding and guiding the band he'd left behind, but more than that: a fulfillment of the same mystic incantation which has since grown up around Elvis Presley's stillborn twin Jesse Gason—the firstborn (one month Ringo's senior, Sutcliffe would have been the oldest Beatle) who dies so that the other might triumph.

Surprisingly perhaps, this particular theme remained undeveloped through the Beatles' lifetime, even among the fervid death-cultists whose convictions prematurely buried McCartney only five years after Sutcliffe was laid to rest.[3] Neither have more recent years, and in particular, the surge of interest in Sutcliffe that accompanied 1994's *Backbeat* biopic, allowed for any subsequent inquiries: John Lennon's death, in December 1980, ensured that.

But Sutcliffe's spirit does linger on. In 1995, New York's Govinda Gallery staged the first-ever exhibition of Sutcliffe's artwork in the United States; the following year, his art and writings were reproduced through a major biography by Pauline Sutcliffe and Kay Williams. His artwork has even appeared on a record jacket by the British band Mansun. He is a tangible presence in the ever-blossoming bootleg market which still surrounds the Beatles; he is seen and heard, too, in the 1995 *Anthology* series. But one also gets the feeling that he would not have lasted the pace.

Like Pete Best, the only other member of the Beatles who summons up any kind of presence in the majority of surviving Hamburg-era photographs, Sutcliffe just did not seem to fit. Black leather and beshaded, so much cooler than his fellows, he disrupted the symmetry, and stole too much thunder. And besides, as the Rolling Stones discovered during Brian Jones's career-long estrangement from the rest of the band, four's company . . . five's just looking for trouble. And trouble, of course, was what the Rolling Stones got.

On the one hand, Brian Jones was the multitalented Lothario who powered the self-styled Greatest Rock'n'Roll Band in the World through its most vital years; the sacrificial lamb led blindly to the slaughter by the greed and guile of the friends he trusted—the original butterfly broken on the wheel. On the other hand, he was a two-faced, conniving swine; greedy, cruel, violent, boorish; and a bitter little boy who never forgave anyone for what happened to the Stones, because he wasn't the one who made it happen. His death was a tragedy, but it was also a release, from his own suffering and everyone else's.

"When I heard that he'd drowned," one former Stones associate remarked, "my

Standing from l.: Bill Wyman, Charlie Watts, Keith Moon, Brian Jones. Sitting from l.: Yoko Ono, Julian Lennon, John Lennon, Eric Clapton (Globe Photos)

only regret was that I wasn't there to hold him under." And the conspiracy authors who have spent the three decades since Jones' death trying to prove that someone in fact was there to do that, certainly pricked up their ears at that. But a police investigation, reopened in the wake of a string of early-1990s allegations, came up blank, and the one man who claimed that he knew all about the murder from the murderer himself, recanted as soon as he was called in for questioning.

According to Bill Wyman, "What happened was, this guy, Tom Keylock, who was a wally in himself, had driven us to some TV show, so Brian took him on as his driver

"Remember when all those people said you were dead? that was a hoax, right?"

and dogsbody. When Anita [Pallenberg, Jones' girlfriend] left Brian to go with Keith, Keith took Keylock to work with him, but he kind of hung around with Brian as well, to do things. So when Brian died, he was on the scene and all that.

"Anyway, he [Keylock] told this author that he went to see Frank Thoroughgood, the builder who was working on Brian's house when he died, and Thoroughgood said, on his deathbed, that he'd murdered Brian. So, that was the story. But the moment it started coming out in the English press, the police got in touch with Keylock, interviewed him, and he denied everything. He said he was just saying that for this author's book, and that was the end of it. But of course, the story just kept going."

Of course it did; how could it do anything else? Like the best-crafted mystery thriller it might still become (fact, after all, has long been exhausted, but fiction has barely had a look), all the composite elements were already in place: greed and jealousy, money and motive.

The Internet, the electronic grapevine of the late 1990s, still crawls with fresh suggestions, solutions, portents, and pointings: the Stones had him killed because they were worried that a solo Jones (he had quit the band just weeks before) might usurp the group; the mob ordered him killed because of a drug bust that went sour. The only suspect missing was Winnie-the-Pooh, in whose house Jones was now living, and who was doubtless shocked to the core of his stuffing by the Bacchanalian excesses to which he was now a spectral witness.

Andrew Loog Oldham, the man who discovered the Rolling Stones, seeing them for the first time ever, in May 1964, remembered his first sight of Jones, seated on a stool, "stage left and smiling, ugly and pretty, hulk more than hunk, shining blond hair on a face which already looked as though it had a few unpaid bills with life round its neck/no-neck. His head slipped straight into a subliminally deformed Greystoke body, while his eyes darted round the room, sussing the reaction before the audience even reacted."

It was the eyes that captivated Oldham from the start, and the eyes remained his only contact with what Jones was really thinking. "His eyes always gave him away. While you were talking, he was planning, and it didn't matter what you wanted to do, he was making up his mind about what suited him." And that was as true the last time Oldham ever saw him, four years later, during the crazy, hazed recording of the Stones' *Their Satanic Majesties' Request*.

"Brian was seriously intelligent," Wyman confirmed, "incredibly well spoken, and he had a great brain, very sharp, very quick." If there were any drawbacks to

Brian Jones (Globe Photos)

these attributes, he insisted, they date back to Jones' days as a struggling, starving bluesman. "When he was living on that level, he used those talents to con people, and steal, and all that kind of stuff, just to get by, to exist. So he got a kind of a reputation of being a bit crafty and a bit that way inclined.

"But I found him on many occasions to be very, very sweet. I used to hang out with him a lot on tour, all the way through the sixties, because Mick [Jagger] and Keith [Richards] would stay in their hotel writing songs, so me and Brian used to loon about, and get all the girls, and go out to all the clubs and sit in with the bands, and do things like that."

By 1966, however, those days were fast receding. Already asthmatic, and increasingly prone to fainting fits, Jones drove his body and soul to the limits. Living a dream even Fellini could not share, posing in Nazi regalia for the cameras, and then picking up groupies with whom he could live out further fantasies, Jones was losing his way, spiritually, emotionally, and physically.

One cold London morning, photographer Gered Mankowitz convened the Stones on London's Primrose Hill, to shoot the cover for their next album, *Between the Buttons*. And it was only later, while he was inspecting the contact sheets, that Mankowitz realized what had been on his mind all morning. "It's strange," he told Andrew Oldham, "but if you look through all the shots, there's one consistent factor in every one: Brian. In every one, it looks like he really wasn't there."

Mankowitz was right. In some shots, Jones appeared to have been superimposed into the group shot; in others, his head might have been cut out of a separate picture entirely, then pasted into place. "In every one, you could see the rest of the Stones work toward, capture, and then slip away from the moment when they and Gered were on," Oldham explained. "Brian, though, I didn't know what he was on, or where he was while he was on it. But in every last picture, the only thing that was clear about him was how absolutely wasted he was."

Wyman had reached much the same conclusion. "Brian got into anything that was stuck in front of him. At first, he'd take it for the fun of it, because he was a party guy, and I saw him in some very strange situations when he'd taken acid and I was straight. He'd be bopping about, saying, 'Oh, look at all the snakes and spiders walking across the pavement,' and I couldn't quite relate to that; it was all like that, 'Look, they're writing in flames on the ceiling, isn't it lovely?' 'Yeah Brian, great.'

"So, he could be really, really great. But other times he could be a real asshole, a real nasty piece of work. He kinda learned to be like that from the poverty period, having a problem with his family, but now, he was kind of ostracized by everyone, including the other members of the band, Andrew, all those people didn't like him. He was browbeaten, trodden down; then he lost his girlfriend to Keith, and then everything went from under his feet. Things got quite nasty at times. I hung around with him as much as I could, to try and keep him going, and Charlie [Watts, drummer] was pretty good as well. But there came a point when you couldn't, because he was so out of it, and it didn't matter who was there."

By mid-1967, Jones's decay was no secret. Neither was his drug use, and over the next year, he would be in and out of the courts, desperately defending himself against yet another possession charge, while a battery of psychiatrists attested to his mental health. Jail, they implied, could easily kill him—assuming he didn't kill himself first.

The Stones, too, were at their wits' end. Jones was still nominally a member of the group, but his contributions amounted to so little, that on the occasions he did turn up in the studio, he was simply left in a corner to sleep off his latest excesses, whatever they were. Occasionally he might be handed an instrument, but he rarely played it—and when he did, it wouldn't be plugged in. On one possibly apocryphal, but certainly realistic, occasion, Jones asked Jagger, "What can I play?" Jagger replied, "I don't know, Brian; what *can* you play?"

Jimmy Miller, the American producer who had replaced Oldham at the helm earlier in the year, once remarked that if he didn't already know otherwise, he'd never have guessed Jones was a member of the Stones. And he regretted until his own dying day[4] that he was never given the chance to work with the guitarist at his peak.

On June 8, 1969, Jones quit the Rolling Stones. A terse press statement issued on Jones' behalf said simply, "I no longer see eye-to-eye with the discs we are cutting."

The previous November, Jones had purchased Cotchford Farm, the sprawling house in Hartfield, Sussex, where author A. A. Milne created Winnie-the-Pooh. It was an idyllic escape, and Jones adored the place. It was there, on the evening of July 3, that his girlfriend, Anna Wohlin, discovered his body lying at the bottom of the swimming pool.

The coroner returned a verdict of misadventure, reporting that Jones drowned "while under the influence of alcohol and drugs." And though it would not be long before the rumors began circulating, Bill Wyman, at least, had no argument with the official findings. "The thing with Brian was just a horrible accident. He was always doing silly things like a lot of sleepers, and then bottles of brandy on top of that, and I know what that can do to people. I've seen it: you just zonk out; so you can imagine what would happen in a bloody swimming pool."

"Remember when all those people said you were dead? that was a hoax, right?"

Jones was a martyr to his asthma and his fainting fits. "It was something you didn't really talk about when people had something weird like that," Wyman admitted. "You kind of left them alone for a few minutes and they were all right again. And Brian really was a bit strange like that. But other people I've heard stories from, said he used to just fall over backwards; he'd be asleep, so they just used to put him on a bed for half an hour, then he'd wake up and he'd be normal. Something like that could have happened in the pool as well.

"But whatever happened, it was just an unfortunate accident. I don't believe there was anybody else involved. I don't see the reason. Why would they? He was a pathetic guy, there was no good motive; he'd left the band, he wasn't interfering with anyone else's life, there was nothing there. He was just a pathetic, wasted guy who had a huge problem with drugs, who had psychological problems, who had health problems." And, with an understatement that could have been Jones' epitaph, Wyman concluded, "He really was quite unwell."

THE WORDS SLIPPED OUT before he even thought of them. When Ronnie Lane got the phone call telling him that his old bandmate Steve Marriott had died in a house fire, his response summed up more than fourteen years of his own suffering, and prefaced another six years more.

"I'm jealous," he said. And he meant it.

One-quarter of the Small Faces, one of the great legends of the Britpop sixties, Lane learned he was suffering from multiple sclerosis in 1977. It was a disease that had afflicted his mother for as long as he could remember—Small Faces drummer Kenny Jones recalled how he and Lane used to carry Lane's mother up and down the stairs at the block of flats where she lived in London's East End, a near-helpless cripple with nothing more to look forward to than the once- or twice-a-year trips to the seaside organized by Britain's Multiple Sclerosis Society. There she would be wheelchaired down to the boardwalk, with a blanket over her knees, and left to look out at the sea until teatime. *"They'd take you off in a Cripples Coach,"* her son would sing years later, *"to sit by the Crippled Sea. Gonna have a Cripple Party!"* Now, as he contemplated his own future, he knew that very soon he'd be attending that party himself.

The illness started slowly, mysteriously: sudden bouts of double vision, a numb feeling in one arm. "You kind of wonder, 'I wonder what that is?' And it would go away, so you wouldn't take much notice. "So next time it came, you'd sit it out and wait for it to go away. And then the numbness, each time it comes back, it's a little bit worse, a fraction worse. Y'know, it's got plenty of time to work on you. It's in no hurry to knock you down straightaway." It would continue working on Lane for another twenty years. By comparison, his career in rock'n'roll lasted little more than a decade.

Yet he crammed a lot into it. With Marriott by his side, Lane wrote the Small Faces into history, as co-author of all their greatest hits: "Itchycoo Park," "Tin Soldier," "Here Comes the Nice," "Lazy Sunday." When the Small Faces broke up in 1969, Lane regrouped their resources around Rod Stewart and Ron Wood, and powered a new band, the Faces, through their finest hours. The boozy-boys-together challenged the Rolling Stones for their rock'n'roll crown, and came closer than most to snatching it. Only when Stewart's solo star wholly eclipsed the Faces' did Lane leave, in 1973. But though he was out, he never was down.

Ian McLagan, Kenny Jones, Ron Wood, Ronnie Lane, Bill Wyman, and Rod Stewart
(Globe Photos)

Ronnie Lane's Slim Chance, a self-deprecating name for a self-deprecating band, was born with high hopes, and though they rapidly subsided, Lane seemed undismayed. A big hit with "How Long" was followed by an ambitious attempt to play rock'n'roll within a traveling circus. Three albums were released to adoring critical praise, and when "The Poacher" became the most incomprehensible non-hit of 1975, Lane simply gave up chasing the charts. He started working when he felt like working, recording new albums when he felt like recording, messing around with Ronnie Wood and Pete Townshend . . . and then he fell ill.

It had started in his left arm and hand. One day he went to add some bass guitar to a song he'd just written, and he couldn't do it. "It was really odd. It was like my arm had become a piece of dead meat that was attached to my body. You go to lift it up or something, and there's nothing there. All of the connections . . . there's no connection to it. It's like a lump of dead meat hanging off your shoulder." At first, MS was only "suspected," but still it was devastating news. Lane was just thirty-one years old. "It's very hard to believe that that's happening to you. It's the kind of thing you'd have nightmares about, I suppose."

Retiring to his farm in Wales, Lane threw himself into a new life, breeding sheep and chickens, only to have the icy winter of 1978–'79 wipe out much of his stock. He sold the farm and returned to London, and it was there that his uncertain future first hit him.

He started drinking heavily, to kill the pain and dampen the despair. What difference did it make, after all? Even when he was sober, his body behaved as though he were drunk, as the disease ravaged his system and left him reeling, slurring, unstable. Kenny Jones noticed, "He seemed very forgetful, slurred his words and tripped up a lot. We accused him of being drunk and having a secret tipple. But he wasn't."

Tentatively Lane tried his hand at a musical comeback, but no matter how high his critical stock could rise, his illness always hauled him back down again. His marriage broke up. He was depressed and antisocial, and on July 31, 1981, a major attack—a complete loss of mobility and power—left him suicidal as well. But he didn't have the strength to do even that. "There was all sorts of people topping themselves quite successfully," he bemoaned. "Keith Moon went.[1] Then John Bonham went.[2] Then Lennon got shot. Believe it, if anybody wanted to get there it was me! And all these fellas was doing it effortlessly!"

Rolling Stone Bill Wyman, one of Lane's oldest friends, visited him toward the end of the year, and was horrified by what he found, a man in his early thirties, reduced to the state of someone three times that age. By the new year, the Stones as a whole were rallying around him, paying for Lane to fly to Florida and take part in a radical new treatment for MS. Fred Sessler's Miami Venom Institute, as its name would imply, utilized snake venom as a remedy for MS, and with some success—Keith Richards' aunt was among Sessler's past clients.

Lane, too, was convinced the treatment was making a difference. When friends asked how it was going, he'd joke, "Well, a mosquito bit me today, and it died." But according to his girlfriend of the time, Boo Oldfield, all it really did was make him smell like a snake. "I really felt he was being poisoned," she admitted. "And he was so enthusiastic about it that he kept on upping the dose! It was terrible! He smelled of a snake! He started smelling of a snake!"

He got his energy back, though, and in April 1982, Lane gave one of the greatest solo concert performances of his life.

The setting was not the most grandiose he'd ever visited. Dingwalls, in north London's Camden Town, was just another of those late-night watering holes to which the British music industry gravitated when there was nothing else to do. But he was alive with passion and conviction, running through a set which seemed to reprise every great hit he'd ever been associated with, from the Small Faces through his recent collaborations with Pete Townshend, and winding up with "The Poacher" and "Debris," the most beautiful of all the songs in the Faces' repertoire.

It was always a sad song—gently nostalgic, regret tinged with evocative sorrow—but there was something about the way Lane sang it that night, a half-cocked smile playing around the words, and a catch in his voice as he clutched the mike stand to steady himself. He usually reserved "Debris" for a simple last encore. Tonight it was more like a good-bye.

In its early stages at least, multiple sclerosis is a cruelly deceptive disease, weakening but never quite flattening its sufferers, always allowing them an element of hope, even defiance. "If you've got a defeatist attitude it'll certainly get you down," Lane swore. "And, of course, the way the disease comes on, it's whole strategy is to make you feel defeatist. You get so weak. You get unbelievably weak! I mean, I've never been a strong man, but I never realized what 'weak' meant until I got MS. You haven't even got the strength to *think* straight!"

Before the show, signing autographs and chatting, Lane gently but brusquely shook off a fan who moved to help him step offstage. Onstage later, he still fought for control, but it was clearly a losing battle. Dingwalls sang along to "Debris," adoring and triumphant, but the lustiest voices had a crack in the back, and a few people coughed so you wouldn't hear them choke. Then Ronnie was gone, from that stage, from every stage. But he never stopped battling.

"The last thing you want to hear [is] the thing that people with MS are being told: 'Relax. Don't do anything. Relax. Don't worry. The wheelchair's in the hall, and it's awaiting you.' The whole thing is crazy! I'd say, 'Nuts! You forget all that! You fuck!' Like, 'fuck!' [You have to] start fighting it, and then I think you've got a chance of getting on top of it. But you don't just let it insidiously crawl all over you, because it certainly will. Cor! I've got a long way to go yet, but I'm gonna beat this thing. I know I am. I think I've got the fight I've always wanted!!"

Lane was equally defiant in August, when *Rolling Stone* journalist Kurt Loder caught up with him, to pen the article that would finally make Lane's sufferings public knowledge. But he also seemed sadly resigned. "How can I describe it? Can you imagine the strands of your hair hurting? That's what happens. And when you blink, it's like your eyelids are made of sandpaper. I was quite prepared to feel bad, like with the flu or mumps. But I've never had anything like this. This is like hell itself."

He was off the snake venom, and trying out steroids. Oldfield said he looked like a hamster with its cheeks full of food. Then he heard of another treatment, involving hyperbaric oxygen chambers (HBOs), and rushed to them with renewed hope.

Long-employed to treat bedsores, gangrene, and the aftereffects of surgical amputations, HBOs were still considered controversial in the treatment of MS. There were two units operating in London hospitals at the time, but both were off-limits to MS sufferers, except under stringent experimental conditions. According to Oldfield, however, "the HBO treatment [is] the only thing I can honestly say [has helped], with diets and everything else. After he had the first twenty treatments of HBO, it's the first time I ever saw anything really positive that's happened to him. Living with it, you watch all the time. You just watch for anything!

"He was up until midnight for about two weeks! He was writing music! He was walking without his sticks! He had enough energy and strength to walk without his sticks!" Even more encouragingly, the effects of the twenty-course treatment lasted for up to two weeks before he began to run down again. So when Lane heard that the Action Research into Multiple Sclerosis (ARMS) research charity was actively trying to raise funds to purchase an HBO unit of its own, he immediately pledged his support.

"I walked around for years wondering why I'd got the bloody thing," Lane cursed, "and suddenly I got the answer: What better fellow to get it? Because I can do something."

Throughout the summer of 1983, Boo Oldfield began rallying support for Lane among his old friends and colleagues. Lane himself was in the dark about her activities for some weeks—Oldfield later joked that he suspected she was having an affair, there was so much whispering and giggling going on.

By August, however, he was fully involved, and the following month, London's Royal Albert Hall played host to the first superstar ARMS benefit concert, headlined by an impressive list of guests: Eric Clapton, Jimmy Page, Jeff Beck, Steve Winwood, Charlie Watts and Bill Wyman all performed, but the highlight—inevitably—was the final song, when Lane himself took the stage, to perform the old Leadbelly favorite, "Goodnight Irene."

In November, the same supergroup convened to play nine shows around the U.S. Two years later, Wyman gathered more of his mates together for the similarly intentioned Willie and the Poor Boys project. Rod Stewart, perennially pilloried for allegedly ignoring his old friend's plight, joined the gang in 1986, when the now wheelchair-bound Lane took the stage alongside him at London's Wembley Stadium. A decade later, Stewart invited Lane to appear with him on a TV special. In a business universally reviled for its selfishness and greed, Ronnie Lane received nothing but goodwill from everyone who knew him.

But goodwill was suddenly all he had. No sooner had Lane announced that he was preparing to leave the U.K. to seek treatment in America, than he learned the country's charity laws forbade the money raised on his behalf from leaving with him. He moved anyway, undergoing treatment in Houston, Texas, but life in the U.S. was no easier than it had been at home—particularly after money raised for an American branch of ARMS disappeared, and Lane was called upon to try and account for it.

Standing in court while the former manager of ARMS U.S.A. accused him of taking "premeditated advantage" of the organization was devastating; even though Lane was swiftly exonerated of any involvement in the scandal, the very accusation affected him badly. For a time he even considered returning to England, though he knew the standards of treatment were vastly more limited than they were in America. But after a brief return to London, he was flying back to Texas.

"I found that Texas was kind of happier, a happier place for me to live with my condition. Even though it's hot, as long as I stay in air-conditioning, it's okay. England is so dreary, you know. We have twenty-four hours of summer, that's all we get in England. And in Texas, you see a lot of sunshine."

He settled in Austin, and over the next few years, he would both relaunch his musical career, yet again, and fall in love once more. Susan, who became his third wife in 1989, was his nurse, and would remain alongside him everywhere: a broadening swath around town; a brief American tour in 1991; and as far afield as Japan, where Lane reunited with another former Small Face, Ian MacLagen, for a short spring tour that same year. But the disease never went away, and when Lane returned home, he was feeling as bad as he ever had. And then he heard about Steve Marriott's death.

Since quitting the Small Faces, Steve Marriott's musical fortunes ebbed and flowed as dramatically as Lane's. On top of the world with Humble Pie, even as Lane was sparking the Faces to glory, Marriott then drifted through the remainder of the 1970s and early 1980s in a haze of well-intentioned but strangely doomed projects. There was Steve Marriott's All Stars; there was the Packet of Three; there was a partial Small Faces reunion; there was even an attempt to resuscitate Humble Pie. Nothing worked. But in 1990, a face from the past rolled around who seemed destined to set the record straight once and for all.

Long before his solo career came alive in 1975, Peter Frampton worked alongside Marriott in the first incarnation of Humble Pie. Now, Frampton declared, he wanted "to form a four-piece band à la Humble Pie, and in looking for the other guitarist/singer/writer, I couldn't help but compare everyone to Steve. So I called him up and asked him what he thought of the idea of getting together."

The pair hadn't worked together in almost two decades, but Frampton flew to England, and he and Marriott reignited their partnership within hours. They wrote a song together that same day.

"Before I headed back to L.A. [in January 1991], Steve played what was to be his last show in England, at the Half Moon [pub in] Putney. I jammed with him that night, and needless to say, I'll never forget that gig. It was great to see Steve play, and unbelievable to be on the same stage, playing together again."

The following month, Marriott and his wife, Toni, joined Frampton in L.A. and over the next six weeks, the pair recorded, pieced together a group, and set up a record deal. Finally, on April 20, Marriott flew back to England to sort out a few things. He would rejoin the guitarist in the studio upon his return.

By the time Marriott and Toni reached their home village of Arkesden, Essex, they were absolutely exhausted, but too excited to sleep. Everything was coming together at last. Instead of going to bed, then, they called a friend, garage owner Ray Newbrook, and asked him to join them at a local restaurant for a celebratory meal.

Humble Pie: Peter Frampton, Jerry Shirley, Greg Ridley, and Steve Marriott
(Hulton Gertly-Liaison)

The party carried on at Newbrook's home, but finally the pair had had enough. "[They] were dead on their feet from jet lag," Newbrook said later. "I put them both to bed, but a few minutes later, Steve got up and said he wanted to sleep in his own bed. I called him a cab and he went home alone. Toni stayed where she was."

Back home, Marriott settled down with a nightcap, a drink and a cigarette.

It didn't even cross his mind that he should probably lay off the alcohol, after the cocaine he'd taken earlier in the evening, and the Valium he'd dropped to help him through the flight, and later it was revealed that the combination of drink and drugs coursing through his system was bordering on lethal in its own right. But he did awake in the night, to discover his bedroom ablaze, and his lungs filled with the choking black smoke.

He leaped out of bed toward the door he thought would lead him to safety, away from the burning room. He leaped the wrong way. According to Police Inspector Martin Reed, "There were doors on either side of the bed." One led to the hallway, the other opened into an airing cupboard. Marriott's smoldering body was discovered there by firemen. The cause of death was smoke inhalation; the cause of the fire was that final cigarette.

Marriott's death plunged Ronnie Lane into one of the deepest depressions he had ever known. It left him mourning a friend, but also mourning the sheer senselessness of the tragedy.

In the months that followed, Lane's health declined rapidly. He was too ill even to sing now, and though he continued to play his guitar, his publicist, Charlie Comer, said, "Every time he struck a chord, you could see he was in torment." While Kenny Jones and Ian MacLagan battled to raise more money to pay for his treatment, fought through the courts to win back years of unpaid royalties from past Small Faces records, all Lane could do was wait—for death, or for a miracle. In his own mind, they were much the same thing.

In February 1993, Lane was back in Houston, undergoing a fresh bout of HBO treatment; a little over a year later, he and Susan moved from Austin to the Rocky Mountain mining town of Trinidad, Colorado. It was there he celebrated his fiftieth birthday, on April 1, 1996. It was there, too, that he would die.

Lane was admitted to the hospital for what would be the last time, in May 1997. Now even his specialists acknowledged there was nothing more they could do for him, and on June 4, he was told he had just two to four months left to live. In fact, he had two to four hours. Lane died at home that same day. He'd finally had enough of other people's promises.

when my time is up, i'll see all my friends

THE STORY OF BRITISH FOLK ROCK is the story of Fairport Convention; and the story of Fairport Convention, as the cliché writers love to say, is the story of tragedy.

It is a legend Fairport themselves have done much to encourage, every year, as they conclude their annual reunions at the Cropredy Folk Festival in England with the one song from their three-decade career that simultaneously symbolizes both the beliefs that kept the musicians together, and the losses that came so close to destroying them.

Perhaps, as countless writers have pointed out over the years, Fairport guitarist Richard Thompson really did write "Meet on the Ledge" about a childhood game which involved climbing trees (and the ledge really was the limb where he always got stuck). But as Fairport biographer Patrick Humphries explained, still, the song "is entwined with tragic memories . . . a song of depth, of parting and reunion, a song of premonition and eventual hope." It was also Martin Lamble's favorite song, the one that would be played at his funeral.

On the night of May 12, 1969, Fairport Convention were returning to London from a gig in Birmingham, England. Singer Sandy Denny was traveling back separately, in a car driven by her boyfriend (and future husband) Trevor Lucas. The rest of Fairport were spread around the band's van: guitarist Simon Nicol, suffering from a migraine, was crashed out on the floor in the back; drummer Martin Lamble, bassist Ashley Hutchings, and the band's American friend, Jeannie Franklyn, sat around him. Thompson was seated next to driver Harvey Bramham, and the moment he realized that something was wrong, felt the van was skewing off the highway, the guitarist grabbed the wheel.

Too hard. With a stomach-churning lurch, the vehicle cartwheeled off the road, somersaulting through the air while its cargo, human and musical, hurtled through windows which suddenly burst, and doors that flung themselves wide. Crashing through the central median, miraculously passing unscathed through the oncoming traffic, the van finally came to rest forty feet down an embankment, upside down on a Mill Hill golf course.

"I can remember waking up while the van was actually somersaulting," Nicol described. "I was the only one in the vehicle." Driver Bramham was lying some ninety feet ahead of the van, thrown through the windshield, and lucky to be alive. Thompson and Hutchings, his face a mask of blood from a broken nose and cheekbone, were simply standing there, dazed. Away in the distance, a shape which resolved itself to be Lamble, lay without moving. Another, Jeannie Franklyn, lay close by. She was already dead when the ambulance arrived.

Lamble, though, still had a chance. Henry Smieth, a seaman friend of the nineteen-year-old drummer, was told how "[the ambulance] took everyone to the hospital in Stanmore, and Martin went straight into surgery. They worked on him for hours, but it was too late, his injuries were too serious." Lamble never regained consciousness, and died in the early hours of May 13.

The band members, who had now been together for two years, scattered to the winds. Producer Joe Boyd, who was in the States at the time arranging for Fairport's debut at the Newport Folk festival, flew home immediately, then returned to L.A. with his shattered charges: Denny and Lucas, Nicol and Thompson. They stayed wherever friends asked them. Hutchings stayed in England, to contemplate alone the horror which had torn apart the band he had dreamed of since he was a child.

The Electric Dysentry Band, Dr. K's Blues Band, Tim Turner's Narration—the revolving door of musicians who would eventually resolve themselves into Fairport Convention went through any number of names. But it was in 1966 that the eclectic brew that fermented in Hutchings' mind finally reached maturity, with the arrival (in the Ethnic Shuffle Orchestra, another of Hutchings' passing fancies) of guitarist Richard Thompson and drummer Martin Lamble.

The band was packing up their gear after a gig in Golders Green, recalled Nicol, "when this chap came up to us in a parka—his Lambretta was parked outside—and announced himself to be Martin Lamble from Harrow" . . . and a far better drummer than the current one. He auditioned the following week, and joined the band on the spot.

Music was only one of the seventeen-year-old Lamble's loves; according to his brother Robin, if he hadn't been a drummer, he would probably have become a railroad signalman. But now the die was cast, and with the addition of vocalists Judy Dyble and Ian Matthews, the newly named Fairport Convention set about establishing themselves on the London underground circuit.

Their first, eponymous album would capture the group's mood-perfect re-creations of the sound (if not the songs) of London's American counterpart, the West Coast confections of bands Jefferson Airplane and Love. Several times, Fairport took the stage as the emcee introduced them, "all the way from Hollywood," and over the next year or so, they played up the comparison for all it was worth. Then Dyble left, to be replaced by Sandy Denny, and suddenly there was nothing Fairport could have been compared to.

The band first saw her, lining up with the other aspirants at the first post-Dyble rehearsal, standing out, Nicol said, "like a clean glass in a sinkful of dirty dishes."

Unhalfbricking, Fairport's third album, and the second with Denny, was just weeks away from release when Lamble was killed; the band was still in America when it appeared, slowly recovering from their disaster. The only consolation, Nicol mused, was that they had already been through the worst thing that could happen to them. Now it was their friends and admirers who were feeling the worst pain, and the flood of sympathy that surrounded the group—a bouquet from the Rolling Stones, a telegram from the Beatles, and benefit concerts the whole country over—only served to remind him of that.

Bit by bit, Fairport reconstituted itself. Drummer Dave Mattacks was recruited from a professional dance band; violinist Rick Grech was borrowed from the rock band Family, before giving way to folk legend Dave Swarbrick. And that fall, Fairport released *Liege and Lief*, the folk-rock album classic which would set the scene for all the band would accomplish over the next decade.

Yet as swiftly as they came to it, both Hutchings and Denny abandoned the course that album carved out: Hutchings to escape the group's electric bastardization of traditional music; Denny to concentrate on her own songwriting, first with a new band, Fotheringay, then across three solo albums. She would rejoin Fairport in 1974 (by which time husband Lucas had been a member for two years), quit again the following year, and Fairport's tongue was only partly in cheek when they placed an ad in the music press searching for a female vocalist who could "sing like an angel, look like a dream onstage, possess that indefinable charisma, and be able to start the chorus at least sixteen bars before anybody else." She should also have her husband in tow; Lucas left Fairport at the same time as Denny.

Through 1976 and 1977, Sandy recorded her fourth solo album, *Rendezvous*, then toured Britain following the birth of her first child, Georgia. She was suffering a cold at the time, but the concerts were a revelation regardless, and early 1978 found Trevor Lucas ensconced in the studio, mixing tapes of the final show for a proposed live album.

He completed work in late March (the album was finally released in 1998!), but behind the scenes, his life with Sandy was collapsing. She never had been a moderate drinker, even while she was carrying Georgia, but now she seemed to spend most of her time at the bar—while the baby sat screaming in the car outside. For Trevor, however, the last straw came when a drunken Sandy fell down the stairs, with Georgia in her arms. He booked an airline ticket back to his parents' home in Australia, packed a few of his own and the baby's clothes, then early in the morning of April 13, he scooped Georgia into her baby carrier and told Sandy he was going to visit his sister in London.

That evening Trevor called a friend, schoolteacher Miranda Ward, to tell her he was leaving Sandy. Sandy rang the same number a couple of hours later, and was given the news. Then Ward drove around to pick her up, and insisted Sandy stay with her for the next few days.

The following morning, Sandy awoke with a blinding headache, the latest in a succession she had been suffering in recent months. She dated them back to a tumble she'd taken at her parents' house, when she cracked her head on a stone floor; foolishly, she didn't do anything about it at the time, but when the next morning—Sunday—brought another onslaught of pain, Sandy finally admitted she should visit her doctor. She made an appointment for the following afternoon.

When Miranda left for work that Monday morning, Sandy was sleeping. When she got home, the singer was in the hospital. A friend, musician Jon Cole, had dropped by the apartment that afternoon and found Sandy unconscious on the floor at the foot of a flight of stairs.

when my time is up, I'll see all my friends

Sandy Denny
(Courtesy Island Records)

All that evening, April 17, Sandy lay in a coma at Queen Mary's Hospital in near-by Roehampton. She had suffered a monstrous brain hemorrhage, and already had been placed on life support. Two days later she was transferred to Atkinson Morley Hospital, home to some of the country's leading specialists, and underwent brain surgery. But it was hopeless. Sandy died a little before 8 p.m. on the night of April 20. The cause of death was "mid-brain trauma." Damage caused by that earlier fall, onto her parents' stone floor, had erupted first in the form of worsening headaches, and then, it seemed, in the blinding flash which had caught Sandy just as she began descending the stairs. She collapsed, and crashed down the remainder of the flight.

Sandy was buried a few days later at Putney Vale Cemetery, piped into eternity, coincidentally enough, by the same traditional lament, "Flowers of the Forest," as had echoed over American singer Phil Ochs' grave, following his suicide in April 1976. Ochs' favorite cousin was Jeannie Franklyn, the artist and tailor who had died with Martin Lamble—and so, as Sandy sang in "Meet on the Ledge," *it all comes round again.*"[1]

There were, within the tangled community of Fairport folkies, rumors that Sandy's accident was not all that it seemed. In 1980, during demo sessions Richard and Linda Thompson recorded two songs Sandy had included on *Rendezvous*—"I'm a Dreamer" and "For Shame of Doing Wrong"; and a new song called "Did She Jump or Was She Pushed?" was the subject of so much speculation that Richard Thompson was constantly required to explain himself.

No, the song wasn't about Sandy's death specifically, but that qualification itself did not put rumors to rest. Neither did his insistence that "[it] is a journalistic song. You're not making judgments, you're recording events, recording someone's path through something—which path people choose to take."

The path Sandy Denny took was that of the greatest vocalist in British rock history, and though the years since her death have tended to bracket her purely within the folk mold her actual repertoire barely hinted in that particular direction.

Her contributions to Led Zeppelin's "Battle of Evermore," a track from their self-titled fourth album, and to producer Lou Reizner's *Tommy* stage-show soundtrack, both highlighted her ability to step completely out of character. She took this process to its furthest extreme when she teamed with a motley bunch of fellow "folkies" to record a tribute to the 1950s rock'n'roll they'd all grown up on, under the pseudonym of the Bunch.

Her four solo albums, too, abound with spectacular moments of musical eclecticism, ethereal and earthy in the passing of a breath. Kate Bush, whose own career got under way, ironically, just as Denny's ended, frequently referenced Sandy as an influence, name-checking her in one song ("Blow Away"); and following Denny's own rearrangement of another song, Elton John's "Candle in the Wind."[2] Linda Thompson, one of Denny's cohorts in the Bunch, expressed a common complaint, however, when she remarked that "a lot of [Sandy's] really brilliant songs got lost because you were listening to song after song that was a wee bit down.

"But when you take them out of that and put them in a different setting, people appreciate them for what they are." Throughout her singing years (she retired in the mid-1980s), Thompson herself rarely sounded more inspired than when she was performing one of Denny's compositions, and she admitted she was constantly battling with Richard to include some of Denny's songs in the duo's live set. She sel-

when my time is up, i'll see all my friends

dom won. "Maybe it would bring back memories for him that he doesn't want to dredge up again."

Dividing his time between Britain and Australia, remarrying, and even rejoining Fairport for occasional shows, Trevor Lucas would expend a lot of time preserving his late wife's memory, most notably compiling the four-CD boxed set, the appropriately titled *Who Knows Where the Time Goes?* Then he, too, passed away early, less than four years after that project came to fruition, and after a few short months of illness. He succumbed to a heart attack at his Epping, New South Wales, Australia, home on February 4, 1989.

Fairport's influence, musical and otherwise, can never be overstated. Singlehandedly, they forced folk music both out of its traditional berth at medieval minstrelsy revival evenings, and out of its more recent insertion into the heart of the transatlantic protest movement.

It was Fairport whose adoption and updating of earlier traditions paved the way for the more esoteric maneuvering of the progressive-rock set; it was Fairport whose absorption of those same techniques into a rock'n'roll framework would father the freedoms that ultimately erupted with the alternative–college radio boom of the late 1980s.

Even before that, however, the likes of Robyn Hitchcock and R.E.M. were incorporating Fairport's researches into their own sonic seminars, and in 1985, Dream Academy scored a monstrous hit single with "Life in a Northern Town," a song both dedicated to, and drawn heavily from, the work of another of the unsung branches of the Fairport family tree, singer-songwriter Nick Drake.

Yet when Nick Drake overdosed and died on November 25, 1974, even his friends and admirers admitted that he was a virtual unknown. Three albums of introspective melancholy, masterminded by Joe Boyd and featuring contributions from as far afield as Richard Thompson and John Cale, had passed by unnoticed; a fourth was in preparation when he died, and would doubtless have suffered the same sad fate.

It would be five years before his record company saw fit to resurrect Drake, responding to a slowly burgeoning cult awareness with a memorial boxed set, *Fruit Tree*, and another decade before that cult itself was finally noticed.

But it was never silent. Beneath the surface, and around the world, Peter Buck, Dream Academy, Lucinda Williams, Kate Bush, Paul Weller, Tom Verlaine, Bernard Butler, and Robyn Hitchcock all lent their voices to the unspoken campaign for

Drake's commercial reawakening. And when it happened, Love and Rockets bassist David J. mused, "It's about time, isn't it? What a gem he was. Cream will always rise."

Yet it is a revival which remains totally uncomplicated by the "what-might-have-beens" that haunt so many other dead artists. As John Lennon's sixtieth birthday rolls ever closer, two decades after his murder, the Internet still buzzes with unanswerable questions about what sort of songs he might be writing now. Five years after Kurt Cobain's death, the hunger for his last demos remains insatiable, in the search for a clue to what he would have done next. Jimi Hendrix's lost fourth album has been "re-created" five times. And spirit mediums still work overtime dictating the music Buddy Holly is writing.

But nobody asks questions about Nick Drake. Nobody wonders aloud about the records would have made as he embraced middle-age in the late 1990s. It is as though the music he recorded between 1969 and 1973 was all he could make, all he needed to make, and the fame attending him in death is simply what he deserved while he lived. "I don't buy the 'posthumous appeal' thing," R.E.M. guitarist Peter Buck explained. "The guitar player from Chicago died,[3] but I don't remember legions of fans going out and buying the first four Chicago albums. The thing with Nick is, I couldn't see him around now, or in the future, age sixty-five and doing the fourth farewell tour. I mean, hindsight is a great thing, isn't it? All the symbols that are there on the records and in the lyrics."

dB's guitarist Peter Holsapple, one of the guiding lights behind a 1997 tribute concert at St. Anne's Church in Brooklyn Heights, continued, "Nobody commits suicide as a career move. The addition of his premature death alongside his beautiful, introspective songs can't help but add a disquieting element to the package. But nobody would remember him had he not left work that was so very moving."

It is that beauty, introspection, and "disquieting element" which marked Drake as something special long before he ever made a record. A tape recorded at Far Leys, the home he shared with his parents in Tanworth-on-Arden, in the English Midlands, around 1966 or 1967, captures the shadow of that melancholy, an English Literature student newly immersed in the music of folk guitarists Bert Jansch and John Renbourne, Tim Buckley and Van Morrison, discovering his own talent for music that had the strength to shake souls.

It was Fairport Convention's Ashley Hutchings who "discovered" the nineteen-year-old Drake, playing solo at a peace concert at London's Roundhouse, in 1968. He got the young singer's number and passed it on to Joe Boyd.

"I've always had a strong taste for melody, and it has obviously been reflected in the people I have worked with," Boyd affirmed. "And it was Nick's melodies that impressed me. There was also a sophistication and maturity about his songs, and the way they were delivered. I really did feel that I was listening to a remarkably original singer."

By the end of the year, Drake's debut album, *Five Leaves Left*, was under way, its title, incidentally, coming from the warning note secreted toward the end of a packet of cigarette rolling papers: only five leaves left. It was only later, after Drake's death, that a more ominous note crept into the picture: At the time of recording, he had only five years left.

"The first strong memory I have of Nick was at the second or third session for *Five Leaves Left*," studio engineer John Wood reflected later. Wood was working with a "well-known" arranger on string parts for a few of the songs, and Drake was growing more and more agitated. Finally, "he dug his heels in, and dismissed the arrangements. He said he'd got this friend, Robert Kirby, [who] would be far more sympathetic to what he was doing. Robert had never before done anything in a studio, but two weeks later we booked him and we were flabbergasted, he was so good."

Nick Drake (Archive Photos)

Having proved he knew both what he wanted and how to get it, Drake would try to retain control of his career, at least, for the rest of his life. He played a handful of shows[4] supporting *Five Leaves Left*, but he hated the experience, admitted that "there were only two or three concerts that felt right," and refused ever to tour again.

Joe Boyd allowed him that privilege; Drake remained in control. It was when that control slipped away, or was taken out of his hands, that he lurched into the despondency which would play such a large part in his death. "Nick's trouble," his actress sister Gabrielle would tell her brother's biographer, Patrick Humphries, "was that he never had [a] tough outside. He was born with a skin too few."

This weakness became especially evident following the release of Drake's second album. *Bryter Layter* was a masterpiece; everyone who heard it said so, with producer Boyd himself convinced that it would make the singer a star. Françoise Hardy, the French chanteuse, was begging Drake to write a song for her, and over at the demo studio where Joe Boyd sometimes recorded reference versions of his clients' songs, a young session pianist named Reginald Dwight let on that he could only dream of writing songs like Drake.

A short while later, Dwight emerged as Elton John, and just occasionally on his first few albums, you could see his dreams coming true.

But though *Bryter Layter* tripled its predecessor's sales of five thousand, it didn't break through, barely broke even, and Drake never recovered from the disappointment—not because he needed fame, friends insist, but because he sincerely believed in the difference that he might make if people heard him.

Drake revealed as much in his first (and only) press interview, with *Sounds*. "I had something in mind when I wrote the songs, knowing that they weren't just for me." Arranger Robert Kirby, too, acknowledged, "He was one of the few people I've met who was ever pure and honest. Maybe he thought that he could change people." And when he realized that he couldn't, he was shattered. Soon after the album's release, with his moods darkening daily, Drake began visiting a psychiatrist.

Counseling didn't help; neither did the course of antidepressants he was prescribed. Drake's father later recalled, "When he did take them, he was a bit better. But then he would stop taking them and say, 'I'm going to get through this my own way.'"

The problem was, he had no idea what his way was going to be. He stopped talking, answering even direct questions with nothing more than a glance, and a mumbled yes or no. After a couple of years living alone in London, he moved back to his parents' home, but a visitor to the house might have thought he was a wax figure, the way he sat without moving in a chair for hours, staring into the distance or down at his shoes.

The only sign of life would be his hands, occasionally twitching as they lay in his lap.

When he did go out, he often returned before he went any distance at all. Other times, he would simply disappear for days on end, driving his family to despair before he wandered back in without a word, as though no time at all had passed since he left. "I just wish I could meet someone who's gone through what I have," Drake told one friend. But what that something was, he never said.

Early in 1972, Drake accepted an invitation to stay, alone, at Island Records head Chris Blackwell's apartment on the Spanish coast. He returned to England strangely invigorated; calling John Wood, he demanded the engineer book him into the studio immediately.

During his interview with *Sounds* the previous year, Drake predicted, "For the next [album], I had the idea of just doing something with John Wood." Now the time was right, and just two nights later, Drake's third album, *Pink Moon*, was complete.

There were no retakes, no arrangements, and only the occasional piano overdub. There weren't many songs, either: eleven titles, but many were little more than fragments, racing by as *Pink Moon* struggled to top 28 minutes. But as Wood himself said later, "If something's that intense, it can't really be measured in minutes."

Years later, Peter Buck would describe the album as Britain's answer to blues legend Robert Johnson's "Hellhound on My Trail"—relentlessly intense, endlessly foreboding. In fact, Drake still had that particular parallel up his sleeve, a tale of pursuit and oppression called "Black Eyed Dog," which, chillingly, would become the last song he ever recorded. But still the comparison is valid. Sparse as its predecessors were lush, bareness replacing baroque, and distant as the horizon he'd spent so many months contemplating, *Pink Moon* was Drake's final word as a living, breathing, recording artist.

Following *Pink Moon*'s completion, Drake admitted himself to a psychiatric hospital, where he spent five weeks before checking out again. He thought about joining the army, but didn't get past his first interview. He started work as a trainee computer programmer, but walked out within hours. He would visit friends, then sit wordlessly for hours, until they forced him to take a walk or play games. One day, John Wood's wife Sheila asked him outright, "If you're so unhappy, why haven't you killed yourself?"

Drake replied, "It's too cowardly. And besides, I don't have the courage."

One night in 1974, Drake returned to the studio with four new songs, the premonitory "Black Eyed Dog" among them. They were the first he'd written in a couple of years, and as he played them through, he acknowledged he'd been having trouble getting his lyrics out. The music was in his head, and he could hear what it wanted to say. But he was numb inside; only he preferred to say he was dead, and now was just waiting to die.

He stopped washing, he stopped eating. He let his fingernails grow long and twisted. The last time Linda Thompson saw him, "I was very shocked, he really did look very ill. I think there's no way Nick could have survived. Absolutely no way at all. He had no survival skills."

Drake's last months read like those of a terminal cancer patient; the gathering gloom, and the sense of an imminent end, and then miraculously, unexpectedly, recovery and remission. One day in October 1974, Drake awoke and announced he wanted to try and live in Paris. He rented a houseboat on the Seine and began learning French. He picked up his guitar again, and talked about writing songs for other people. So what if his own records didn't sell? Maybe someone else's would.

He returned home in early November, and still appeared happy, now disturbed only by the insomnia which had, in any case, haunted him for years. Of course he was still taking his antidepressants, but only because they helped him sleep, he said. And that was what would kill him, an overdose of the Tryptizol he took every night when he climbed into bed, and which kept him sleeping late every morning. What he didn't know—what his doctor neglected to warn him, and nobody else even dreamed of—was how easy it would be to overdose on those tablets. Just one pill over the limit was all it took.

Long after his parents went to bed, the night of November 24, 1974, they could hear Drake moving around his bedroom, working at the old schooldesk that sat in one corner, listening to the Brandenburg Concerto on his record player. Around midnight, he wandered down to the kitchen for a bowl of cereal. His mother, woken by the sound of his footsteps on the stairs, rolled back over and returned to sleep. It was another normal night.

It was noon the following day before she went upstairs to awaken her son, and found him still in his bed, lying beneath his favorite painting, of a wild sea storm. She spoke to him; he didn't respond. Then she realized how utterly, breathlessly silent the room was.

The assistant coroner would later bring in a verdict of suicide, and while Drake's family would contest his findings vigorously, sister Gabrielle now acknowledged, "I personally prefer to think Nick committed suicide, in the sense that I'd rather he died because he wanted to end it, than for it to be the result of a tragic mistake. That would seem to me to be terrible, for it to be a plea for help that nobody hears."

And of course, that tragedy would be amplified, every time it happened again.

7

NICO WAS UNIQUE. She styled herself, or allowed herself to be styled, as an enigma. She had nothing to do with rock'n'roll, but she exerted a fascination which few rock'n'rollers could ever aspire to. And when she died, her legacy left more questions unanswered than she had ever asked in life.

Born in Cologne, Germany, on October 16, 1938, the former Christa Paffgen never surrendered an iota of her true identity. To her friends, to her fans, even to her family, she was simply Nico— named by Chanel, filmed by Fellini, discovered by Andrew Loog Oldham, enshrined by Andy Warhol.

She had a son, Christian Aaron, or Ari, by French film star Alain Delon, and once conducted a wild affair with Iggy Pop. "She taught me how to eat pussy," Pop revealed, but she taught him a lot more than that—she taught him how to perform.

"She would tell me edgy things. 'I think you should be more poisonous as a performer. You are not yet totally poisoned.' The more we were together, the crazier she seemed and the crazier I became.

Nico and Andy Warhol (Globe Photos)

She wanted me to throw glasses into the audience, act mad, angry, violent." Pop drew the line at that, but he did cut himself up onstage, so the principle remained. "She was completely out on a limb," Pop concludes. "She was a pioneer." And she would soon become a legend.

As an actress in the early 1960s, Nico studied under Lee Strasberg, but she drew her lessons from elsewhere, from the superficiality of a society that prized her because she was beautiful. She never made it to Hollywood.

As a model, she flaunted her charms with the best of them, but when the scene began to bore her, she was out of it like a shot. And when she started life as a pop singer, she didn't expect that to last for very long, either.

"I was acting a role that I had to do," she said of her first recordings. "It was like being back with Strasberg. It was fun, really. But I was not acting a role on a stage or on a record. I was acting for contracts. I was too shy to be me, and it's easier to play someone else, isn't it?

"But it's okay, because you become a success and you can live your real life out of sight. That's what Garbo did, and Dietrich. That's what I could do"—and it is, to an extent, what she did. She could have been, with her classic, icy beauty and impenetrable mystique, another Marianne Faithfull, and Andrew Oldham, signing her to his Immediate label in 1965, certainly thought so. But the world to which she was exposed, and which existed within her, could not tolerate such an easy option.

Nico drifted between careers. In 1966, Warhol drafted her into the nascent Velvet Underground, pitching her into the already unstable brew of John Cale and Lou Reed, Mo (Maureen) Tucker and Sterling Morrison,[1] and made sure they gave her some songs to sing. Leaving the group after just one album, she then starred in Warhol's film *Chelsea Girls*, and released a solo album of the same name.

She drifted between lovers—Bob Dylan, Jackson Browne, Brian Jones,[2] Jim Morrison. Four years after she and Morrison exchanged blood, two years to the day after Brian Jones' death, Nico was in Paris when she saw the now fat, bearded singer pass by in a car. "I signaled, but he did not see me. He was looking straight ahead, facing death. He died that night in his bath, of heroin. But I knew his spirit entered me and it was an unbearable load. It meant nothing but pain. Thoughts were flying round my head, male and female. And then you can say that heroin became my lover."

She drifted between her responsibilities. Young Ari was shuttled among friends and family, with his mother the Valkyrie looming into his life on an irregular basis, and taking him away someplace else. Finally, upon his fourteenth birthday, in August 1976, his paternal grandmother applied to formally adopt him. Permission was granted.

And Nico drifted between situations. In 1974, she had a deal with Island Records, an album and a tour. Four years later, Patti Smith came across her in Paris, a penniless junkie who had just lost her last meaningful possession in the world, the harmonium whose droning dominated her records. Smith promptly bought her a new one.

Though any number of established rock idols offered to help her, Nico rejected their offers out of hand, then mocked them in the press. David Bowie, she swore, fantasized the song "Heroes" about her, and pursued her love across Berlin. Leonard Cohen, she said, scared her: "He always behaves in an odd way to me. He always

Sterling Morrison (left) and Nico with the Velvet Underground (Pictorial Press Ltd.)

the dum dum boys

imagines that I would be the ideal girlfriend for him, that I should become his wife or something." And when, shortly before her death, Marc Almond did persuade her into the studio, to record a duet, she dismissed the end result as "a dreadful song by an idiotic man."

Only John Cale, with whom she'd worked in the early Velvets, possessed either the temper or the temperament to successfully capture Nico in the recording studio. Tony Secunda, producer of Cale's classic re-creation of "Heartbreak Hotel," enthused, "Cale was great with Nico, he was the only person who she listened to." And after listening to the three albums Cale and Nico recorded together—*Marble Index* (1969), *Desert Shore* (1970), and *The End*, so titled for its nightmare re-creation of Jim Morrison's oedipal title track (1974)—you couldn't imagine anyone else working with her. "Those albums are so incredible," Lou Reed marveled. "The most incredible albums ever made. [But] you try to get a copy. You can't get 'em, you can't order 'em. They've disappeared off the face of the earth. Nico doing 'The End' is so unbelievable."

It was just another irony in a life full of the things, then, that prompted Nico to title her fifth solo album—and her first without Cale since 1968—*Drama of Exile*. She had been exiled, her music had been exiled, and the fact that the drama itself would go on for five years, and encompass not only Nico's banishment, but also her return from a decade in the critical wilderness, only compounded the pertinency.

Nico first started talking about what became *Drama of Exile* in the spring of 1978, three years after *The End* terrified a generation of blissful, sun-soaked, mid-1970s hippies. She was surprisingly buoyant; in 1978, after all, she had no record deal, she had no musicians, and the handful of solo shows she'd played over the last few months ended in humiliating chaos. The Velvet Underground were widely regarded among the most influential groups of all time, but Britain's punk-rock community, faced with the reality of the Velvets' own Femme Fatale, alone onstage with her pumping, droning harmonium and the spartan peaks and valleys of her voice, reacted as though they were under attack.

They might as well have been. "If I had a machine gun, I would shoot you all," Nico threatened the crowd as a hail of cans and spit forced her offstage when she opened for Siouxsie and the Banshees in the Welsh capital of Cardiff. "John Cale was born just up the road," she mused a few years later. "I expected more from those people."

She got her revenge in London, supporting the Adverts. According to vocalist Tim "TV" Smith, "All I can remember is, we were really pissed off with her because she went on and on for hours. All our fans were waiting for us to go on, it was one in the morning, she'd been on for two and a half hours, and she still hadn't stopped."

It was Nico's meeting with a young Corsican reggae musician, Philippe Quilichini, that changed Nico's fortunes. He moved her into the London apartment he shared with his girlfriend Nadett' Duget, and photographer Antoine Giacomoni, and together they conspired Nico's next comeback. It would be her most powerful yet.

Nico had always been capable of songs of iridescent beauty: "All That Is My Own," "Secret Side," "Mutterlein," "The Falconer." But she was equally capable of frightening intensity. She sang of the desert shore, and conjured up a bleakness nature could never compete with. She recorded "Das Lied der Deutschland"—the über alles anthem Germany banned in 1945, to atone for its recent Nazi past—and dedicated it to terrorist Andreas Baader.

Songs for other people's funerals . . . . The Banshees audience was not alone in its fear-stricken response to her: rock'n'roll itself never had much time for Nico. But that's because Nico never had much time for rock'n'roll.

Drama of Exile was going to change all that. "It was really boring, all that quiet stuff," Nico said of her past albums. "And having been a member of the Velvet Underground, rock'n'roll is something I have to do at some point, even if only for one album."

Aura label head Aaron Sixx financed much of the recording, and was already preparing his promotional campaign when he received word from the studio that Nadett' Duget, acting as Nico's manager and "executive producer," was planning a double-cross. She and Sixx had never signed contracts; Duget was now intending to make off with the completed album tapes, and resell them to the highest bidder.

Moving just hours ahead of Duget, Sixx himself went to the studio and removed the tapes. He then contacted Nico, and worked out a deal with her alone, paying her $1,000 for the rights to *Drama of Exile*. Sixx admitted that Nico "didn't give a shit what happened to the LP, she just wanted the money for drugs." Yet despite these unconventional circumstances, *Drama of Exile* would see Nico receive some of the best reviews of her career.

Nico's timing could not have been more fortuitous. The early 1980s saw the British underground firmly in the grip of the so-called "raincoat brigade of dour, unsmiling, and stereotypically, dark-raincoat clad" bands like Echo and the Bunnymen,[3] Joy Division, and Doll By Doll, whose own frames of musical reference drew a straight line from Jacques Brel to recent (*Low*/*"Heroes"*-era) Bowie, and thus bisected Nico at a dozen different spots. Nico responded equally enthusiastically, giving some of the most lucid interviews of her career, and devising a live set that embraced every aspect of that career, from the Velvets on.

Amid so much activity, the demand for a fresh Nico project was immense, but little was forthcoming. In 1983 Philippe Quilichini returned to the studio, and continued work on *Drama of Exile*, an album he still considered incomplete. But the drama continued, as he and Nadett' Duget were involved in an horrific traffic accident just as the revamped album was wrapped up. Quilichini was killed; Duget died three years later, having remained in a coma since the crash.

Nico took Quilichini's death in stride, just as she had accepted the flood of past friends and lovers who had fallen dead around her. "It doesn't mean I don't miss them," she explained in 1983. "Just that I understand why I miss them."

She began work on a new album, *Camera Obscura*, soon after, reuniting with John Cale even as she abandoned a near-lifelong heroin habit for a methadone substitute; soon she would be cutting back on that as well. She was writing songs which were, if not the best, the most commercially viable of her career; and she had finally found an audience who accepted her on her own terms, the doomed, dark denizens of the incipient gothic scene. Cale was especially enthusiastic. "Nico's got a lot of depth in her personality that she didn't have before," he remarked at the time. "Lyrics and sensibility; she's not as abrasive as she used to be."

Dissenting voices, however, were already charting what would swiftly be revealed as her decline. Her notorious unreliability still unnerved promoters and rattled record companies—one label executive went so far as to admit, "We'd only sign Nico if she dropped dead beforehand. That way, at least we'd know where she was."

The British music press still ridiculed her, that doomy old dame with her songs of woebegone weariness. Concert promotors viewed her as a high-risk proposition. Her own keyboard player, James Young, was compiling the damning dossier which would eventually be published as *Nico: The End*—a vicious examination of her last tours and business arrangements, and a portrait of a decaying junkie queen, living out the last act of a play that had gone on too long. Yet even Young admitted that Nico's death shocked him. "I thought she'd see us all out. Tougher than the leather of her boots, I could see her at eighty, a terrifying old bat in a black cloak, swooping down on her latest victim."

Journalist Dave Thomas, reviewing a 1985 Nico concert in *Melody Maker*, had already arrived at the same conclusion. "She might be pushing fifty, but she still looks a debauched thirty. Not for Nico the ravages of time. Perfectly preserved, she'll run forever, baffling twenty-first-century anthropologists with her note-perfect impersonations of an industrial computer with a Garbo fixation."

But Nico herself wasn't so sure. Pondering both her past and her future, she mused, "I have a habit of leaving places at the wrong time. Just when something big might have happened for me." And as the 1980s drifted toward their end, that "something big" was suddenly lurking just around the next corner.

In early March 1987, Nico played a tribute concert to her sixties mentor, Andy Warhol, who had died following a routine gallbladder operation on February 22. It was one of a string of gigs enacted around the world for the peculiar little man who revolutionized the art world, and, through his dilettante patronage, the music world as well. On the other side of the Atlantic, John Cale and Lou Reed were formulating what would become their *Songs for 'Drella* stage show and album, and taking the first steps toward what would eventually emerge, five years later, as a Velvet Underground reunion. Nico, however, would be missing from the lineup.

For a year after the Warhol concert, Nico worked toward a new album, previewing songs in a string of sometimes stunning, sometimes less so, concerts around Britain and Europe, and in early July 1988, she and the twenty-five-year-old Ari decamped to Ibiza, Spain, where she intended to get on with more songwriting.

On July 17, with the mercury hovering around the 90-degree mark, Nico announced that she was going into town to buy some marijuana. Seated in front of a mirror, she spent close to an hour patiently winding a heavy black scarf around her head, to complement the heavy black clothes she habitually wore. They suited her temperament, she said; they suited her mood.

Then she climbed onto her bicycle and headed off down the hill. After she was gone, Ari glanced at the typewriter whose keys she had been pecking at earlier in the day. Nico had written just one sentence: *The last days of a singer*. He would never see his mother again.

The coroner blamed Nico's death on a cerebral hemorrhage, exacerbated by the heat, but exaggerated by the most appalling medical neglect. Still alive, still conscious, Nico was found by a passing taxi driver, lying on the side of the road, her bicycle upended beside her. He placed her in the back of his cab, then drove to the nearest hospital. They refused to admit her because she was a foreigner and did not have the necessary health coverage.

It was the same story at the second hospital. At the third, she was turned away as a case of heat stroke, an old beatnik who'd had a touch too much. Finally, losing patience with both the doctors and his quickly vanishing working day, the driver cajoled a fourth hospital into taking the burden off his hands.

In a chilling echo of blues singer Bessie Smith's sordid death, refused treatment after a car crash because she was "a nigger," Nico was bundled onto a gurney, briefly examined—again, a nurse diagnosed heat stroke—and left until morning. Not until then was she seen by somebody who finally realized something more serious was going on.

The doctor readied a series of injections, to stabilize Nico's worsening condition, then looked at his assistant in confusion. After years of intravenous drug use, every one of Nico's veins had collapsed in her body. Finally the doctor admitted defeat.

Nico hung on through the day, but was weakening. While Ari frantically called around her customary haunts, searching for his mother, Nico lay on a hospital gurney, slipping in and out of consciousness, horribly aware of where she was, but unable to speak, unable to ask why nobody was helping her. At eight o'clock that evening, alone on her trolley, and three months short of her fiftieth birthday, the woman who was once described as "the most beautiful girl in this world" slipped into the next one.

Later, Nico's English associates would complain that not one of her so-called American friends showed up at her funeral. She, however, would not have been surprised at that. Cale aside, Nico had skillfully distanced herself from even the closest allies of her past, and they from her.

In 1974, Lou Reed turned down her request that he produce her, claiming he didn't have the time. ("Lou's got a problem," Nico explained. "He wants to be black.") Her friends in the Doors appeared to have deserted her around the same time she started insisting that the group re-form, with her replacing Jim Morrison ("We have the same voice").

And in Berlin in 1977, she was spurned by Iggy Pop who was staying with David

Bowie while he recorded his latest album, *The Idiot*. She left a note on the door to their apartment saying, *I want to see you*. A note came back: *I don't want to see you*. She was not to know, of course, that at that precise time, Iggy was exorcising demons of his own.

In 1968, while the Velvet Underground was cauterizing the intellectual flesh of America's college underground, "assaulting the sensibilities of teenage America," as John Cale so memorably put it, halfway across the country in Detroit, Iggy and the Stooges were having much the same effect on the physical well-being of the midwestern bar circuit.

If any band epitomized the sheer nihilistic tendencies for which rock'n'roll was spawned, it was the Stooges. Howling out of Ann Arbor, Michigan, in 1968, fronted by Pop's maniacal frenzy, and playing shows even their fans acknowledged were closer to Armageddon than anything else, the Stooges may not have chosen deliberately to walk so close to the edge of self-destruction . . . but they did it anyway.

In 1977, however, with a long history of heroin addiction behind him, and the Stooges having finally shattered on a broken-glass-strewn stage in Detroit, Iggy himself was ready to finally cauterize the madness with a new song, "Dum Dum Boys." While co-writer Bowie tortured unimagined chords from his guitar, Pop intoned a simple paean to comrades past and present, the ones who went straight . . . the ones who went back to live with their mothers . . . and the ones who never got the chance to do either. Dave Alexander was one of the latter.

Alexander was bassist on the first two Stooges albums, slobbering slabs of protopunk metallisms which leaked onto the fringes of the American mainstream in 1969 and 1970. Razor-sharp-edged, capable of both the most intricate patterns and the most mindless riffs, Stooges roadie Billy Cheatham recalled Alexander as simply "crazy. He was a juvenile delinquent, a great guy, one of those guys you thought you could size up by looking at him, then realize later there were so many facets to him. But he was nuts, deep down, just a crazy kid."

Which is why he fit into the Stooges so well.

Neither *The Stooges* or *Fun House*, the original lineup's sole offerings to the world, would impact beyond the closeted audience that the Stooges' savage appeal—and more savage reputation—had already carved out for them. Despite later protestations to the contrary, the Stooges never were cut out for mainstream success, and—even at the height of their late-seventies infamy, when their name was being dropped by every safety-pinned crustacean to crawl out from Planet Punk—Iggy also knew why. They were simply too far ahead of their time.

"I saw a superficial correlation between punk and what the Stooges had been doing, and I knew exactly what was happening," Iggy explained in 1993. "Accidentally, the superficial aspects of noise, energy, aggression, irresponsible negative preening, and emotional exhibitionism were finally being adopted by the mob and their various frustrated mentors who couldn't create anything themselves."

The Stooges swung into action in 1968, coincidentally but not accidentally, with the dawn of the era of rock-star excess. Led Zeppelin's fabled coupling of groupie and fish was still a sordid rumor waiting to be told, and Keith Moon's limo in the swimming pool was a novelty, not a way of life. But the Stooges saw which way the breeze was blowing—and rented a roomful of wind machines.

"[We] did it to the point of parody," Pop reflected. "Other people drove their cars into swimming pools. We couldn't afford cars, so we drove other people's cars in. Then, when others started doing that, we went beyond it again. We'd throw ourselves in the pool and drown." He smiled nostalgically. "We were a very nasty little band.

"The only people who responded to what we did early on, were the avant-garde and the deviants, the arty sickos. And kids and high-school dropouts, the real dregs, the young sickos."

Which means, as Stooges drummer Scott Asheton put it, if Dave Alexander had never been in the group, he'd have loved them nonetheless. "[Dave] lived north of Ann Arbor, in a lake community; he came into Ann Arbor a spoiled child and a wild thing. He was drinking and smoking, was this happening guy; he had long hair which came from the surf style, and we were dancing to Phil Spector and the Motown beat."

Even amid the Stooges' school of wild experimentation, Alexander was a born leader. According to Cheatham, "He was first to experiment with anything that came along, he was [always] ready to go all out"—even to the detriment of the band.

Though Iggy, with his own acts of autodestruction, would get whatever headlines the Stooges received (and even more once their legend took off), it was Alexander who set the chemical precedent, right up until the group played the Goose Lake Festival, in Saginaw, Michigan, in 1970. Ron Asheton alleged, "Dave got really drunk and smoked dope and he sort of froze onstage and forgot all the tunes. After the gig, Iggy said, 'Hey, you're fired. We don't want to play with you anymore.'"

"Goose Lake is kind of a blur to me," Cheatham admitted. "There was a lot of drugs there, a lot of coke, we played relatively early, and I seem to remember something about Dave fucking up. He wasn't doing heroin," he said, contradicting a popular legend. "But he was drinking pretty heavily."[4]

Dave Alexander's departure from a band that was already disintegrating did not initially impact upon their lifestyle. He'd already begun to distance himself from the others; in keeping with their image, the Stooges and their crew lived together in one big communal, free-for-all crash pad. Alexander, however, was rarely there, preferring the company of his parents to that of his bandmates.

"I think that more than anything was what took him out," Cheatham speculated. "He stopped talking, pretty much. He had this defensive way of laughing things off. If you started to talk to him, then he'd find a reason to leave." Ron Asheton agreed, but the last time he saw Alexander, the bassist wanted to stick around.

The Stooges had shattered, re-formed, then broken up again so often that the next time they did it, at the end of 1973, Ron Asheton grabbed his guitar and formed a new group, New Order (no relation to the past Joy Division dance band, of course). That way he'd be busy the next time they came knocking.

"I saw Dave when I came back to Detroit once, when I was living in L.A. I played him my New Order tapes, and he was saying, 'Man, that is great.' He was really into it, we smoked some dope and stuff, and he wanted to ride along when I went to the airport. My thing is, when you drop me off at the airport, I don't want anyone to come in, I am on my thing, I want to be alone. But he goes, 'Please let me come in,' so he came in, [and] when I got up to the gate, he looked at me and said, 'I'll probably never see you again.'"

Asheton laughed his concern away. "I said, 'No man, I'll be back in a couple of months.'"

But Alexander was right. Just a couple of weeks later, on February 10, 1975, he died from the pneumonia years of heavy drinking had allowed to run rampant through an already frail body.

Scott Asheton said, "Both Dave's parents drank, and when I met him, I must have been about fifteen or sixteen, and he was eighteen or nineteen, probably eighteen, and he had a real nice fast car, he was all up on the clothes thing, having the right wardrobe, the happening thing for your image, and he was drinking. And when I got to know Dave later, when he was much more of a friend, I found out that his parents drink, and since . . . a very young age, they let him drink.

"And so Dave practically drank his whole life. He started when he was like ten years old, died when he was twenty-seven. But those are growing years, you don't need alcohol in your body when you're ten years old."

It only compounded the tragedy, then, that after years of drifting and indecision, Alexander had finally found his niche in life. Former Stooges manager Jimmy Silver got a call from his old friend just weeks before his death. "He said, 'My folks have inherited some money, and I've been playing the stock market with it.' I was later told that he had made hundreds of thousands of dollars!"

i know i'm small but i enjoy living anyway

MARC BOLAN *WAS* GLAM ROCK. Others rocked harder, others glittered brighter. But it was Bolan who showed them how to do it, and Bolan remained the model to match. Four number ones, a string of number twos, Britain's first new pop idol of the 1970s, Bolan's transition from underground antihero to superstar demigod not only shattered all predictions and preoccupations for the new decade, it launched British rock'n'roll to its most invigorating high of all time.

The genre Bolan so effortlessly created was essentially one of pure narcissism, nothing more or less. Aided by British television's recent conversion to color (*Top of the Pops* finally dropped the monochrome in 1970—not at all coincidentally, the year of Bolan's breakthrough), Glam revolved around looking good, sounding good, and being good. Bolan could do all three.

"Glam" meant projecting glamour—not as the nebulous property of some Hollywood screen goddess, although that was part of it, but as something tangible, something that could be encapsulated in a word, in a gesture, in a chord. But most important of all, it meant offering up something that could be emulated.

Like Marilyn Monroe's beauty spot or Jean Harlow's platinum-blondeness, Bolan's image was a series of carefully calculated visual hooks: his mane of curling hair, the glittering eye paint, the elfin smile, the metallic green and electric blue in which he dressed—everything was designed to catch the eye. Bolan might have been short, but he would stand out in any crowd.

Verbally, too, he was brilliant. He wove legends like he wrote songs; he seldom lied but he always economized on the truth, playing up one angle, playing down another (and then telling it the other way around the next time he spoke). You believed in everything he said, and after a while, it seemed he did as well.

A night spent in Paris in the arms of a gay conjurer became a great mystical experience involving wizards and the invocation of evil spirits. A solitary session with producer Joe Meek was enlarged into a musical masterpiece—many people still believe Bolan was responsible for "Magic Star," a vocal version of the "Telstar" smash, which Meek produced for Kenny Hollywood. And six months with his first band, before he faded gracefully off the scene, became two stormy weeks with an equally stormy conclusion. Bolan's first manager, Simon Napier Bell, never lost his admiration for the singer's storytelling abilities. "He really knew how to treat journalists."

Bolan's private playground, of course, was always one of pure imagination. The very notion that he could become the biggest rock star ever seemed a fanciful dream during the hazy days of his acoustic folky duo Tyrannosaurus Rex, but he believed it, and he made it happen.

It took him one hit to make it, one hit to consolidate it, and after that, he could do what he wanted. Even after glam rock exploded like acne across the teenage British scene, Bolan's initial impact was still so great that he both encapsulated and transcended the rest of the pack. For a couple of years, he ruled the world. The only problem was, he never figured out what to do with it.

In 1965 Bolan was an itinerant folkie with a Donovan cap. By 1966, he was the autodestructive heart of protopsychedelic mod mobsters John's Children. And in late 1967, solo again, he decided to form his own group.

Napier Bell recalled, "He got a gig at the Electric Garden, then put an ad in *Melody Maker* to get the musicians. The paper came out on Wednesday, the day of the gig. At three o'clock he was interviewing musicians, at five he was getting ready to go onstage. That was all there was to it. He didn't audition anybody, he just picked people who looked good or who had nice names. Marc thought he could just magic it all together. His theory was that you just went onstage, told the audience what you were going to do, then you did it, simple as that. And he genuinely believed that it would all come together, and that he would wake up in the morning as a superstar."

Instead, "it was a disaster. He just got booed off the stage, but he still didn't think he'd done anything wrong; it was the musicians who were incompatible. The fact that they hadn't rehearsed or anything had nothing to do with it. So he went out, bought himself a rug and an incense stick, and then he and Steve Took went out as a duo."

At nineteen, a year younger than Bolan, Steve Peregrine Took, was one of the musicians onstage at the Electric Garden that fateful night, and the only one with whom Bolan felt any camaraderie whatsoever. After all, the pair looked great together: Took with flowing silks, bongos, and the name he borrowed from *The Lord of the Rings*, a Shakespearean pixie with the broadest smile ever; Bolan with corkscrew curls and acoustic guitar, and he was elflike, too, with a quavering voice that scarcely sounded English, and lyrics that sometimes weren't. Set adrift within the psychedelic potpourri of Aquarius, with their pixiephones and one-stringed fiddles, Tyrannosaurus Rex flourished from the start.

"And Marc hated it, hated every single minute of it," insisted Napier Bell. "He'd do a gig and the promotor would say, 'oh, sorry, we can't pay you. Have a couple of joints instead, or a couple of sugar lumps,' and Marc would have to say, 'Oh yeah, cool man,' but inside he'd be really seething. And the more it went on, the more he hated it, because he was trapped in this horrible hippie thing, because he'd gone out of his way to attract an anti-commercial hippie audience."

Tyrannosaurus Rex signed with the Straight Ahead management and production team of Tony Secunda and Denny Cordell in early 1968. They were dispatched immediately into the studio, kick-starting a relationship with producer Tony Visconti which would endure for the next seven years, and give him a firsthand glimpse of the demons which drove Bolan.

"Marc was in rivalry with everybody," Visconti insisted. "He was a total megalomaniac, God bless him, which is what a lot of stars are made of. You have to have a huge ego to be a huge success, Marc's was simply huger than most.

"He used to do things like buy ten albums a day, James Burton guitar-player records, then come round to my flat, play them, and ask me what I thought. So I'd say, `Pretty good, that's a good solo,' and he's say, 'Yeah, but I'm better.'

"Once I was listening to a John Williams album, I was off in a reverie somewhere, going, 'Oh, what marvelous technique,' and Marc said, 'I could play like that in two weeks.' He was in rivalry with everyone. He couldn't stand competition. He'd meet it head-on, even if he had to make the most outrageous claims. He'd have the bravado to do it."

With the three Tyrannosaurus Rex albums released during 1968-1969 having unearthed, or at least identified, an audience, Bolan would spend the next year or so both enlarging on, and experimenting with, its limitations. The duo's first U.S. tour, in mid-1969, not only found Bolan experimenting with an electric guitar, it also saw Took exchange his bongos for a full drum kit. In 1969, in a moment of pure prescient enthusiasm, *Melody Maker* tagged the duo "electrified teenybop," and, had things not gone so horribly awry between Bolan and Took, all that Marc was to achieve in the first years of the next decade might instead have happened for him during the final years of the sixties.

"I met Steve Took at the Festival of the Flower Children at Woburn," underground journalist Steve Mann once remarked. "And even then it was obvious that he and Bolan cordially detested each other." And the reasons for the mutual hatred were plain. Tony Secunda explained, "Basically, Bolan was unhappy about Tookie's drug habit. They hung out with very different crowds, Bolan living quietly with [wife-to-be] June Child, Tookie stuffing himself with chemicals, and spending his time with like-minded fellows."

Even when the two musicians visited their management together, they would separate immediately. "Bolan would be into the office to talk money and percentages, Took would disappear onto the roof for a joint which he'd roll from the stash he kept in a bag around his waist."

"I used to go out and jam occasionally with the Deviants and the Pretty Things," Took agreed in 1972. "[But our] management would come and say, 'Boy, don't go and jam with this group, it's bad for the image.'" And Took would simply stare at them incredulously. "What image? I'm Steve Took, well-known drug addict!"

"Steve . . . was always a bit of a dipstick," June Child herself added. "Rather sad. Very kind, terribly nice, came from an awful household south of the [Thames]. Another acid casualty." Bolan, on the other hand, would "hold a joint because people expected him to. But he . . . never smoked, never. He didn't like what it did."

For a time, Bolan tolerated Took's proclivities. But, according to Secunda, that was to change the night somebody spiked his drink with acid. Bolan freaked out completely, a nightlong trip which culminated with June driving him around a darkened Hampstead Heath while Bolan tried to eat his own hand. And while no one knew for sure who exactly had done the deed, Bolan himself had no doubts. Took had long since earned (and rejoiced in) the nickname of "The Phantom Spiker." Well, this time the Phantom had spiked the wrong person.

Against this festering backdrop, the duo's American tour, which kicked off in San Francisco on August 6, 1969, was ill-starred from the outset, and could only get worse. Took almost missed the flight out of London, oversleeping until some friends bundled him into a cab and off to the airport, while the duo's New York debut, at the Club Au-Go-Go, coincided with the Woodstock Festival, and was even more sparsely attended than the rest of the shows.

But, according to Bolan, Took remained the biggest obstacle. Several gigs were marked by his penchant for stripping naked onstage; at others, he indulged in what Bolan described as "musical sabotage," playing one song midway through another, missing cues, fluffing breaks. Finally with the last date behind them, Bolan and June Child flew home alone. By the time Took returned to England, he was already history.

It was Took's acrimonious departure that gave Bolan the final push he needed to "go heavy," as he called it. Promptly recruiting a new percussionist, Mickey Finn, Tyrannosaurus Rex recorded what would become its crowning achievement, the monumental *Beard of Stars* album—a set that not only echoed Bob Dylan's four-year-old decision to "go electric," but which was also destined to echo the repercussions.

While Bolan's underground following was still shouting, "Judas," his ambition gained momentum. Because his next single, he knew, was going to be a hit. "He recorded 'Ride a White Swan' convinced that it would either make him or break him," Napier Bell insisted. "But he was so scared of it bombing out, that he was going around telling everybody that he disowned the record. What he really meant was, that he disowned it if it was a flop. And when it was a hit, it simply wasn't worth the bother of trying to explain all that crap to people who said he'd sold out. Because now he was God, and whoever heard of God selling out?"

"Ride a White Swan" soared to number two in December 1970. Bolan abbreviated the band's name, then expanded its lineup, adding bassist Steve Currie and drummer Bill Legend in the early new year. In March 1971, "Hot Love" stormed to number one, and stayed there six weeks. Five months later, "Bang A Gong" (Get It On) ruled Britain for a month and stormed the American Top Ten. *Electric Warrior*, his next album, would remain on the British charts for close to a year, and two decades later, appeared in *Rolling Stone* magazine's "all-time greatest albums" survey.

Recruiting Tony Secunda to act as his business manager, Bolan landed a new record deal, and his own record label. T. Rex Hot Wax premiered in January 1972, and the new year began where the old one left off. And then the chart-toppers stopped—overnight, it seemed. Bolan's bubble had burst—and was going to keep on bursting. He sacked Secunda, and started hanging with yes-men. He ran out of ideas and began recycling old ones. Now new stars were bringing along new tricks, and Bolan couldn't compete. One look at the charts spelled out Bolan's rivals: David Bowie, an old friend of Bolan's from his Tyrannosaurus Rex days; Roxy Music, an explosion of high art and sexual tension; the Sweet,[1] arch bubblegum musicians with a heavy-metal obsession; Gary Glitter, a silver-clad caricature of every rock star there ever was; Alvin Stardust . . . Suddenly everybody was overtaking him, and they had his blueprints with them.

The magic Bolan promised was delivered not only through his music, but across every level on which he operated. Even a simple photograph captured it—Bolan was absurdly photogenic, a trait that, above all others, was to be emulated by all the glam rockers who surfaced in his wake. But his own novelty was wearing thin. Bolan's early 1973 releases were little more than sad attempts to recapture the glory of the previous two years, and by the time 1974 rolled around, T. Rex was pretty much spent as a commercial force.

Still, Bolan put a brave face on his failings. "I was allowing the madness to move away," he explained. "I'll accept that I'm blatantly commercial, because I enjoy it, but I would like to do something beyond the simple Bolan rock'n'roll. And if only a quarter of the kids come with it, it wouldn't matter." He concluded, "I enjoyed the madness and being born to boogie, but I can see more clearly now."

But when Tony Secunda caught up with him again, in 1974, he was amazed he could see anything at all. "Marc had started getting heavily into coke on the 1972 American tour," he recalled, but now cognac joined it as Bolan's only other principle form of nourishment. Fat, bloated, and directionless, Bolan himself addressed his decline only after he and a fortuitously passing journalist, Roy Carr, caught sight of his corpulent mass in a hotel mirror. "Oh God, just look at the state of me," Bolan groaned. Over the next six months, he would work hard to exorcise that demon forever.

Marc Bolan and David Bowie (Archive Photos)

The ghost of his decline in popularity, of course, could not be so easily dismissed, but Bolan worked at that as well. And, as suddenly as he'd lost "what it takes," he got it back again. June Child explained, "He only used to do things he liked. He would never construct records for the market, and when he tried deliberately to write songs . . . they lacked his intuitive thing, and he then became desperate." When he stopped trying so hard, everything came flooding back.

Regaining enthusiasm as he reshaped his body, that spring of 1975 saw Bolan preface his *Bolan's Zip Gun* album with "New York City," a frivolous piece of non-sense about women with frogs in their hand which bore all the hallmarks of vintage T. Rex, while still managing to sound fresh. It was a hit. A year later, the sublime "I Love to Boogie" followed a similar pattern, with the accompanying tour proving Bolan once more capable of harnessing and sustaining his reemergent talents. Even more impressively, he managed it without any of the fabulous team that had sustained T. Rex through the glory years; Steve Currie, the last surviving member of the classic lineup, quit in 1976 to work with guitarist Chris Spedding.[2]

By early 1977, Bolan's star was truly ascendant both personally and musically. He was a father at last: he and June had broken up in 1973; now Marc was living with the American singer Gloria Jones, and their two-year-old son, Rolan, was his pride and joy. *Dandy in the Underworld* was his most enjoyable new album since 1972's *The Slider*. And his British television series, *Marc*, not only tooted the old Bolan horn of old (and provoked a timely reunion with David Bowie, filmed just days before Bolan's death[3]), it also acknowledged the growing importance of punk rock, both on the streets and within Bolan's own canon.

"Celebrate Summer," the next T. Rex single, was still new on the shelves when Elvis Presley died in the bathroom of his Graceland home. Maria Callas, the opera singer, passed away the same day; and Bolan, in conversation with his publicist, B. P. Fallon, admitted, "I'm glad I didn't get killed today. I wouldn't have got the front covers."

He outlived Presley (and Callas) by just four weeks, and got all the front covers there were. Returning home from a club in the early hours of the morning of September 16, 1977, the car in which Bolan was a passenger, crashed into a tree on Barnes Common in southwest London. Bolan was killed outright; Gloria Jones was critically injured.

There was a chilling piece of irony, too, awaiting the first journalists on the scene. A copy of that week's *New Musical Express* lie open to an interview with the Who's Pete Townshend. The headline was paraphrased from "My Generation": "Hope I get old before I die." Two weeks shy of his thirtieth birthday, that was one thing Bolan would never get to do.

Neither, as it transpired, would Steve Peregrine Took.

Since his departure from Tyrannosaurus Rex, Steve Took had done little more than drift through a bewildering succession of would-be bands, and an equally chaotic chain of high hopes and dashed dreams.

Together with the flamboyant former Pretty Things drummer Twink, and Deviants vocalist Mick Farren, he was there at the birth of the Pink Fairies, scheming the high-octane madness which would eventually resolve itself into one of the key acts of the British hard-rock underground. But as Farren reflected, schemes are one thing; actually putting them into practice is something else entirely.

"It's the difference between the star and artist. A lot of people—and Tookie is the obvious example—as long as they can maintain some resemblance of the tactile experience of being treated like a star, they go on doing it. But the fact of actually creating something, the reality of creation, dislodges the mythology of stardom.

"He'd had a bit of a lark with Bolan, having really only thrashed around in somebody's garage before that, then literally within three months they were on TV, and the whole question came down to, could he do it again? And the reality was, when he split with Bolan, Tookie couldn't even play the guitar. He did learn fairly rapidly, and he wrote some good songs. And he was hanging out with Twink, so they would go down to the Speakeasy in their pink velvet capes and show off, and it didn't matter that they didn't have a pot to piss in.

"But the fundamental problem with Tookie was that he absolutely couldn't finish anything, because that might finish him. There was this process where he'd come round, he'd sit on the floor and play this fucking thing on the guitar, and it'd get better and better and better, and then he'd get into the studio and he'd show up fucked-up, and that would be it."

In 1972, for example, Took entered the studio with Pink Fairies Duncan Sanderson and Russell Hunter, and David Bowie's old guitarist, Mick Wayne,[4] under the auspices of Bolan's own recently dismissed manager, Tony Secunda. Nothing happened. "Tony was putting him in the studio, and it wasn't some hole-in-the-corner place that Tookie was paying for out of his own royalties," Farren asserted. "It was the real deal. And mysterious swellings would appear on Tookie's left hand so he couldn't play. He was at the point where his phobia about not finishing things became psychosomatic."

Determined to record Took, Secunda then set the reluctant would-be superstar

The wrecked, purple Mini in which Marc Bolan died
(Archive Photos/Express)

up in his own basement, with a mini-studio at his beck and call. "I'd leave him down there, come back later, and all he'd managed to do was record himself falling off the chair," Secunda sighed. "He'd be playing back this tape, he'd start playing, and it was going along and suddenly, this fucking great crash. 'What was that?' 'Ah yeah, I fell over.'" Finally, even Secunda gave up.

Took drifted through the 1970s, then a sad, shadowy, figure. He arranged a handful of London club shows, but they tended to be disastrous, if he even bothered turning up at all. Strumming his guitar, mumbling into his mike, photographer Steve Sparks encountered him just before he died, at London's Dingwalls nightclub. "'Grrbllhh, Steve . . . terrible, man. Ggrrbbllhh.'"

"Tookie lived in my house for about two years," remembered Hawkwind's Nik Turner, "and I looked after him, and tried to get him off drugs, and it worked. I weaned him off, but as soon as he got back to London, he was right back onto it. He was among all his friends, who were saying, 'Go on, Tookie, have this one, have that one, have them all . . . . You can take more drugs than anybody I know.' And he'd do it."

Mick Farren continued, "One of the things Secunda did for Tookie was, he sorted out his royalties. As soon as Bolan got big, someone got Steve out of his head on acid, and had him sign away his rights. Secunda got them back for him, and that's how he came to die. A royalty check came through. There were these long moments of poverty when he couldn't afford many drugs, and that was when he was at his most together. Then the royalties came through and he'd completely fuck up."

Took died on October 27, 1980. Sure enough, a check had arrived, and he spent a chunk of it on a cocktail of morphine and magic mushrooms. Awakening in the night, he began picking at a bowl of cherries he'd left beside the bed—and fell back to sleep with a mouthful. One fruit lodged in his mushroom-numbed throat, and when he was found the following morning, Steve Peregrine Took had choked to death.

Bolan's death made headlines around the world. Took's at least hit the music papers in Britain. There was one glam-era idol, however, who passed so silently that even his friends didn't find out for days—even years—and his fans wouldn't know for a decade. Yet, had self-belief, and a cool million dollars of record company money counted for anything, Jobriath would have been bigger than everyone.

TODAY, JOBRIATH IS AN ICON. The first openly gay musician in American rock history, the Pet Shop Boys love him, and Morrissey has been photographed clinging lovingly onto one of his albums. The Pop Group's Mark Stewart thinks he was wonderful; Jayne County called him America's premier glam-rock idol; and both Peter Frampton and John Paul Jones played on his albums.

It's just a shame that very few people were listening at the time.

Jobriath was born Bruce Campbell in King of Prussia, Pennsylvania, smack in the heart of Amish country, and he always stood out from the crowd, even when he moved to New York for a stint in the original, Aquarius Theater production of *Hair*. Decca Records certainly thought he possessed something, and signed his group, Pidgeon, in the late 1960s, while former Jimi Hendrix manager Mike Jeffrey was so impressed that he was actively courting the young singer. Had Jeffrey lived,[1] maybe the Bruce Campbell story would have turned out different somehow.

But the people who knew him weren't so sure.

In 1973, with Campbell recording demos under the name

no rest your weary bones,
no need to suffer anymore

Jobriath, one of his tapes made its way into the office of Columbia Records president Clive Davis. It was he who uttered the words that alerted the world to the fact that Jobriath was something special.

"Clive thinks Jobriath is mad and unstructured, and destructive to melody," a record-company staffer remarked, and entrepreneur Jerry Brandt, passing through the Columbia offices at that precise moment, just smiled and said, "Oh yeah?" Legend insists that he signed Jobriath on the spot.

Brandt's scheme was simplicity itself. Jobriath would be aimed unequivocally at the center of rock'n'roll's showbiz heart, and after the buildup he received in that direction, there was no way he could have succeeded in any other.

It was the era of David Bowie's Ziggy Stardust–Aladdin Sane extravagances, but Brandt wasn't phased by any of that. Bowie played at bisexuality; Jobriath was rock's first avowed homosexual. Bowie said he was a space invader; Jobriath was the real thing. Or, as Brandt so succinctly put it, Jobriath was as different from Bowie as "a Lamborghini is from a Model A Ford—they're both cars; it's just a question of taste, style, elegance, and beauty."

By the time Jobriath was ready to be introduced to the world's press, then, he was being projected as the ultimate glam-rock Missing Link—the intellect of Bowie, the craziness of Slade, the joy of Bolan, the theater of Alice. When comedians Cheech and Chong recorded "Earache My Eye" under the name Alice Bowie, they were making a similar projection. But their idea lasted the length of one single. Jobriath was intended as a way of life.

He did no interviews, and he had no past. According to Brandt he was a star of Garboesque proportions, and when was the last time Garbo spoke of her past? There was that turn in *Hair*, of course, but Jobriath was fired because he kept stealing the show. There was Pidgeon as well, but their one album had been buried because nobody understood it. No, Jobriath was unique, and though Clive Davis was still convinced he was mad, and A&M Records thought he was a joke, Brandt—a man who worked with Del Shannon, Mick Jagger, and Carly Simon, and who thus should have commanded at least a little faith from his peers—was not to be deterred.

Using his own money, he had Jobriath and his latest band, the Creatures, record an album, then put on a live show which would prove once and for all that the kid was everything Brandt cracked him up to be, that he really could "paint, sing, dance, write, compose, arrange, conduct." Within two days of Jobriath's media launch party, at New York's Bottom Line, Elektra Records took the bait. Politely, Brandt forbore from reminding them they'd already turned the singer down once in the past.

Photographer and journalist John Michael Cox Jr. recalled his first encounter with the phenomenon that was Jobriath . . . or rather, with the phenomenon's manager. "Jobriath was going to appear that weekend at a popular club in New Jersey called the Joint in the Woods, in order to get a reaction from the crowd and to warm up for the Bottom Line. [Brandt] said he wasn't informing the press about this, and he didn't want me to go. Whoops! I was the only official member of the press the club knew, and I was always over there shooting. I didn't need his permission, a

Jobriath

(© John Michael Cox)

now rest your weary bones, no need to suffer anymore

press pass or anything else. So of course I went, and had the great joy of seeing, and photographing, Jobriath and the Creatures' first public concert."

Over the next year, until well into 1974, Brandt and Elektra were to sink over a million dollars into Jobriath, most of it on advertising. No cheap *Rolling Stone* and *Melody Maker* spreads for this boy; Jobriath was pushed through *Vogue* and *Harper's Bazaar*. When he toured Europe, he opened at the Paris Opera House.

He threatened to take a giant penis on the road with him and announced he was God. He talked openly about his sexuality, and claimed that his ambition was to be kidnapped by extraterrestrials. He went on the U.S. music television show *The Midnight Special* dressed as a vacuum cleaner, then moved into a custom-built pyramid atop the Chelsea Hotel in New York City. Naturally, when the British BBC made a documentary about that august pile, Jobriath made one of the star turns.

Billboards were erected across North America, screaming his name at passersby. In London, every other bus carried his face on its front. And Brandt sat in the center of the storm and laughed. "I don't know how to define hype," he explained, "but if it means using the media to project an artist to the public, then I'm going to produce the biggest hype you've ever seen."

Jobriath cut two albums. The eponymous first featured guest appearances from Peter Frampton and Peggy Nestor; the second, the conceptual *Creatures of the Street*, boasted Zeppelin's John Paul Jones and the Jobriath Symphony Orchestra. Asked to describe them, Brandt refused to mince words. "It's Bing Crosby, Elvis Presley, the Beatles, and Jobriath," was one of his favorite comments. Another was, "David Bowie? He's tacky and he can't pirouette."

Unfortunately, Brandt could find few to agree with him. Both of Jobriath's albums were thoroughly enjoyable, but both were savaged by the critics. They sold to the curious, to people who ran across bargain-bin copies of the "Liten Up" single and were entranced by the spelling; who heard "Scumbag," with its slurping, slopping, slovenly noises, and thought it was good for a laugh.

Within months of their appearance, both albums were deleted. Brandt dropped Jobriath from his roster midway through an unspectacular tour, and the star was next heard of auditioning for the role of Al Pacino's gay lover in *Dog Day Afternoon*. He didn't get it.

Cox caught up again with Jobriath a few years later, "doing cabaret as Cole Berlin. I photographed him atop the Chelsea Hotel in his pyramid home. With no makeup on, he looked like a young Robert Redford. I engineered a great deal of press for him, with layouts in gay publications around the world." But the two drifted apart again, and it would be years before Cox discovered that Jobriath had not simply retired. He was dying.

He had contracted the AIDS virus—all but unheard of at that time, outside of medical circles, but no less virulent for its obscurity. Setting up a home studio, writing and recording between the increasingly lengthy, and ever-more-debilitating illnesses that now wracked his body, Jobriath devoted his spare time to creating a rock musical, *Pop Star*.

Through his final year, 1983, Jobriath worked, when he could, at a piano lounge in New York, and it was only when he didn't show up there for a few days that anybody thought to drop by to check if he was okay. A friend went over to the Chelsea, and up to the pyramid on the roof. Jobriath's body was waiting for him there.

It is not difficult to pinpoint the reasons why Jobriath failed to become the biggest star ever. In directing his attentions toward what he considered a "classy" market, Jerry Brandt immediately alienated a vast proportion of his audience. The mainstream pop press covered Jobriath, but as a joke, rehashing the press releases without ever giving anybody a glimpse of something they might actually want to buy.

Matters were made worse by Brandt's refusal to allow Jobriath to be interviewed. David Bowie's manager, Tony DeFries, put him through a similar period of invisibility, but only once he was certain people wanted to talk to the boy in the first place. Brandt did not give people that option, and the rock press retaliated by labeling Jobriath a lost cause before they even heard him sing, let alone speak.

Brandt wanted to develop a mystery; he wound up creating a pariah. There is a thin line to be walked between giving people what they want, and giving them a hard time, and Jobriath wasn't even close to keeping his balance.

It is ironic, then, that today, after years during which his memory was invoked almost exclusively by rock historians searching for an adjective to replace "tacky" and "kitsch" in their vocabularies, Jobriath is finally beginning to win the fame that, two decades ago, not even a million dollars could buy. It is even more ironic, and unfathomably tragic as well, that he is no longer around to accept that applause.

Of course, the annals of music history are littered with similar (if perhaps not quite so resounding) failures, and it is true, too, that it is the very fact of that failure which elevates such artists from cults to heroes.

Ramases appeared on the European underground scene in 1968, with a couple of singles ("Crazy One" and "Screw You"), and the seemingly unshakable belief that he was the reincarnation of the Egyptian pharoah after whom he was named.

now rest your weary bones, no need to suffer anymore

Recorded with his wife Selket, neither record sold, and for a time the pair vanished.

In 1971, however, Ramases and Selket decided the time was right for their second coming, recording the *Space Hymns* album with four itinerant Manchester session men—Graham Gouldman, Eric Stewart, Kevin Godley, and Lol Creme (soon to emerge in their own right as the band 10cc)—and impressing everyone they met with their unmitigated sincerity.

"Ramases had a vision," Gouldman recalled. "We would sit down on the floor with acoustic guitars, that kind of vibe, very hippie and mystical; he would sing and we would sit cross-legged at his knees. There was a great atmosphere when that record was being made."

Space Hymns did little business, a fate which also awaited a second album, 1975's *Glass Top Coffin*, and Ramases and Selket soon vanished again, their whereabouts a mystery even to their friends. Sometime early in the 1990s, however, it was reported that Ramases was dead, a disillusioned suicide doomed to remain unknown outside of a select band of vinyl archivists.

Gouldman, however, never forgot him. "Ramases was a very strange and interesting man—he was always strange, he was fascinating. I remember one night we were at my house, Kev, Lol and myself, Ramases and his wife, and we just sat there for hours and hours, and he explained everything about Egyptian mythology, and it was just brilliant. He was totally convinced that he was the reincarnation of Ramases, quite genuine.

"He was actually a central-heating salesman from Sheffield, but that was just his day-to-day job. He had to earn a living! He really believed in the Egyptology thing, and if you sat down with him, you'd believe it."

Like Jobriath, Ramases overestimated the gullibility of the record-buying public. No matter how sincere his own beliefs, reincarnated Egyptian pharoahs are ultimately no more palatable to the public at large than men dressed as vacuum cleaners. But it is also true that some performers really are simply caught in the wrong place at the wrong time. And in those instances, it is doubly tragic that once again it takes a death to make people realize that.

Certainly that was the case with Gary Holton, a successful television actor at the time of his death in 1986, but a decade before that, the leader of one of the most exhilarating—and overlooked—live acts of the time, the Heavy Metal Kids.

It was that dual career which both highlighted and hampered his efforts. Was he, as the Kids' detractors assumed, simply an actor "slumming it" with a bawdy rock-

'n'roll group? Was he, as his fans swore, a rock'n'roller who just happened to act well? Or was he, Holton himself insisted, "just a guy who wanted to do it all, and was lucky enough to find people who let him"?

By 1978, when Holton and the Heavy Metal Kids re-formed after a two-year hiatus, the question was even more complicated. Holton had landed some cinema success by then, in the disco movie *Music Machine*, and via a role in the upcoming and much-hyped film version of the Who's epic, *Quadrophenia*. The Heavy Metal Kids, too, were being reassessed; no longer a fish out of musical waters, now they were acknowledged as one of the sparks which lit the whole punk-rock fire. But did they still possess that incendiary streak? On the strength of the handful of shows which they played that summer . . . no, they didn't.

T. V. Smith, a friend of Holton's throughout the Kids' heyday, reflected, "The Heavy Metal Kids were one of these bands who fit perfectly as a pre-punk band, but once punk came along, they were blown out of it, a bit like the Doctors of Madness and Cockney Rebel.[2] Coming back, they suddenly looked a bit dated—they were so far ahead of their time beforehand, but they were dated afterwards."

A child star with the Sadlers Well Opera Company and a graduate of both the Old Vic Theatre Company and the Royal Shakespeare Company, Holton joined the British touring company of *Hair* in 1972, when he was seventeen. It was there that he began making the contacts which would serve him in such good stead when he left two years later and formed the Heavy Metal Kids.

A raucous blend of streetwise rock, reggae, and balladry, permanently wrapped up in a Dickensian image of street-urchin chic—homage to another of Holton's childhood gigs, playing the Artful Dodger in a production of *Oliver*—Smith recalled, "They cared about their look, wearing makeup onstage, dressing up special for gigs, which was the kind of stuff we were looking for before punk. Silly lyrics, funny, energetic onstage."

Former Damned guitarist Brian James agreed. "The Heavy Metal Kids were great fun. Gary used to take the piss out of himself so much, and they kinda filled a little bit of a gap, among all that pomp of the early 1970s. You had the hippie side, you had the glam thing that was taking itself so very seriously, and then there was Gary and his boys, just being silly." He, too, believes "they were ahead of their time."

Holton himself, however, would simply snigger, "It's the performance that counts. That's what you're up there for. What you do offstage is boring, no one really cares. So what you have to do is, make what you do offstage as exciting as what you do when you're on, or at least make people think that's what you're doing."

The Heavy Metal Kids lived up to that dictum with a passion. But they weren't saddled only with a tricky reputation. They had a very dubious name as well.

The Heavy Metal Kids had nothing whatsoever to do with Heavy Metal, and they would pay dearly for the confusion. In an art form where you're only as strong as your last lowest common denominator, it was too easy to take their name literally, and when the band toured America in 1975, they shortened it to just "the Kids."

"All these headbangers were coming up after shows," Holton once laughed, saying, 'You Limey motherfuckers, what kind of Heavy Metal . . .' and we'd try to explain, tell them to go and read William Burroughs, that 'Heavy Metal' has been around for years before KISS. But after a while it was easier just to shorten the name." They kept the abbreviation when they toured Britain with Alice Cooper that fall, and released their second album (*Anvil Chorus*), but Holton later admitted that only added to the confusion. "Now the old fans didn't know who we were, either."

Holton quit the Kids in 1976, amid a tidal wave of recriminations and drug-tinged accusations. He was always a drinker, but drugs brought a new—and troubling—influence into play. "I don't think he was really into drugs while the band was happening," Smith acknowledged. "I think it was what came into his life afterwards, after things started to sour the first time around."

Another friend blamed the American tour, where the very nature of the venues where the Kids were booked lent themselves to such introductions. Whatever the cause, however, it appeared to be a mere passing fancy, and after two years on the sidelines, with punk historians paying increasing tribute to the Heavy Metal Kids' original power and influence, Holton rejoined the group in 1978.

With Holton dashingly cloaked and behatted, "they did some dreadful comeback gig at the London Marquee," Smith cringed, "and dragged Gaye [Advert] up onstage because we were in the front row. But . . ." The reunion didn't last, and Holton moved on.

In December 1978, the Damned sought him out to stand in for their temporarily errant vocalist Dave Vanian, for three shows in Scotland. There wasn't time to rehearse beforehand, but with an eight-hour bus drive ahead of them, the Damned handed him a cassette tape of their live set, and told him to learn the songs. Unfortunately, they also handed him enough alcohol to blot out a bar, and by the time the group reached the first show, Holton had less idea of what he was meant to be doing than ever.

Somehow he was hauled onstage; somehow, too, he got through the set. But sympathy surely played as big a part in the audience's reaction as appreciation for the night's entertainment. The Damned explained away Vanian's absence by telling the crowd he was dead.

With Holton putting the Damned behind him, acting resurfaced to consume his time. In 1979, he landed a role in the punk hit flick *Breaking Glass*,[3] and starred in the kids-on-the-rampage BBC TV movie *Bloody Kids*. But he also came close to scoring a hit single, when he joined with ex-Boys guitarist Casino Steel for a phenomenal reworking of Mel Tillis's "Ruby, Don't Take Your Love to Town," (also recorded by Kenny Rogers in 1969), and he was firmly in line to fill the late Bon Scott's shoes in AC/DC,[4] a role which would have stretched both his, and the Australian rockers', talents to the limit.

"All that fuckin' racket," he cackled one night. "I mean . . . strewth!" Roughly translated, this meant he was overjoyed when the job went to Brian Johnston, and by 1983 Holton's musical career was based almost exclusively in Norway, where he proved the perfect frontman for Casino Steel's latest project, CCCP.

In mid-1984, Holton finally broke into the big time when he appeared in British television's *Auf Weidersehn, Pet*, a light drama dreamed up by *Quadrophenia* director Francis Roddam. With the show itself centering around the exploits of seven British construction workers employed on a building site in Germany, Holton all but played himself, an extrovert Cockney rough diamond named Wayne, who wasn't above a bit of petty larceny but essentially had a heart of gold. It was, after all, a cliché Holton himself deliberately reveled in all his life. "He was always smiling, always had that cheeky grin," laughed T. V. Smith. "And he could have sold you your own mother"—a characteristic which the makers of Pilsner lager obviously picked up on as well, when they recruited Holton to star in a series of TV commercials.

In September 1984, Holton returned to the stage, appearing in the London cast of the 1950s Americana musical *Pump Boys and Dinettes*, and remaining in view whether he was on- or offstage. During the intermission, he could be found sitting in the stalls, his back to the stage on the top of a seat, puffing a cigarette and talking to fans, as though he'd known them for years. Then he'd saunter back onstage for part two, and it was like he'd been a midwestern grease monkey for years.

Late the following summer, Holton was recalled to *Auf Weidersehn, Pet*, to begin work on the long-awaited second series, this time set on a building site in Spain, and simply picking up where series one had left off. He was still at work there when he died at age thirty-one on October 25, 1985, the victim of a heroin habit which even the gossip-ridden London underground scarcely remembered.

now rest your weary bones, no need to suffer anymore

For a time, it looked as though work on the show might stop then and there, but the team was persuaded to at least complete the second series. (A projected third season, however, was canned at its shocked stars' insistence.) A mere handful of episodes remained to be shot, and watching the show when it was aired the next spring, Holton's absence was barely noticeable. With a look-alike stand-in maintaining a safe distance from the cameras whenever "Wayne" was demanded onscreen, Gary Holton had died as he always wanted to live, as Jobriath and Ramases, too, had schemed their careers. By steadfastly refusing to allow reality to impinge upon the performance.

"MY NAME IS ALEX HARVEY, and I would like to introduce you to my band. The Sensational . . . Alex . . . Harvey . . . Band." For five years in the early to mid-1970s, at the sound of those words, a club, a theater, an entire stadium full of fans would rise and roar, secure in the knowledge that for the next ninety minutes, they would be experiencing one of the greatest concerts of their lives.

It takes a lot of nerve to name your band something that unequivocal, a lot of nerve and a lot of self-belief. Alex Harvey boasted both. For many musicians, if success is going to strike, it's going to strike early. Even among those artists whose pre-fame history reads like an eternity of near misses and unlucky breaks, few seem to be out of their mid-twenties when they do finally make it.

And though there's always an exception to prove the rule, rock-'n'roll is adamant about one thing. If you're still struggling when you're thirty, nothing's going to change. Alex Harvey, the exception, was still struggling at thirty-seven, and already he was resigned to nothing really changing. "I never wanted to be a star," he once said. "I just wanted to be happy."

He spent the 1960s following that dream, in a string of projects dating back to the earliest days of British skiffle, stretching forward through blues, R&B, and psychedelia. He usually worked with his brother Leslie, ten years his junior and as hot a guitarist as Alex was a singer. Alex admitted there were times when it was only the younger Harvey's enthusiasm that kept him going. So when Led Zeppelin manager Peter Grant[1] snatched up Leslie's own latest group, Stone the Crows, and set them off on the road to stardom, Alex wasn't far behind.

Fronted by the twin dynamite charges of Leslie Harvey's guitar and singer Maggie Bell—herself one of Alex's own discoveries—Stone the Crows put two tight and soulful hard-rock albums behind them within a year. By the end of 1971, Stone the Crows were firmly established among the premier live attractions on the British college circuit; their third album, *Teenage Licks*, was selling up a storm, and Bell was winning the Top Female Singer award in the music papers' annual polls. Watching from the sidelines, Alex discovered the impetus he'd been seeking.

Late in 1971, he was introduced to Tear Gas, an equally directionless Scottish underground combo, and within the space of a single rehearsal, a union was forged. With one eye on the increasingly theatrical glam-rock scene which was exploding all around, and the other eye on his own comic-book mythology (he was a fervent fan of the U.S. comic book *Sergeant Fury*), Harvey began honing Tear Gas into a solid rock'n'roll act, complementing his own onstage dynamism with a showmanship that swiftly justified his choice for a new name. They truly were the Sensational Alex Harvey Band.

But the group was not in for an easy ride. The Sensational Alex Harvey Band had been playing together for just two months when Leslie Harvey was killed, electrocuted by a "live" microphone during a Stone the Crows show at Swansea University, on March 3, 1972. Les was twenty-seven.[2]

It was a devastating blow, to Stone the Crows—who came close to folding on the spot—and to Alex, who came just as close to quitting the music business for good. He relented, but it was sheer bloody-mindedness that kept him afloat over the next few months, for there certainly was no solace to be found in work.

Early audiences hated the Sensational Alex Harvey Band (SAHB), unable to comprehend why such a seemingly traditional rock group should so readily have embraced glam-flavored gimmickry. Guitarist Zal Cleminson even wore makeup, for heaven's sake, the thick white mask of a Pierrot.

Harvey later agreed that it was the hatred of the band that turned things around for them. People couldn't believe what they were seeing, so they brought their friends back to show them for themselves. By the end of the summer, SAHB was ranked among the biggest draws on the London club circuit, and as their audience grew, so did their fan base. In the early fall of 1972, the group signed to Vertigo, and went straight into the studio. Five days later, SAHB emerged with their debut album, *Framed*.

The album took its title from the Leiber-Stoller song already established as the centerpiece of SAHB's live show, a song which would become increasingly more elaborate as time passed. With a silk stocking pulled over his head, Harvey acted out the part of a hard-done criminal as though his life depended on it; mid-song, the stocking would disappear into his mouth (!) as he busted his way through a polystyrene brick wall, to plead his innocence before the audience. "But . . . no one believes him," *New Musical Express*'s Charles Shaar Murray wrote. "'Sure he did it, man, just look at him!'"

Framed remains an epochal album, with Nick Cave's cover of "The Hammer Song" on his 1990 album, *The Good Son*, sending a whole new generation scurrying back to rediscover Harvey. "Which was what I intended," Cave admitted, because his own first group, The Boys Next Door, idolized Harvey to the point of obsession. "Alex was everyone's favorite, and we used to do maybe eight or nine of his songs. We did just about everything off the first album."

Chris Bailey, singer with fellow Australians the Saints, shares Cave's enthusiasm. "Alex Harvey is an artist . . . . That band made some absolutely wonderful, wonderful records, and I remember I really pissed off someone, some quite prominent

The Sensational Alex Harvey Band

journalist in England, by suggesting that the Sex Pistols were a bad Alex Harvey cover band with cockney accents."

More tours, more albums; by 1975, SAHB were among the biggest concert draws in England, and at last the inevitable happened. SAHB scored a hit single, a cover of Tom Jones' "Delilah," and six months past his fortieth birthday, Harvey rolled out to appear on *Top of the Pops* for the first time in his life. But he continued harking back to the maxim which supported him through his years of struggle: "I never wanted to be a star. I just wanted to be happy." In November 1976, with SAHB's seventh album, *SAHB Stories*, gnawing the Top Ten, Alex announced he was quitting the music industry.

"I don't wanna be a rock'n'roll star," he told *National Rock Star* magazine. "I'm not saying I haven't had a good time. I'm not knocking it. I can still get a terrific buzz out of performing with guys who really know how to play. But I don't wanna crash through walls onstage anymore."

The recent death of SAHB's manager in an air crash had affected Harvey deeply, but he stressed that wasn't why he was packing it in. Neither was he tired of his bandmates. "I'll always be with them. They're my boys. Maybe I'll be doing other things, but I'll always be involved."

Harvey gave notice of their next project, an album and tour under the ungainly name of SAHB—without Alex—then listed his own immediate itinerary: a solo album, a musical, and a spoken-word album narrating the legend of the Loch Ness Monster. But he also spoke darkly of health problems, the chest pains which led to a heart-attack scare, and the sheer hell of trying to keep the show going when he was feeling like hell himself.

For close to a year, at a time when the punk-rock movement was finally bringing to fruition the dreams of rock revolution he had been nurturing so long, Harvey was off the road, out of commission, and in and out of the hospital as his chest problems continued to baffle his doctors. But when he did return to the fray, in August 1977, it wasn't because his own energies were returning, but because someone else's had finally expired. Like the recently deceased Elvis Presley, Harvey was forty-two; unlike Elvis, he didn't want to live out his last years in a world of twilight legend. Ill health or not, he was going back on the road.

The revitalized SAHB debuted at a Belgian festival, then followed up with a showing at the Reading Festival. But the album which they spent much of September recording, *Rock Drill*, was at best a pale imitation of the original SAHB—and at worst, the sound of a sick man trying to sound like every breath didn't hurt.

"I think he came out of the hospital too early," bassist Chris Glen said later. "And during the weeks that followed, he was expected to do too much. It just came to the point where he felt he couldn't do it any more." The failure of a new single, "Mrs. Blackhouse," followed by the delayed release of the album itself, only compounded Harvey's renewed disillusionment. In October, during rehearsals for a BBC broadcast, *Sight and Sound In Concert*, the singer walked out of SAHB for the last time.

Harvey, however, was neither down nor out. Dismissing his record company's insistence that he had finally retired, he publicly resurfaced in February 1978, and announced that he would be performing at the London Palladium on March 5. Later in the year, he previewed an album's worth of unheard songs at the London Venue.

Nothing came of it, however, and over the next two years, Harvey seemed content simply to wander, a musical itinerant caught between the energy of the protopunk he once was, and that of the new punks who had conquered the music industry in his wake. But his confidence was returning, and in May 1979, he appeared alongside the best of the new breed at a Rock Against Racism festival at Alexandra Palace, performing a stellar version of Bob Marley's "Big Tree, Small Axe." Shortly after, Harvey released his first solo album in ten years, *The Mafia Stole My Guitar*.

The album showed that Harvey had lost none of his crooked wit. The title track was just as great as its title demanded it should be, while a fiendish reworking of Johnny Kidd's "Shaking All Over" paid tribute to one of Harvey's greatest fallen idols. But just six months later, a new recording of "Big Tree, Small Axe" closed Harvey's recording career forever.

Throughout January 1981 Harvey was on the road in Europe, looking frailer than people liked to remember him, but loving every second, and lapping up the affection. He talked of the demos he'd been recording at home, and his hopes for a new album soon; he mentioned another possible reunion with at least a few of the SAHB crowd. If there was any indication of his newfound straitened circumstances, it was that he wasn't flying to shows anymore. He'd catch the Zeebrugge ferry back to England. And it was on the dock there that he died at age forty-five, suffering a fatal heart attack while he waited for his ship to come in. As journalist Pete Frame later put it, "Rock lost one of its greatest characters."

Of all Harvey's accomplishments, both before and during his 1970s heyday, perhaps his farthest-reaching influence was his patronage of Jacques Brel. Other rock artists had toyed with the Belgian songwriter: Scott Walker, who recorded a succession of Brel's songs during his own mercurial phase of teenybop success through the late

1960s; and David Bowie, who regularly dropped his name in interviews around the time of his *Ziggy Stardust*-era breakthrough in 1972.

But Walker, by 1972, was yesterday's news, an aging teenage idol now best known for popping up and crooning on teatime TV variety shows, and Bowie dropped so many names it was hard to keep them straight. Besides, "his version of [Brel's] 'Port of Amsterdam' always sounded like he took too many acting lessons," said Saints singer (and fellow Brel enthusiast) Chris Bailey. Bowie himself would later make amends, debuting a dramatic drum-and-bass version of "My Death" during his American tour in the fall of 1997. But still, Bailey insisted, "If you wanted to hear what Brel really meant, Alex Harvey was your man."

"Next," the title track to SAHB's second album, was a dramatic version of Brel's "Au Suivant," transformed into an apocalyptic tango, a bloodcurdling reminiscence of mobile army whorehouses, gonorrhea, and queer lieutenants. It was demented, dramatic, and it was utterly without precedent, a confession Harvey himself used to make when he introduced the song during concerts. "Rock'n'roll comes in many strange forms. This is one of them. And it was written by this Belgian man . . ."

From Harvey and Bowie, to Echo and the Bunnymen and Pulp's Jarvis Cocker; from Marc Almond and Gavin Friday, to Chris Bailey and Momus—Jacques Brel straddles rock history like a colossus. On the surface, which (of course) is all most casual listeners paid attention to, he was just another in a long line of swarthy-faced Gallic balladeers; a little quirkier than some, a little harder than others, and his accent was tougher than most—a little sadder, more bitter.

But from any number of starting points over the last forty years, Brel has woven his way into modern rock culture, and if his influence can be felt moving elsewhere as well, in the breast of MOR, for example—Frank Sinatra and Rod McKuen, through Terry Jacks' eternal renditions of "Seasons in the Sun" (Brel's "Le Moribund") or another nightclub throwaway of "If You Go Away" ("Ne Me Quitte Pas")—then that only exacerbates his impact. He retired in 1967; he died in 1978. But he has never, ever, gone away.

Born in Brussels, Brel was already into his twenties and married, a father of two with a respectable job, when he cut his first single in the summer of 1953. By September, he had all but fled Belgium, his family, and his life, to sing in Paris. "I think that talent really means wanting to make a dream come true," he reflected later. "The rest is sweat, perspiration, and discipline." Once in Paris, he demonstrated all three.

In 1955, still a struggling performer at the foot of city bills, Brel was booked onto a countrywide package tour. It was there that he met François Rauber, who would become his arranger and lifelong friend. Interviewed shortly after Brel's death, Rauber recalled simply, "I met him under the bandstand. There was this young guy hunched really intently over his guitar. He sang three songs. This was Brel."

Suzanne Gabriello, a singer appearing on that same tour, and one of several mistresses Brel would take over the years, continued, "He was shy and rather a strange character. We were all a bit intrigued by this Belgian straight out of Belgium. [His act] was pretty hard-hitting and unusual for 1955. He accompanied himself on his guitar and he held a sort of special fascination for the audience. He sort of took them by storm."

Inhabiting that strange half-world of shadowy figures that musical history insists existed on the eve of the rock explosion, close enough to what would soon be happening that he would both influence (and be influenced by) it, but undeniably a part of earlier traditions as well, Brel was the consummate protorock performer. America had Elvis Presley; France had Jacques Brel. There was the same connection between soul and audience; the same implied but rarely stated sexual energy; the same broaching of "forbidden" subject matter. Television footage from the period supports this. When Brel performed, there was an intensity which radiated tangibly from him; and though he barely moved, the way he held his guitar, the way he carried his body, and the utter joy that could flow from him, were quite unlike any other performer of his age.

But he was more than Presley. He was Presley possessed by the pen of Cole Porter. Had Brel not been born a Belgian, had those same dreams, emotions, and visions been present in a singing, songwriting American talent, who knows what might have become of him?

As it was, Brel would visit America only twice, for two one-off New York performances, in 1963 and 1965. Both were triumphs, but the first remains a milestone, for the single, ad-libbed moment at the end of the show when Brel, instead of offering the encore a packed Carnegie Hall demanded, merely asked one simple question: Had anybody understood a word he sang? Up on their feet, roaring applause, the audience responded with a rousing "*No!*" Years later, Love and Rockets bassist David J., himself an avid Brel fan, admitted the same thing. "But you don't have to understand the language. You understand what he's singing anyway."

New Yorker Eric Blau was the first writer to try and introduce Brel to an English-speaking audience, in 1961. Blau himself discovered Brel through his wife, singer Elly Stone. "[She] told me that he was not only great, but also the most important songwriter of the century."

Intrigued, the couple began translating Brel into English, completing two songs,

"If You Go Away" and "Carousel," in time to incorporate them into the musical revue *O Oysters*. (A third song translation, "Marieke," was later added to the show.) The first underground rumblings began, and they would not remain isolated for long. By 1963 Rod McKuen, too, was courting Brel, but from a very different direction than that employed by Blau and Stone.

Brel's magic, McKuen believed, was in conveying moods, not simple words; that was what Carnegie Hall responded to, that was what attracted McKuen himself. He couldn't understand French, but he didn't need to. His attempts to render Brel into English were not so much translations as they were transpositions, and if "Seasons in the Sun"—so freely adapted from Brel's prototype—were all the Belgian was honored for today, then his reputation would be sorely misplaced.

Fortunately, however, there was far more to come. Reworked from the Blau's earlier effort, McKuen's translation of "Ne Me Quitte Pas" was first covered by Damita Jo in 1967. Three decades later, this most exquisite of love songs has been rendered by everyone from Sandy Shaw to Frank Sinatra, soul group the Dells to muzak king Tommy Garrett, from folkie Judy Collins to country star Glen Campbell, and ultimately, by Marc Almond. And not once has it lost its beauty, its pain, its sheer devastation.

In 1966, Brel found himself the object of another American songwriting hero's attentions. Mort Shuman was twenty-eight, but already he and partner Doc Pomus[3] had written for Elvis Presley, Ray Charles, and many more. It was lucrative work, but, as Eric Blau explained, "after hearing Brel and getting to know Brel's work, Mort turned off rock. Brel [knocked] him out, and Brel was for Mort, a bridge to his own future work. And that's not a small thing, because Shuman [was] an intensely gifted man."

Shuman was one of the rapturous hoards who caught Brel at his return to Carnegie Hall in 1965; he also attended Brel's first and only London show, at the Royal Albert Hall in 1966. Now he, too, wanted to widen the songwriter's appeal. The result, in tandem with Blau and Elly Stone, would be the stage show, *Jacques Brel Is Alive and Well and Living in Paris*.

Brel announced his retirement from music in 1967, a year before *Alive and Well* opened. He intended to focus now on theater and movies, a decision that caused uproar, in France at least. In Britain and America, however, it was barely noticed, for even as Brel took the last bows at his last major concert, at the Paris Olympia in early 1967, on the other side of the English Channel, Scott Walker was debuting him to an entire whole new audience—one who would have a decade's worth of catching-up to do before they ever noticed Brel was gone.

■ ■ ■

One-third of the teen sensation Walker Brothers, now striking out on his own solo career, Walker discovered Brel through a girlfriend. The girl was soon forgotten, but the music never would be. Instantly Walker identified with Brel's work, the themes of anger, love, and world-weariness which so succinctly summarized his own emotions. Walker remembered, "It was one of the happiest days in my life when a girlfriend gave me the first translation I'd seen of Brel's lyrics."

Brel was equally taken with Walker. Although the two never met—Walker apparently refused to be introduced, for fear that his idol might disappoint him—Brel personally ordered Mort Shuman to hand over the proposed *Alive and Well* translations to the young Californian. Between 1967 and 1969, across three albums, Walker would record nine of Brel's songs and even within the confines of the "popular entertainer" mold into which his record company forced him, he set a standard for Brel's work within the world of rock.

Both David Bowie and Alex Harvey would learn of Brel through Walker's recordings, and based their interpretations upon his own; they in turn created their own precedents, prompting their listeners, too, to dig deep into a new idol's influences, with Marc Almond emerging as Brel's most loyal, and effective, disciple. In 1982, even as he topped the chart with Soft Cell's "Tainted Love," Almond's Marc and the Mambas alter-ego reappraised both "If You Go Away" and "The Bulls." And though at the time the entire project was considered darkly uncommercial, a decade later Almond would throw such condemnations back in his accusers' faces by topping the charts once again, with Brel's own "Jacky" ("Chanson du Jacky"). And between times, he recorded an entire album of Brel songs, under the logical title *Jacques*, bringing brand-new meaning to a clutch of familiar songs.

Working with arranger-translator Paul Buck, Almond commissioned fresh English interpretations of some songs, and first-time versions of others, creating a work of such daring that Buck himself would later state, "Jacques Brel died in 1978, just as Marc Almond started out as a singer. I'd like to suggest that some of Brel's spirit transferred itself during that October night."

Brel, had he lived to see it, doubtless would have remained unimpressed. His musical retirement in 1967 coincided with his discovery by the English-speaking world. In 1974, when Canadian singer Terry Jacks' recording of "Seasons in the Sun" presented Brel with his biggest success yet, the singer announced he was going to retire from public life altogether and sail around the world.

He neither needed this new fame, nor cared for it. Brel was tired—of his reputation, of the French and Belgian media which hounded him even after he gave up performing, and now, of the realization that his own mortality was catching up with him.

In August 1974, Georges ("JoJo") Pasquier, Brel's friend, confessor and confidant for the past twenty years, passed away.[4] The following month, Brel discovered that he himself was suffering from lung cancer. He halted his globetrotting long enough to undergo treatment, having the diseased lung removed so that the other might stand a chance of recovery, but he could not—would not—remain still. Within six weeks, he was back aboard his yacht; within a year, he was looking for a home on the Marquesas Islands, in the South Pacific.

Accompanied by his current mistress, Madly Bami, Brel set up house in a white bungalow, surrounded by islanders who liked him for the man he was, not for the star he had become. He began writing again. Far from the maddening frenzy of the Parisian paparazzi, he composed the songs that would become his first new album in a decade, *Brel*. Then, contacting his old arranger, François Rauber, plans were made for Brel to travel quietly to Paris to commence recording.

Jacques Brel backstage after his farewell concert in May 1967
(Archive Photos/Paris Match)

The sessions were difficult. Despite Rauber's insistence that Brel call his family, with whom he had remained so close despite years of philandering, his wife and children never did find out that Brel was back in Europe. That caused tension; so did Brel's still-fragile health. So, too, did his refusals to remain in Paris to promote the record, and to seek medical advice. Rather, he fled back to his island home, instructing his record company not only to leave him alone, but to leave the album alone as well. Not only would he not promote it; they shouldn't, either.

The label carried his instructions out to the letter . . . after a fashion. As its fall 1977 release date approached, *Brel* was hyped not with the traditional praise for its contents and form, but with tales of its maker's own demands for secrecy. Advance copies were shipped to the press in padlocked boxes, whose combination would not be revealed until the day before the album's release. Magazines, unable to actually play the album, instead reviewed its mystery, speculating over the contents of a record which took ten years to gestate. Brel's disappearance, coupled with salaciously dramatic accounts of his continued ill-health, only added to the furor.

On November 8, 1977, *Brel* was released, and immediately catapulted to the top of both the French and Belgian charts, setting a new world record for first-day sales. In Britain, Brel's historical resonance was sufficient for the music press there to swoop on the record, even at the height of punk rock. In terms of iconography, Brel's French label, Barclay, boasted just one other release that year, which even threatened to rival the excitement surrounding *Brel*. It was by the Sex Pistols.

In July 1978, Brel flew from his home to nearby Tahiti for a series of routine tests. The results were grim. After two years in remission, the cancer had spread to his other lung. He was faced with no alternative but to return to Paris for treatment, but of course there was no rest there. The press hounded his every move, camped outside his hotel, waited outside the hospital. In August, *Paris Match* magazine ran a three-page picture exclusive of Brel, bandaged, broken, and barely able to walk, as he departed one day for treatment.

He vanished underground, to a secluded house in Provence, and briefly enjoyed another respite. But early in October, he relapsed, an attack which spewed so much blood into his one bronchial tube that first he almost drowned, and then almost suffocated as it began to coagulate. The forty-nine-year-old Brel was rushed back to Paris, to the Franco-Muslim Hospital, and it was there that he would die, in the very early morning hours of October 9, 1978. His last words, unutterable until a nurse removed his oxygen mask to allow him a sip of Coke, were one last whispered rasp of defiance: *"Je ne vous quitterais pas."*

11

this isn't au revoir, this is good-bye

THE HEADACHES HAD BEEN WORSENING for weeks. His business, a small, independent delivery company, was going through hard times; he wasn't sleeping well. So when he told friends he was feeling ill, they all thought it was stress and carried on with their own lives. Instead, it turned out to be a brain tumor, and less than ten weeks later, Howard Pickup was dead.

Adverts guitarist Howard Pickup never won a "best guitarist" award in the music polls. He never received an instrument custom made to his specifications. And he only occasionally attracted that ubiquitous knot of fans who'd stand by the stage to study his technique.

In a group which already boasted two all-consuming focal points, punk pinup bassist Gaye Advert and dervish vocalist TV Smith, Pickup was content simply to remain in the background. Yet without his tight, economical guitar, weaving between Advert's auteur bass lines and Laurie Driver's piledriving percussion, Smith swore, "the Adverts would have been a very different band, with a very different sound. Basically, Howard could play pretty much anything we wanted him to."

Howard Boak—his surname, he proudly attested, was a quaint northern England colloquialism meaning "vomit"—was born in Yorkshire, England, in 1946. "It was the classic story," longtime friend Pam Hardyment relates, "playing guitar from the age of ten. He'd played folk clubs, been in bands, done everything, and he knew his guitar." When he spotted an ad in the *Melody Maker* classifieds that summer of 1976—"Special band seeks not-so-special guitarist"—he also knew he'd found the group he was looking for.

With a repertoire blistering with ready-made punk anthems—"One Chord Wonders," "Bored Teenagers," and "Safety in Numbers"—the Adverts' early shows were chaotic but exhilarating. Veteran journalist Miles was impressed enough that he would eventually produce the Adverts; the Damned's Brian James offered the band both live shows and an introduction to his record label; and publishing magnate Michael Dempsey became the group's manager, and would remain by their side for the rest of his life.[1]

Within a year of coming together, the Adverts had scored their first hit single. "Gary Gilmore's Eyes" was inspired by convicted American murderer Gilmore's insistence that he be executed, and that his eyes be donated to medical science for transplant ("I don't think the heart will be any good"); it was followed into the chart by "No Time To Be Twenty-one," and by the Adverts' debut album, in February 1978, *Crossing the Red Sea with the Adverts*.

It was a devastating record. Twenty years on, both *Rolling Stone* and *Q* magazines were still ranking it among the finest releases of the 1970s, but in 1978, even with the full weight of the music press and another sell-out British tour behind it, the album sank almost without a trace. It spent just one week in the Top 40, trailing in the slipstream of "No Time To Be Twenty-one"'s Top 50 success, then fell away.

The year began with disappointment and only got worse from there. Both drummer Driver and his replacement, John Towe, quit before the Adverts settled on Rod Latter. Their record label folded, removing *Red Sea* from the shelves altogether, and as for manager Dempsey's promise that the group's next stop would be America, where they were going to be "bigger than Beatlemania"—the farthest west the Adverts got was the coast of the Irish Republic.

They began work on their second album anyway; *Cast of Thousands* would finally appear more than a year later, by which time the Adverts were already over.

Neither could they discern any breaks in the gathering gloom: a movie made for German TV, *Burning Boredom*, was never released outside of that country; money problems were constantly to the fore; tempers were flaring; rehearsals were replaced by arguments. The only place the Adverts could get it together was onstage, and even that security was growing increasingly shaky. One night in September 1979, Pickup packed up his gear and went home from a show . . . and never came back again.

"Howard had been getting rather vague," Smith confirmed. "As soon as a gig or a rehearsal was over, he'd just go off immediately, then one day he didn't even turn up and we never saw or heard of him again. I think basically, he was pissed off with never having any money—we never got any."

In fact, he was fed up with the entire music industry. Pam Hardyment remembered, "He was just fed up with the backstabbing that went on, the lies and all the shit that comes with trying to make music. He dropped out completely. I used to say to him, 'Come on, play your guitar,' but he would say no. He wouldn't do it in front of anyone; he'd just play quietly to himself."

He did talk occasionally of getting back into the business, and he looked back on the Adverts with a great deal of affection. It was an indication of his disillusionment, however, that even after he learned of his illness, he never made any attempt to contact his former bandmates. They themselves only learned of his death from a mention in *Melody Maker*.

John Towe ran into him a few times in the early 1980s, playing golf, and operating a taxi service; when that fell apart, Pickup opened a delivery company. Then, in early 1997, the headaches started.

Hardyment continued, "His delivery company was on its last legs, with the recession and everything, and that's when he started getting stressed out, so when he said, 'I'm feeling ill,' that's when I said, 'Oh, it's stress, it's stress.' We all kept ignoring it, because he was quite a stressed guy. But it was a brain tumor, and within ten weeks, he was dead.

"As soon as they knew what was wrong with him, he went in for the radiotherapy. But he should never have bothered. All that shit did was make him feel worse."

Admitted to the Royal Marsden Hospital in early July, Pickup was due to be released home on July 12. Hardyment was intending to visit him that day. "I thought, 'Well, I'll just go home and change first,' and then I thought, 'No, he'll be out tomorrow' . . . and that was it. He died that same day. But I think he just wanted to go. With the radiotherapy, you get epilepsy, then they pump you full of morphine, you've got no chance anyway. He might just as well have died gracefully by himself, at home. Instead he died in this fucking hospital, and there was no one there.

"He was a great guitarist. He used to play at home, and compose in his own way; he had his own setup there with a computer and everything. He was very much a loner, but he couldn't give it up, he kept saying, 'Ah, maybe I'll start again,' and then it was too late. He was serious; he'd had enough of his business, it wasn't going anywhere, and I told him, 'Just do your music again, you never know.' But of course, he never did."

Pickup and the Adverts' importance in the British punk scene has never been in doubt. Along with the Sex Pistols, the Clash, and the Jam, they were—and remain—a genuine force of motivation in a genre that otherwise might have been drowned simply by its own self-imposed limitations. It was the Adverts who proved that not every song needed to be played at breakneck speed; not every chord had to jar your teeth; and not every emotion had to be negative and destructive. That much of their legacy, at least, did filter down through the ranks.

Yet if ever a musical genre seemed destined for protracted self-destruction, it was punk. Self-mutilation was already a part of it—albeit of the sort of now tame-sounding piercings of mouth, nose, and cheek—and self-degradation was natural, a given. It was inevitable, in the public mind, that death would swiftly follow.

Interviewed by journalist Terry Southern, asked whether he found "anything really new, or innovative, in the so-called 'new wave' music," Rolling Stone Keith Richards subscribed to one of the oldest urban myths around when he replied, "I did hear about this one guy . . . who pissed straight into the middle of this monstro amp, and got electrocuted—had his back to the audience and it knocked him right out into the third row. I mean, I wouldn't've minded seeing that."

But taking the stance to its furthest extreme only worked as a slogan, never a career move, and wearing a T-shirt emblazoned PLEASE KILL ME was only successful for as long as everyone who saw it was in on the same postnihilistic joke it punctuated.

When Richard Hell, the New York-based creator of that particular T-shirt, was confronted onstage in England by a fireworks-wielding fan, the fear in his face, said journalist Julie Burchill, was palpable. And when the fictional archpunk Norman Sleek died onstage every night during theatrical mavericks Albertos y Los Trios Paranoias' post-Presley *Sleaze* presentation, his demise drew a line everyone understood.

this isn't au revoir, this is good-bye

Sleaze was the story of a fantasy rocker, Sleek, who kills himself onstage to ensure his lasting fame. But all Sleek's nightly fate really proved was, that however artistic death might appear, it is still death. It doesn't matter how high your record sales go. If you can't reap the benefits, what's the point?

Even within punk's most devoted circles, where the New York Dolls' very name remains immersed in posthumous glory, few people remember drummer Billy Murcia, who overdosed at a party in 1972; fewer still recall Rick Rivets, their original guitarist.[2] Life went on, the Dolls went on, and even David Bowie had quit playing "Time," the song he dedicated to the late "Billy Dolls." Live fast, die young . . . and before you're cold, you're ancient history.

Sid Vicious notwithstanding, few punks died in the manner the media preordained for them. For all the tabloid terror about a cult of glorified self-immolation, only Darby Crash and G. G. Allin ever succeeded in (or even attempted) turning their final breaths into their final performances.

Mike North of the shortlived Watford-based Bears perished in a motorcycle accident in September 1977. Zenon De Fleur, the Polish-born guitarist with the R&B-based punk group Count Bishops, died in a car accident in March 1979. And then, of course, there was Stiv Bators.

Bators had been hanging himself onstage for years, suspending himself from his mike cord, then collapsing to the ground as the last chords of the night rang out, lying there while the roadies scurried to carry him off. It was effective, it was theater, it was part of the show. But one night at Amsterdam's Melkweg club, it didn't seem such a good idea. He'd been depressed all day, and as his band, the Lords of the New Church, prepared to take the stage, guitarist Brian James (formerly of the Damned) took the wiry little singer aside for a moment.

"Don't do the hanging bit tonight, okay? You don't really know what you're up to. You're a bit out of it." Bators kept walking, and didn't say a word. He rarely did when he was in that kind of mood.

The Lords were on their last legs, even they admitted that. Four years had elapsed since their last album, 1984's *Method to Our Madness*—years during which all the band's earliest promise and vicarious thrill slipped out of sight for all but the most ardent fans. Of course Bators was depressed. Everybody was.

The show raced by, somewhere between spontaneous inspiration and tired repetition, and then Bators started to choke himself, wrapping the cord around his neck, tighter and tighter, pulling the lead with one arm, while the other hung loosely beside him. Then a sudden jerk, a convulsive shudder, and he slammed to the floor.

Stiv Bators

(Jon Hammer/Archive Photos)

But was it the other musicians' imagination, or did he hit the ground just a little bit harder than he normally did?

The roadies appeared, took his arms and legs, and carried him into the wings. That was where he would normally spring back to life, but tonight he lay there still, unmoving, unflinching, even when he was laid on a backstage bench, and the room filled up around him.

The Lords' road manager, Ivor, poked him. "Stiv?" Behind him, James looked on, trying to disguise his mounting alarm with laughter and threats. "Better get up, Bators, or we'll leave without you." He leaned over to try and catch the singer's breathing. It was barely detectable. He slapped the singer's face a few times. Still nothing. If this was a joke, it was Bators' best one ever. But if it wasn't . . . Somebody suggested calling for an ambulance; somebody else took them up on it.

James made last one attempt at rousing his stricken partner. "Stiv, we've called the fucking fire brigade. If you're fucking with us, now's the time to get up, because there's a lot of drugs here, everybody's worried . . . . Stiv . . ." Then there was a knock at the door.

"Stiv waited," James marveled. "The bastard waited until not only were the fire brigade in the room, they were all around the bench, all ready to do the whole fucking lifesaving bit, and then he sits up, laughs, and goes, 'Fucked ya! Fucked ya!'"

Was it any wonder, then, that when James and Lords bassist Dave Treganna traveled to Paris for Bators' real-life funeral, they couldn't help wondering whether he was going to do it again? "We went down to view the body on the morning of the funeral, and I was fully expecting for this to be the end of another put-on, and for him to just sit up and say, 'Fucked ya!' Because he'd cried wolf so many times."

On this occasion, however, Bators wasn't joking. He really was dead.

Bators was one of the powerhouse frontmen of the 1970s East Coast punk explosion, rocketing out of Cleveland at the helm of the Dead Boys, who in turn would unleash one of the great debut albums of the era, *Young, Loud and Snotty*, before collapsing in disarray just two hellacious years later.

Born Steven J. Bator Jr. in Youngstown, Ohio, on October 22, 1949, and undecided whether to call himself Stiv Bators or Steve Machine, he joined Rocket from the Tombs—the self-styled "World's Only Dumb Metal Mind Death Rock & Roll Band"—in 1974. He didn't last, though: According to guitarist Peter Laughner's wife Charlotte, "He could hit the notes all right, but everything he did came across like an Iggy parody."

And why not? One of Stiv's favorite legends revolved around one night at a Stooges show: "You know that famous Stooges gig when Iggy smeared himself with peanut butter? It was me that handed it to him. I had this jar of peanut butter with me, and I wanted to see what he'd do with it."

But Stiv—why take peanut butter to a Stooges gig?

"I was only fifteen. They wouldn't let me take beer."

Bators walked out of Rocket from the Tombs and took half the band with him: guitarist Cheetah Chrome and drummer Johnny Blitz joined him first in Frankenstein, and then the Dead Boys, a band whose name came from an old Rocket from the Tombs song, "Down in Flames," and whose repertoire was drawn from that source as well. But their attitude was all their own.

"Stiv understood the importance of creating an image," explained a friend, John Donovan. "The whole band did. Out of all the American bands at that time, the Dead Boys were the only ones who had that British thing of attitude. You saw it at photo sessions. Other bands went and had their pictures taken. The Dead Boys had their attitude's picture taken."

It was Joey Ramone who discovered the Dead Boys, after his own band played a show in nearby Youngstown, then followed the Dead Boys back into Cleveland. "They were doing ninety miles an hour, then all of a sudden Bators climbed out of the driver's-side window, and he's still driving at ninety. Then he mooned us."

Ramone had never seen the Dead Boys play, but he was impressed all the same. The moment he got back to New York, he told Hilly Kristal, owner of the CBGBs nightclub, to book them, and by August 1976, the Dead Boys were firmly entrenched in the New York scene.

Bators was hanging himself back then, as well. "And the only time he ever thought twice about it," a friend once said, "was the night Peter Laughner died. It was like, 'Do I really want to be doing this?' And the next show he played, he went out, and did one of the best hangings of his life."

Like Bators, Peter Laughner had been around the Cleveland scene since the early 1970s. It was he, in fact, who formed Rocket from the Tombs, and when that band split and half the group became the Dead Boys, Laughner led the remainder into Pere Ubu, sonic art-terrorists whose initial statement of intent, "Final Solution," remains a classic of the age.

They, too, would swiftly hightail it to New York, but Laughner—already combining near-lethal combinations of drink and drugs in an orgiastic blitz of near self-destruction—didn't spend much time around them. Having already composed his own epitaph, the chilling "Ain't It Fun" (co-written with Cheetah Chrome, recorded by the Dead Boys, and later repopularized by Guns N' Roses), he was now furiously mythologizing himself via occasional writings for the rock magazine *Creem*. But he was also in and out of the hospital with a regularity that scared even his friends, martyr to a battery of drug-induced ailments.

"Peter was cool," Stiv Bators recalled half a decade later. "Peter was the one who made me believe in myself, told me not to let anyone else hang me up, that I should just get out there and play. He brought New York to Cleveland, and he got me and Cheetah together because he knew we'd work with each other. But you didn't want to hang out with him too long. There was a side to him you just didn't want to see too much of. The point was to be in control, no matter how out of your head you were, and Peter didn't get that."

Journalist Lester Bangs received a late-night phone call from Laughner around the fall of 1976, in which the guitarist casually let it slip that the doctors had warned him to quit shooting smack and drinking, or else he'd be dead before he knew it. Laughner seemed to have taken them seriously. "It's gonna hafta be Valium and grass from here on out," he conceded. "Shit, you gotta have something."

But he didn't quit the other stuff, and friends began to drop him. Bangs, no saint himself,[3] stopped letting Laughner stay over at his apartment; told him outright that if Peter wanted to kill himself, that was fine, but no way could he drop dead on Bangs' floor.

Laughner returned to Cleveland, checking into a hospital with another textbook full of ailments, and there he died, on June 22, 1977. But the coroner's verdict of "acute pancreatitis" only told half the story. Lester Bangs had the real scoop. With his death, Laughner finally had proven his commitment to the causes he deemed most sacred. Writing Laughner's obit in the September 1977 *New York Rocker*, Bangs opined, "He killed himself for something torn T-shirts represented in the battle fires of his ripped emotions." It was as simple, and as committed, as that.

Stiv Bators was fighting those same battles in 1981, two years after the Dead Boys self-destructed, when he formed the Lords of the New Church with Brian James, Sham 69 bassist Dave Treganna, and Barracudas drummer Nicky Turner. Describing how the band got its name, Bators explained, "it's a sort of swipe at born-again Christians. The label wanted to call us the Lords of Discipline—I liked the 'Lords' bit, it put me in mind of a New York street gang. Then one day we were talking about religion, and how rock'n'roll has come to replace it: people look to songs for guidance like they used to look to the Bible, they take slogans and wear them on buttons and T-shirts, and they live by them, they die by them. Rock'n'roll's become the new church, and I just thought, `Yeah, the Lords of the New Church.'"

Across three albums from the early to mid-1980s, the Lords pursued that belief relentlessly, until every frown of disapproval was treated like a triumph. The idea of the Lords as societal outcasts, a lone voice of reason speaking amid a web of political and social conspiracy, intrigued Bators from the start, even as he struggled with his own personal belief system.

Brian James revealed, "Stiv came from a very strong Catholic background, and he was constantly at odds with himself in the sense that he wanted to be open-minded and free about things. But at the same time, he had a real Catholic upbringing, and once you're brainwashed to that extent, it's very Jekyll and Hyde. So Stiv had one side of himself saying, 'Ah, everybody thinks for themselves, do your own thing,' and the other side's like this devil pulling him into the unquestioning religion side of things, because he'd been so conditioned as a kid.

"He became obsessed with [conspiracy theories], and you could understand, you could look at it with an open mind and say, 'That's possible, anything's possible,' and you'd run with it. But at the same time, we'd say, 'Stiv, you've got to keep an open mind about it.' The whole point of the Lords was not to preach, but to offer options and alternatives, to make people think for themselves: 'Don't believe what you read, don't believe what you're told.' So Stiv was caught in the middle, pulling in two directions inside himself."

Bators reacted against his upbringing in every way he could, then, but he seldom took his rebellion to the point of no return. On May Day 1981, for example, Bators wed girlfriend Stacey in a Wiccan marriage ceremony, one which bound them together for a year and a day, but would never be acknowledged by societal law or religion.[4] Later, on the Lords' final album, *Method to Our Madness*, he defused the conspiratorial legends he spun in song by recruiting manager Miles Copeland (famously, the son of an American CIA agent) to contribute a few lines of "warning" to the title track. Always, Bators left an exit open.

This tug of war could only pull the Lords down with it, escalating as their own popularity slipped (the victims, of course, of the controlled media's resistance to them), and climaxing when the group toured Spain in 1989. The shows were intended as the first leg of a European tour they only agreed to because it would pay off a monstrous tax bill. Bators, however, "got really crazy. He wasn't a drinker, but he'd be downing tequila like there was no tomorrow." James was coming off the drink at the time, "and I was saying, 'No, no man, this is sensible Brian here, remember?' and once in a while, Stiv listened to me. But he half killed himself while we were out there, and there was no way he could do the tour."

The rest of the shows were cancelled, and as the Lords finally broke down, Bators returned to Paris, where he and his new French girlfriend, Caroline, had moved the previous year. France, Bators stated, was the only country in the world that hadn't tried to suppress him. It was all the more ironic, then, that Paris was where he should meet his end.

He was scheming a new group at the time, tentatively called the Whores of Babylon, and linking him with Dee Dee Ramone and Cheetah Chrome, among others. But on June 4, 1990, Bators was out shopping with Caroline, waiting outside a store while she ran in to pick something up. Suddenly a passing motorist lost control of his car, mounted the pavement, slammed into Bators, and knocked him to the ground.

The singer seemed all right at first. An ambulance was called, but although he was in considerable pain, Stiv refused to go to the hospital. It was a typical Stiv performance, always the showman, always the hero. Brian James reflected, "Everybody wanted him to go to hospital, but he was too cool for that: 'No, I'll be all right.' He went home, went to bed, and died in his sleep from massive internal injuries.

"For anybody else, just being knocked down like that probably wouldn't have had the same effect. Stiv was just hollowed out from the amount of speed and shit he'd done throughout his life, and his body couldn't take it. At the same time, though, it wasn't like an out-and-out, 'This is an OD.' It wasn't the way people expected Stiv to go, so that was nice. Because it means Stiv is still saying, 'Fucked ya, fucked ya, fucked, ya!' "

OVER THE COURSE OF eighteen months, from the fall of 1978 until vocalist Malcolm Owen's death on July 14, 1980, the Ruts established themselves amongst the most compelling of all the groups on the British punk scene.

Politically aware but rarely sloganeering, operating on the very fringes of the genre's outrageous public self-consciousness, the Ruts stood at the crossroads of punk, reggae, and that peculiar brand of skinhead chanting known as Oi!, and gave their heart to all three. The fact that they accomplished it all with just one official album and a handful of singles, only emphasizes their power; the fact that Owen was spiraling out of control even as the band's fame grew, only accentuates their tragedy.

The first song the Ruts ever recorded, Owen's anti-heroin anthem "H Eyes," set the scene. Through a chilling attempt to isolate in his own mind what it was that he found so compelling about the drug, Owen counseled, *"It's gonna screw up your head, you're gonna wind up dead."* He knew what he was doing to himself, but he simply couldn't stop.

Even as the Ruts' appeal grew, through the heavy dub of "Jah Wars," the fiery punk of "Babylon's Burning" and the querulous pop-rock of "Something That I Said," the singer was engaged in his own private battle. As early as 1977, when drummer Dave Ruffy, guitarist Paul Fox, and bassist Vince Seggs first met Malcolm, he was blithely combining the roles of club DJ and small-time drug dealer. His plunge into a heavier dalliance was inevitable even then.

Not one of his bandmates sensed that, though. "He was a very well connected young man," recalled Ruffy, "very handsome; he had this fantastic woman named Rocky who he married"—in other words, he had everything going for him, and as the Ruts took off, he had even more. But it turned out that he wanted even more than that.

"He wanted to be a rock star," attested bassist Seggs. "Malcolm wanted to be a pop star. He wanted a lame jacket for a laugh, to earn money, and take taxis. And he was hanging out with Phil Lynott of Thin Lizzy[1] who was a lovely man, but was maybe not the best kind of influence for someone like Malcolm to be around."

For a time, through 1979 and a succession of ever-more-incredible triumphs, Owen kept his demons at bay. "There were a lot of other different things around," Ruffy reflected. "We were big on drinking, we were big on spliff, like most young men given the chance, and though we signed a dogshit of a record deal, somewhere along the line it all started going off for us. And that's when smack got into the equation."

"When we first started playing," Seggs continued, "he used to be late sometimes, because he'd have fifteen whiskeys down the road, because that was the way he performed. In a similar way, that's what the smack did, only it took over. And in the end he wasn't that dynamic person I first knew. He was a gray, struggling person in the end."

Seggs detailed the next stage. "You tell someone to get themselves together, and they can't. And what happens is, they lie. Malcolm and I used to share a hotel room, and when the little bag came out, I'd tell him, 'You're not doing that in my room.' So he'd go, 'Okay,' and a while later, he'd off into the toilet and do it. Then I caught on to that, so he'd go off and do it somewhere else, and it just became seedier and seedier.

"We'd get to a gig and just before the soundcheck, he'd disappear. He always said he'd never do it before a gig, but then sometimes we'd be waiting twenty, twenty-five minutes to go onstage, and he'd come out of the bathroom, his eyes pinned, and say, 'Ah, I couldn't get me laces undone,' and we'd just be, 'Oh fuck.' Or in the studio, he'd disappear to the toilet with his bag—'Just going for a piss before this take'—then he'd come back twenty-five minutes later, out of it. You'd go in there, there'd be blood in the toilet and the little cigarette filter. It was so sad."

When the Ruts first came together, Owen's pride and joy was a massive, and massively expensive, stereo system, with a vast, eclectic record collection to go with it. Early band meetings would be held at his house, simply listening to music nobody else but Owen owned. He sold it all for smack, and the rest of his possessions followed into the void. So, early in 1981, did his loyal wife, Rocky, finally driven away by Owen's heartless quest for the only thing he now cared about.

"The band was really suffering badly," Ruffy said with regret. "Even getting Malcolm to rehearsals was difficult. He'd turn up five hours late, or not turn up at all and make some bullshit excuse, or other times he'd come in with his face smashed up, because he hadn't paid someone."

That spring, the Ruts went into the studio to begin work on their second album. It was a disaster from the start, but they persevered—according to Ruffy, "because this was a bloke that we loved, there was the four of us, we were like a family, we'd been together about two years. But it just wasn't working."

One song gave them a glimmer of hope, "Love In Vain," a B-side documenting both Owen's addiction and the breakup of his marriage. Ruffy remembered, "When we did 'Love In Vain'—that line *I don't want you in my arms*'—smack was taking its toll, and Malcolm didn't really want to be into it anymore. So he wrote that because he was splitting up with Rocky as well, and the song was the romance and the heroin at the same time. He said, 'Yeah, it's really, really bad, I'm going to clean up.' And we believed him."

But it wasn't as easy as that, as Ruffy soon discovered. "Like a lot of junkies, he just gave us a complete load of bollocks. It was well-meant but we'd go on tour, we'd be at gigs, and he had a fucking secret compartment in his shoe! We'd be, 'Malcolm, come on, we're going on,' and he'd be in the toilet. . . ."

"And the only way we dealt with it," admitted Seggs, "was—we couldn't. We tried to help him, and it didn't work." By the time the Ruts' spring 1981 tour reached the south-coast town of Bournemouth, England, the singer was in a bad way. "He was so out of it," Seggs mourned. "Someone had to keep giving him lines of coke; they kept coming out with lines of coke for him, so he could go back onstage, just to keep him going.

"He'd become like an old man. All his hands were withered and everything. He lost it. He got a nodule on his throat, and in the end he just collapsed." The Ruts were in Plymouth, England, facing a sell-out crowd, and Owen was completely out for the count. "He couldn't get up for the gig." The show was canceled; so was the next one, and the one after that. Almost overnight, the remainder of the tour was wiped out.

"You wanna know if I'm a heroin addict, right?" In an interview with the British music paper *Sounds* that May, Owen denied the rumors that had finally escaped the Ruts' own circle, and were swarming around the media as well. "I'll tell you the truth, the same as I told my mum when she rang up, scared to death. I've dabbled a bit in anything you could name. But everything's all right now, so don't worry."

Behind the brave words, however, it was crisis time. Ruffy said, "His voice was shot, but as far as he was concerned, everything apart from smack was irrelevant. It was really sad, this remarkable man, who was really loved and respected by everybody, was just becoming an asshole, basically. All he cared about was smack. Nothing else mattered, all the stuff we did together didn't matter.

"So we thought, 'The only way we can confront this is to say, "fuck you, we're not gonna do this anymore, we're not gonna be the Ruts, you can fuck off.' Because he kept saying he'd stop, then you'd see him and he'd be all pinned out, and it was still going on. So we said, 'Okay, we'll knock it on the head.'"

It was the most brutal shock treatment they could imagine, all the more so because they meant it. Virgin Records, the Ruts' label, had already given their blessing to the Owenless team continuing as a trio, and studio time was booked. Whether they remained the Ruts or not, the group would go on. "And it really did Malcolm in," declared Ruffy. "Suddenly he went into rehab for a couple of weeks," and from there, he retired to his parents' house to convalesce.

"I went round me mum's, and she locked me in for a week," Owen told *Sounds*. "Literally. I stayed in bed shivering and moaning, but it worked. I'm totally free of the filthy stuff now." He celebrated his recovery by going into the hospital for another reason entirely, for the removal of the nodules at the back of his throat. Without them, he was confident, he'd be singing like a bird. On Friday, July 11, he arranged a meeting with his estranged colleagues.

"He'd done a clean-out, and said, 'Look, lads, I'm okay now,'" Seggs recalled. "He had the old sparkle back in his eyes, he was the old Malcolm, and he said, 'Look, how about one last farewell gig?' And we were, 'Shit, okay!' He'd been off the smack for three weeks, he was clapping his hands: 'I'll get the band back together.' And we said, 'You know, maybe we will get the band back together; maybe splitting the band was the best thing we could have done.'"

Owen spent that night at the house Ruffy and Seggs shared in South London, and the following morning, his father came over to drive him home. Then, at some point over the next day or so, while his bandmates were in the studio recording the demos they now desperately hoped they would never need, Owen borrowed seven hundred British pounds from his father, to pay off his drug dealer and finally close the book on his habit forever.

What happened next is anybody's guess. According to Andy Damon, the Ruts' manager, "He was feeling so great when he paid the dealer, he must have thought, 'Aw, it won't hurt to have another hit.'" Returning home with his booty, Owen sat on it for one night, maybe two. But that Monday morning, July 14, he ran a bath, got out his works, and he fixed what had been his usual dosage.

Ruffy documented the inevitable conclusion. "Someone had gone round to meet Malcolm for a lunchtime pint, turned up and waited in the front room, because Malcolm was having a bath. His dad's looking all sheepish, and the friend says, 'What's going on?' and his dad says, 'I can't get any answer from Malcolm.' So he got a ladder and went up the side of the house." Owen's body lay submerged in the bath.

"They kicked the door down, but by then it was too late." The sudden massive infusion of smack into Owen's detoxed body knocked him unconscious, and slowly the singer slipped beneath the cooling water. The actual cause of death was drowning.

The following week's music press would give Malcolm Owen all the headlines they could, but all Seggs could see was hypocrisy. The Ruts were never critical favorites, he said, "and I got very, very annoyed afterwards, because they were always slagging him off in the press while he was alive, then he died and suddenly our new single ["West One"] got 'Record of the Week.' Everybody was saying he was great, and how he died for his art and all that. And he didn't. He didn't die for his art, because we weren't doing fucking art. We were a noisy punk band. He died because he couldn't handle the heroin."

"But that's what death can do," Ruffy concluded. "It turns whatever you did do when you were alive into something else entirely different. It makes people look at everything in a different light"—which is exactly what Germs vocalist Darby Crash was banking on when he slammed a few hundred bucks' worth of smack into his body, then lay on the ground in the shape of a cross and waited for death to resurrect his career.

Years earlier, Darby Crash's stepbrother Bobby had died from a heroin overdose; years earlier, too, Crash and guitarist Pat Smear had discussed taking the same way out themselves. "We had always talked about suicide, and doing it at this certain time, this certain time of your life," Smear admitted fifteen years later. It was just coincidence, he mused, that "when [Darby's] timetable came up, he was fucked-up enough in the head to want to do it."

Then again, was there ever a time when Darby Crash wasn't fucked up? Certainly his fans didn't think so, basing their beliefs on experience, which went back to the first-ever Germs show, opening for the Weirdoes at the L.A. Orpheum in 1977, through almost everything the singer did from then on.

That first night, he covered his entire body in sticky red liquorice, then stood as it melted beneath the hot lights, while the rest of the Germs played the only two songs they'd bothered to learn . . . over and over again. And as the Germs' repertoire grew, so did his. For Crash (originally known as Bobby Pyn), it was calculated role-playing, a game anyone could play. Punk was irresponsible; punk had no rules; punk would accept you, whatever you wanted to do. Crash just took that philosophy to the limits.

His first group, back at University High School, when he was still called Jan-Paul Beahme, never even existed outside of its members' heads, but they were enthusiastic enough to give it a name—Sophistif and the Revlon Spam Queens—and keen enough to go out one day, intending to get some T-shirts printed. The name changed when the printer got out his price list, and they discovered he charged by the letter. So the Revlon Spam Queens held a hasty conference, then returned home with a new name. They were the Germs, they said, because they made people sick.

Even by punk standards, Los Angeles punks were outcasts. In the home of the megabuck major labels, not one even sniffed at a punk possibility, so Pat Smear formed the band's own What Records with Chris Ashford, and released their sole classic single, the immortal rough cut, "Forming." It was what punks did.

Gigs were hardly any easier to find than record deals, so the bands created their own. They were banned from the Starwood, so someone opened the Masque. They were banned from the Troubadour, so someone else opened up their basement. And the savage, iconoclastic Germs, played every last toilet in town. That, too, was what punks did.

Other bands were better players, others wrote better songs. But for sheer input and intensity, the Germs left everyone bleeding behind them, onstage and—when the mood hit them—off. Down at the Oki Dog diner, nine nights out of ten, you'd find musicians and fans just hanging around, giving themselves a trademark

"Germs burn," a lit cigarette on the inside of the wrist, held in place long enough to make the flesh sizzle. It hurt like hell, but according to their own myth-making, that's what the Germs were all about.

Crash knew no pain, felt no shame: If it moved, he fucked with it; if it didn't, he took it. Groupies would line up just to be abused by him, the story went, but he very rarely slept with them, and that added to his mystique as well. Whether one appreciated what he was doing or not, in terms of punk iconography, he was riding a winner all the way—and had been ever since Sid Vicious checked out.

Overdosing on heroin supplied by his very own mother,[2] the death of the former Sex Pistols bassist, on February 2, 1979, made an enormous impression on Crash. So did the Danteesque drama that had begun four months before, one October morning when a hapless Vicious awoke in a hotel room in the infamous Chelsea Hotel in New York City, to find his girlfriend, Nancy Spungen, lying murdered in a pool of her own blood. Sid's knife, bought a few days earlier while out shopping with Stiv Bators, lay sheathed in gore nearby. So far as the NYPD was concerned, it was an open-and-shut case.

Of course it wasn't, and Spungen's murder was never closed. But that, too, became part of the ongoing tragedy; a saga that could be dated back to the days when the newly rechristened John Beverly learned that with a nickname like Sid Vicious—and friends like the Sex Pistols—there were certain reputations that demanded to be upheld.

Pistols vocalist Johnny Rotten shrugged, "He believed his own hype. He was called Vicious because he was such a wanker. He couldn't fight his way out of a bag [of chips]." But Sid read his own press and believed it. Of course it was only a matter of time before he started to upstage it and other people wanted to raise the stakes even higher.

In New York, out on bail following Spungen's murder, Vicious picked a fight with Patti Smith's brother, Todd. "That was actually quite frightening," Smith recalled. "My brother [was] a tough kid but he's very pacifistic. He was a real peacemaker type of guy. I think Sid Vicious was just crazy. He just went crazy in this bar and my brother almost lost his eye. He didn't provoke him or anything. But Sid Vicious was fairly out of control then, because he died soon after that. He was another kid who was really talented but he didn't keep his balance. That whole story is tragic. Both of them [Sid and Nancy] lost control and it's sad."

Even today, the most famous photos of Vicious are those where he's covered in

Sid Vicious

(Pictorial Press Ltd.)

blood; even today he remains the last vivid stitch in rock's revolutionary tapestry—not because of what he did, but because of what he didn't do.

Wholly absorbed in his own sordid image, Vicious was never able to strip away the mask and figure out where the mythmaking ended, and real life began. Neither, fifteen years later, could G. G. Allin, the self-consciously apocalyptic postpunk showman who claimed his greatest ambition was to set fire to his audience, but ended up bowing out in bed with a needle in his arm. And neither, sandwiched between the two, could Crash . . . . Except maybe, right at the very end, he did.

By the summer of 1980, the Germs were on the verge of collapse. Bassist Lorna Doom quit; drummer Don Bolles and manager Nicole Panter were sacked; and Crash was in London, seeking new thrills. The L.A. punk scene was collapsing around him; too many years of police repression, too many years of vicarious thrill-seekers waiting for him to hurt himself for them. He needed a break, and a brand-new direction, but when he returned to L.A. with a foot-high Mohawk haircut, and plans to form a new, eponymous band, his friends weren't overly impressed. He was, they reflected, "a little weird"; he looked "a little silly."

Retaining only guitarist Pat Smear from the Germs, the singer led his Darby Crash Band through a handful of poorly received live shows before he acceded to the inevitable. On December 3, 1980, the Germs played a reunion show, at the Starwood, and for a while, it was just like old times again. (Two songs from this performance are included on the Germs' *What We Do Is Secret* EP). Then the show ended, and Crash discovered what else had changed in the years since "Forming." "See you at the Oki Dog," he called to the crowd as he left the stage, because that was where people went after Germs shows. But when he got there later, the place was deserted.

Four days later, on December 7, Crash turned up at girlfriend Casey Hopkins' home on L.A.'s North Fuller Avenue, with a bag of china white in his pocket, and a suicide pact in his head. Scrawling out a final note, Crash and Hopkins slammed $400 worth of smack into bodies already pricked and kicked to their limit. Hopkins would survive; Crash did not.

In life, as that last show proved, Darby Crash was old news. But in death, he became a new hero, and today, in the eyes of a still-adoring audience, his demise remains the ultimate rock'n'roll death trip: heartless, senseless, and best of all, painless. Dying not for what he believed in, but for all that he didn't, Crash's choice of exit ensured, deliberately and knowingly, that whatever else his life was remembered for, the sheer eloquence of its ending would be remembered more.

**Sid Vicious on stage
with the Sex Pistols**

(London Features)

Because if it was sordid, it also had style—for the first time, a rock "star" who lived up to his own hype; for the first time, a martyr who did it for himself. Cynics, and there were many, argued that in life, the Germs produced little of lasting artistic merit, and that Crash himself was simply the luckless fool who took the bus out of town before he was unmasked.

And maybe, had the Darby Crash Band crashed and burned, had he been consigned to the comeback circuit for the rest of his days, eking out an increasingly pathetic existence on the back of long-irrelevant oldies, that would have been the case. In death, however, he not only validated his stance, he also ensured that he would never be asked to explain it again. More than any lyrics, any song, his death confirmed everything he'd been trying to say in life.

Plus, he did the one thing which no other punk rocker ever managed to do. He beat a Beatle to the finishing line. John Lennon was murdered the following day.

Darby Crash's suicide would be lost in that chaos. While Lennon grabbed the front pages, Crash was in the back. While Lennon's records topped the charts, Crash's weren't even on sale. Not until Germs guitarist Pat Smear joined Nirvana (and later, Dave Grohl's Foo Fighters) in 1993, was there more than a ripple of interest in Crash and an underground cult of worshipers. There was, however, what he would have wanted—speculation, admiration, and very little information. Some secrets are best left untold.

this is the hour when the mysteries emerge

IF EVER A GROUP WAS made for enshrinement, it was Joy Division. While bassist Peter Hook looked back and marveled at the reputation the band has lived with in the years since its demise, wondering "why people thought we were so miserable, because I thought it was quite exciting," still, the weight of so much critical opinion crushes that excitement into barely tangible dust.

Joy Division played their songs in a slow, minor key, insists the perceived wisdom of twenty years' worth of critics. Their lyrics were doomy, relentless and black. And then their singer killed himself. Even in the most optimistic world, that is not the hallmark of happiness.

And so the confusion remains, and grows stronger every day, nurtured by the icy drone which was Joy Division's signature sound, and blossoming through the lyrics which Ian Curtis laid out as though they might someday become his own valediction. Because when they did, the synchronicity cut like a knife. Today, Joy Division's entire oeuvre is described as a spiraling darkness, dense and despairing, hopelessness hamstrung by its own inevitable destiny. And the records don't disagree.

Curtis, however, would. Seated with the three friends who joined him in Joy Division, all he would say, in the same soft-spoken monotone he always adopted for interviews, was that things were not always what they seemed. "Some people have said [our music] is all about death and destruction. But it isn't, really. There's other things. None of the songs are about death and doom; it's such a heavy-metal thing, that." And Hook, speaking almost two decades after Curtis's suicide, continued, "Students, young kids, people still play that music to each other, because it's got a power that seems to open people up. Ian left a legacy that lasts to this day. All right, he couldn't do it himself, but he left music that still gives hope to loads of people."

It just didn't give much hope to Curtis.

On the evening of Saturday, May 18, 1980, Curtis left his parents' house, and headed over to the home he had recently been sharing with his ex-wife, Deborah. He wanted to watch Werner Herzog's *Stroszek*, without disturbing his parents; they had never showed much interest in subtitled art-house movie classics, even ones whose culminating horror, as an artist tries to choose between two women in his life and can't, found an uncanny echo in Ian Curtis's own affairs. He and Deborah married young, just nineteen when they tied the knot, but after four years together, Curtis fell in love with another, Annik Honore, who worked for Joy Division's Belgian record label.

Curtis' comrades tried to stay out of the triangle. Friends with Deborah, and uncertain how important Honore really was to Curtis, they watched from afar, and it was only later, rereading the lyrics Curtis was writing, that they understood just how deeply the conflict was affecting him. But it was Deborah Curtis herself, writing a decade later in her *Touching from a Distance* autobiography, who noted most publicly that "Ian's personal life was disintegrating, as his professional life was flourishing." But it was not only his love life which was falling apart.

On December 27, 1978, as Joy Division still struggled to escape the cult confines which early singles had erected around them, Curtis discovered he suffered from epilepsy. Traveling home from their first-ever London gig, trying to sleep in the back of the van, guitarist Bernard Sumner suddenly became aware of Curtis tugging at his sleeping bag. He tugged back, and the two began to struggle, with Curtis all the while wrapping the sleeping bag around his own head.

Drummer Steven Morris pulled the van over to the side of the road, watching in bemusement as Curtis, still encased in the sleeping bag, began lashing out with his fists, slamming them against the windows with increasing, and then just as suddenly, diminishing strength. Finally, as he calmed, Morris restarted the van, and drove to the nearest hospital.

Back home in Manchester, Curtis's own doctor placed him on a waiting list to see a specialist; meanwhile the fits continued. One day he returned home from walking the dog, looking as though he had been beaten up. On another occasion, he slipped into an immobile silence from which he could not be roused. Both events were seizures, extremities which matched the wild mood swings his newly prescribed medication could so easily set off. "The whole thing about epilepsy," Peter Hook explained, "[is] they can treat it so much more easily these days. Back then, it's amazing the guy didn't rattle, he was taking that many pills."

Joy Division released their debut album, *Unknown Pleasures*, in spring of 1979, to a firestorm of stunned reviews. Suddenly, the Manchester quartet that had started life listening to Iggy Pop's harrowing album *The Idiot* and had been refining its effect ever since, was suddenly teetering on the brink of a major step forward.

Sounds described *Unknown Pleasures* as the last record you'd play before committing suicide, and headlined its review "Death Disco." (John Lydon's—formerly known as Johnny Rotten—Public Image Ltd. would later turn that title into a hit single.) *Melody Maker*, whose reviewer had just relocated to the city, compared it to a tour of Manchester: "endless sodium lights and semis seen from a speeding car, vacant industrial sites . . . gaping like teeth from an orange bus."

Names like Ultravox, Orchestral Manoeuvers in the Dark, and Gary Numan's Tubeway Army[1] all could be referenced as bands working in the same musical sphere as Joy Division—that was undeniable. Where Curtis and company distinguished themselves was lyrically, and in allying those lyrics to the power of their music. There, names like Peter Hammill, Richard Strange, and, in later critical retrospectives, Nick Drake, could, and would, be dropped as potent forebears, distinctly English romantics who understood the emotional equation that gave them that distinction in the first place. Like them, Joy Division's music possessed an innate changeless timelessness; like Drake in particular, Curtis operated from a position of absolute isolation.

Six years earlier, reviewing Drake's *Pink Moon* swan song, *ZigZag* magazine remarked, "The album makes no concession to the theory that music should be escapist. It's simply one musician's view of life at the time, and you can't ask for more than that." That same observation was echoed time and time again as *Unknown Pleasures* made its presence felt.

"It's funny, isn't it," mused Peter Hook later. "Americans have this thing where they can sing about what a beautiful day it is. Whereas with the English, its always a really rotten day." John Cale, discussing the commercial failure of Nico's *Marble Index* album, once opined, "It's an artifact. You can't package suicide." Joy Division, it seemed, suddenly proved that you could.

The group's sudden elevation shocked them, all the more so since they so disagreed with the pedestal upon which they now rested. With supreme understatement, Hook continued, "It was very unsettling. To go from being nothing, to being lauded as one of the darkest groups known to man, was a trifle confusing."

Joy Division adapted to their reputation, though, just as Curtis adapted to his illness, subconsciously but nevertheless effectively, incorporating his seizures (or at least, their appearance) into his stage act. "During the set's many 'peaks,'" *Sounds* journalist Mick Middles wrote, "Curtis often loses control. He'll suddenly jerk sideways and, head in hands, he'll transform into a twitching, epileptic-type mass of flesh and bone." And just as suddenly, he would recover again. It was an unsettling display, all the more so since his comrades were never certain exactly what was going on. Was he simply dancing? Or was this the real thing?

Nobody could be sure. When Joy Division appeared on BBC-TV's *Something Else*, the station switchboard was swamped by viewers complaining about Curtis's appearance, with opinion divided over what they were most offended by: The fact that he looked so stoned? (He wasn't.) Or his tasteless impersonation of an epileptic fit? But even as the band tried to keep Curtis's condition to themselves, the singer's onstage behavior continued to attract attention. Years later Bernard Sumner detailed one evening when some fans approached Curtis with one simple question: "Are you the singer that has fits?" "I felt like fucking killing them," he admitted.

At the same time, however, Hook acknowledged that the true extent of Curtis's illness remained an abstract thing to his friends. "I couldn't see his illness, to be honest with you. We were so young, and so caught up in what we were doing. Now you could stop that; it would be the easiest thing in the world to stop someone who was that unhappy, and that unwell. But at that time, it's just all down to experience."

He counseled, however, that the group was not alone in the darkness. "It wasn't as if it was just us four beer-swilling knobheads from Salford who couldn't see what was going on. There was a lot of professional people who didn't spot it either, and he was being treated by doctors and psychiatrists and they didn't seem to spot it

either. And you can sit there now, and say, 'Fucking hell, how did you miss that, you dozy bastards?' But I think there's a lot more education these days, about depression and mental illness."

In July 1979 Curtis's specialist committed suicide.

It was their fall 1979 tour supporting the Buzzcocks that lifted Joy Division into the mainstream consciousness, as a brand-new audience caught them in concert. By the spring of 1980, it was as if the entire nation was awaiting their second album, *Closer*, and with it, a new single, "Love Will Tear Us Apart." An American tour, too, was imminent, and a European one after that. Had Joy Division only wanted to, they could have started filling up their schedules well into the next year.

To friends and family, however, it was also apparent that there was a chilling finality creeping into Curtis's life. Peter Hook outlined one facet of the singer's dilemma. "The thing was, he desperately, desperately wanted to do the things he wasn't meant to do. He wanted to play in a group, he wanted to push himself that much, and that made him ill, the exertion. The flashing lights made him ill. He liked the touring around—that made him ill, because he was always tired. He wasn't supposed to drink, he wasn't supposed to stay up late. He wanted that life, and his illness wouldn't allow him to do it. It was obvious, really, that something had to give."

Deborah Curtis, too, remained convinced that her husband finally had endured enough, that he had already developed a timetable, and knew exactly how, and when, he would enact it. Both as a posthumous hit single, and the inscription on his gravestone, "Love Will Tear Us Apart" would become Ian Curtis's epitaph. First, however, he had a movie to watch.

The artist, *Stroszek*'s hero, is in America when he finally makes up his mind about his two lovers. He decides that he cannot, and will not, decide. Then he kills himself. Curtis, for whom the looming U.S. tour was itself a source of considerable dread, could not allow himself the first luxury. But he apparently had no fear of the second. The last two months of his life convinced him of that.

Joy Division was scheduled to play two shows on the night of April 4, 1980. The first, at the Finsbury Park Rainbow, would see them opening for the Stranglers; the second, across North London at the Moonlight Club, placed them top of the bill at a record-company showcase. Looking back, everybody concerned agreed that they shouldn't have played either concert. Instead they did them both.

Curtis suffered one fit at the Rainbow, spinning around uncontrollably until he

slammed into the drum kit. The other musicians carried him offstage, still convuls-
ing, and locked themselves away with him until the seizure was over. Then they drove
to the Moonlight Club. Five songs into the set, Curtis suffered a second episode.

The seizures were coming faster. On April 8, at a show in Bury; a week later in
Derby; two weeks later in Birmingham. The group was collapsing around an illness
medical science could not control, and which was pushing Curtis to the edge of
despair. On April 7, the night before the Bury concert, Curtis overdosed on
Phenobarbitone, one of the drugs that was apparently doing such a poor job of controlling his seizures.

But he told Deborah what he had done; she called an ambulance, and he was
rushed to the hospital to have his stomach pumped. A few nights later, spending
time at Sumner's house, he talked about what happened.

The guitarist thought he understood. Echoing one of Curtis's own recent lyrics,
the opening line of the new album's "Colony," he suggested that it was a cry for
help. Curtis's response would remain with him always. "No it wasn't. It wasn't a cry
for help. I knew exactly what I was doing when I took the tablets. But when I'd
taken them, I realized that I didn't have as many as I thought." He'd summoned
help because he didn't want to risk brain damage. But he never explained why he
tried to kill himself, and Sumner admitted that they never really found out why he
did it again, six weeks later.

The movie over, Curtis placed his well-worn copy of *The Idiot* on the turntable, and
waited for Deborah to arrive. Their marriage had broken down completely since his
overdose. She was staying with her parents now, and when he called and asked to
see her, she thought he wanted to try talking things through. She'd be there later
that evening, after she got out of work.

Ignoring his insistence that she bring their baby daughter, Natalie, with her,
Deborah got to the house in the early hours of the morning. She left again when it
became apparent that there actually wasn't that much left to say.

Curtis drank some coffee, then finished off the whiskey he found in a cupboard.
He wrote a letter to Deborah, talking about their old life together, and the love he
still held for her, despite Annik, despite everything. By the time she received the
note, he continued, he'd be away; he was meeting up with the rest of Joy Division
at ten the following morning, and the day after that, they'd be boarding their plane
for New York. He just wanted to say good-bye before he went.

It was Sunday lunchtime when Deborah arrived back at the house, and saw the note on the mantelpiece. Her first thought was one of pleasure, how nice that he'd written to her before heading off. Then, out of the corner of one eye, she saw him still in the kitchen.

"What are you doing now?" she snapped, but something about the position he was in made her feel uneasy, even before she'd completed her sentence.

"His head was bowed, his hands resting on the washing machine. I stared at him, he was so still. Then the rope—I hadn't noticed the rope. The rope from the clothesrack was around his neck." Behind her on the turntable, *The Idiot* was still spinning around.

"I've thought about Ian's death countless times"—in 1997, on the eve of the release of Joy Division's *Heart and Soul* boxed set, Bernard Sumner revealed that he still speculated on the reasons for Curtis's suicide. "It could have been his epilepsy, that he didn't want to go on with it.

"It could have been that he couldn't face his relationships crumbling. It could be that the [medication] he was on for epilepsy affected his moods so much—and they really did. It could be the fact . . . that he was a suicidal personality.

"But I tend to think it was a combination of those things coming together at the same time. The one thing I would say about Ian Curtis is that his ambition wasn't—as many singers' ambition is today—to get on *Top of the Pops* and be famous. That wasn't it. He had something to express. It wasn't a show, it wasn't an act. He wasn't seeking attention. Ian Curtis was the real thing."

Joy Division's final recording session took place two weeks before Curtis died. Ensconced within the ironically named Graveyard Studios in Prestwich, with producer Martin Hannett,[2] they chipped away at the two most recent songs they'd written. One was "Ceremony," the other was called "In a Lonely Place."

It was a melancholy piece, and foreboding as well, as Ian Curtis ad-libbed one of the most haunting lyrics he would ever create, one which would certainly haunt his colleagues as they faced a new life without him. It painted a waiting hangman, and the moment of death as the cord pulls tight.

this is the hour when the mysteries merge

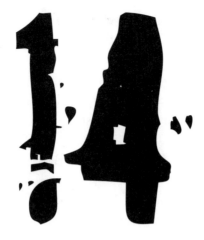

fuck with us and die

IN EARLY SEPTEMBER 1992, a Nick Cave gig in London
exploded out of the self-mythologizing milieu that was the
Australian vocalist's traditional stage show, and into the realm of
rock'n'roll legend.

A decade earlier Cave had been leader of the Birthday Party, one
of the most astonishing groups of their era, a mélange of paranoid
fantasy and mutated poetry, hanging by its splintered fingers to the
very edge of a ghostly tune. They toured constantly, and spat out a
string of albums and a singles, a potent stream of inviolate violence
which captivated some souls, but alienated far more, and by the
time the Birthday Party broke up, in 1984, a lot of people had heard
of them, but few possessed the courage to actually check them out.
Now, eight years later, Cave was letting the fainthearts know what
they missed.

It was a brief but effective moment: three vintage songs performed by a now-vintage lineup but, as even the most starry-eyed
observers acknowledged, something . . . someone . . . was missing—

bassist Tracy Pew, the man who Cave himself once described as "the only male genius I've ever met."

Tracy Pew began playing bass alongside Cave at high school, and throughout Cave's own gestation as a songwriter, the punk-inspired thrashing of their first band, Boys Next Door, and into the full-fledged goth histrionics of the Birthday Party, Pew remained the anchor from which the rest of the band's flights of fancy erupted.

He was always a great bass player—better, even, than the Birthday Party's admirers gave him credit for. "For someone who had never previously owned a bass guitar, let alone practiced, he was just magic," recording engineer Tony Cohen recalled. "He was an absolute natural; he never needed a drop-in or a retake, he just played and that was it."

The four albums' worth of material the Birthday Party released between 1980 and 1983 beat out their own testament to such praise; the recordings are dominated by his playing, as surely as the Birthday Party itself was dominated by his presence.

Like his partners, Pew was raised in Melbourne, Australia, and Cave detailed the impact of their immediate environment. "There was a river that divides the city, and there was the side of the river I was on, which was St. Kilda, which was where the junkies and the prostitutes hang out . . . it was that kind of area, and that's where we grew up. But we were also middle-class kids, who'd kind of left home and gone and lived down in that area. On the other side of the river, it was where the universities and so forth were, and [the two sides] loathed each other. The other side of the river was to make music that had a point. My side of the river was just about taking drugs and making nasty music."

Punk rock, exploding out of Britain and the U.S. in 1976, attracted them right away. But, Cave insisted, "we were also listening to a lot of country music, and other stuff, like blues, so there was all that kind of mixed in together."

Pew absorbed these influences both musically and personally. Onstage, he defied punk's media-ordained uniform of tight pants and leather by turning out in purple polyester suits with wide flares and platform boots.

But he could also turn fashionably violent if the occasion merited it. In Cologne, during one German tour, a helplessly drunken fan began pissing on Pew's leg. The bassist retaliated by cracking his instrument over the offender's head. A year later, in the same city, he watched as a skinhead poured a pint of beer over the Party's tour manager's head—Pew then laid out the miscreant with a bottle. The rest of the band, awed by his sheer muscular presence, called him Boss Shitkicker.

He could also be relied upon to provide ample on-the-road diversion, both sober—he spoke Latin, not fluently, but enough to converse in the language with Cave, a delightful distraction for anybody hanging out backstage with the band—and drunk. One night in the studio, after a particularly potent drinking session, he collapsed in a stupor on the floor. When he came to, it was to discover that his bandmates had piled everything they could lay their hands on around him, then sat back to watch him disentangle his way out of it.

On another occasion, during Birthday Party's 1979 Australian tour, he and Cave were arrested for urinating out of the back of the van, into the path of a car being driven by a local policeman's wife. Convinced that the two men were masturbating rather than micturating, she had them pulled in.

Early the following new year, Pew was arrested again for drunk driving—his fourth such offense—and simultaneously nailed for two recent counts of theft: a sewing machine and clothes the previous month; frankfurters and rice four months before. Jailed for eight months, his biggest regret was the disruption it caused the Birthday Party.

"The band was due to leave for America about a week after I was locked up, which was a little awkward," he told Britain's *New Musical Express* in 1983, then mused, "I often seem to be doing things like this to inconvenience the rest of them." For their part, the Birthday Party replaced him temporarily with bassist Barry Adamson, and simply carried on.

"The jails in Victoria aren't bad," Pew reviewed later. "I got sent to a nice little prison farm. It certainly cleansed my body, I was off the piss, exercised a lot, worked every day, did weight lifting—that way you could sleep really well, so time went a lot quicker." In fact, it passed even quicker than he expected; after serving just three months of the eight-month sentence, Pew was released for good behavior, and immediately went to London to rejoin the Birthday Party.

Yet Pew was not the wild man subsequent Party legend has painted him. He was, for instance, very well read; as soon as the band got paid, he would be out scouring local secondhand bookstores, and though he offered little direct input into either the Birthday Party's personal politics or its public output, on the occasions when Pew and Cave did collaborate on a song, the results would be startling.

"She's Hit," one of their earliest efforts, for example, was a brooding blues ballad Cave biographer Ian Johnstone later singled out as both "ample evidence that the

Birthday Party were much more than a mere thrash band" (a common criticism during their early years), and an indication of Cave's developing lyrical style.

"Tracy was very important in a number of ways," guitarist Rowland S. Howard averred. "Just through his presence, he changed the way Nick [Cave] acted. Nick and Tracy would become this mischievous pair that didn't care what they said or did. In a lot of ways he was the heart and soul of the group." And when he began to lose interest in the group, both heart and soul went with him.

In 1982, bored with the fickle provincial mentality of the London scene, the Birthday Party shifted their base of operations to Berlin. "We abhorred everything about London," Cave later complained. "We found it to be one of the greatest disappointments of our lives. After living in Australia and reading constantly about London, what an amazingly exciting place it was, we finally got there and found this horrible, very constipated society."

Berlin was brighter, freer in a way, but the optimism the move initially prompted, wouldn't take hold. Internal relationships were deteriorating. Cave was searching for a new direction; Pew was constantly looking homeward. Yet it was guitarists Mick Harvey and Rowland S. Howard who quit first, on either side of one more tour; Cave and Pew simply followed their leads.

The break was not permanent. By January 1984, just months after the Birthday Party's dissolution, Pew rejoined Cave, Harvey, Barry Adamson, and Australian guitarist Hugo Race for a handful of Australian shows under the name Nick Cave—Man or Myth? Pew, however, was at great pains to ensure that he wasn't about to remake that same old career. He was planning to enroll in Melbourne's Monash University, studying philosophy and politics as part of a general-arts course. When Cave and Company returned to London, Pew remained in Australia.

He played one more tour; in February 1984, he went out with the Saints, the most legendary of all Australian punk bands. Then he sold his bass, and settled down to study.

Pew did not completely fall out of touch, of course, and would be recalled in early 1986, to guest on a couple of tracks on Cave's all-covers album, *Kicking Against the Pricks*. But again it was no more than a fleeting visit, complicated this time by illness.

Shortly before Christmas, Pew suffered what was swiftly diagnosed as an epileptic seizure, powerful enough to stop his breathing. Early in the new year, he endured three more fits, each as bad as the first, and was promptly placed on medication. The condition continued to worsen, however; five times he was treated for a dislocated shoulder, suffered during one of his fits, and by the following summer, Pew was even forced to defer the completion of his university course, as he battled his fits with powerful sedatives.

Yet he seemed resigned not only to this fate, but also to that which he apparently knew was just around the corner. Rowland S. Howard later received a page from Pew's diary, and revealed, "The gist of it was, every day when he looked in the mirror and he looked older, it delighted him and it all took him closer to death. He was interested in pursuing some strange idea he had."

On November 7, 1986, he got that opportunity. Visiting his girlfriend's house, racked by another violent fit, Pew keeled over and caught his head on the side of the bathtub, knocking himself out cold. Once again he stopped breathing, but this time, for the first time, there was nobody there to revive him. Hours later, his body was found still on the floor where he fell.

The Birthday Party "reunion" six years later was one of two headline shows that year in which antipodean musicians gathered together again, to mourn a fallen fellow: On February 16, 1992 members of the New Zealand new-wave group Mi-Sex convened at a benefit concert aimed at raising money for their vocalist, Steve Gilpin, lost deep within a coma following a road accident a month before.

Alongside Midnight Oil, Mental As Anything, and the Angels, Mi-Sex ran through an emotional greatest-hits set at a massive benefit show, at Sydney's Hordern Pavilion. But though the receipts would keep Gilpin alive, the singer would never recover, and on November 25, he died at the Gold Coast Hospital in Queensland.

Almost exactly five years later, tragedy again struck the Australian music scene, in the rumor-strewn shock of the suicide of INXS vocalist Michael Hutchence on November 22, 1997.

Discovered kneeling naked beside the door of his Sydney hotel room, his leather belt round his neck, and its broken buckle hanging from a door hook, Hutchence's body was still warm when the first titillating allegations stirred, that he had been engaged in the masturbatory act of autoerotic asphyxiation when he died.[1]

Hutchence's fiancée, Paula Yates (ex-wife of former Band/Live Aid founder and Boomtown Rats singer, Bob Geldof), was swift to refute the charge. "It's killing [me] dealing with [stories suggesting] Michael was having a fucking wank on a

Michael Hutchence (Nick Towers/London Features)

door. He wasn't." But the stories continued circulating, even after her unequivocable denial was backed up by the coroner's investigation: a cocktail of alcohol, cocaine, Prozac, and depression had sent the singer over the edge. There was nothing more to his death than that.

But devouring the headlines as it did, Hutchence's death and its sordid aftermath obscured another fact—another death—and one which, ironically, impacted as hard on the former members of the Birthday Party as either Pew's or Hutchence's (Nick Cave was godfather to Hutchence and Yates's daughter, Heavenly). November 22, 1997, also recorded the passing of Epic Soundtracks, drummer with Rowland S. Howard's These Immortal Souls, and before that, Crime and the City Solution.

Throughout his career, Birmingham, England-born Kevin Paul "Epic Soundtracks" Godley remained one of the unsung legends of the postpunk era and beyond. At age twelve, in 1972, he and brother Nikki Sudden formed Swell Maps, a precociously experimental combo which started out from a spot mapped out by Germany's Can, and kept going from there. By the time punk exploded onto the scene in 1977, Swell Maps might not have released any records, might not have played many high-profile gigs, but their reputation had long since preceded them.

Swell Maps swiftly became a fixture on the London scene: their debut single, "Read About Seymour," was an independent chart hit; their first album, *A Trip to Marineville*, was the second-ever release on the then-fledgling Rough Trade label, one of the landmark projects which placed that company on the map.

Rough Trade label founder Geoff Travis told the *New Musical Express*, "They were a wonderful band and played great gigs. I always thought Epic was an incredible drummer. He was so in love with music in a genuine and refreshing way. His kind of joy and love is what really fuels the whole music world. It motivated him to compete with his heroes"—and it motivated others to place him in the same lofty pantheon. Years later, chronicling Swell Maps' acknowledged influence on the "alternative" underground of the late 1980s, Sonic Youth's Thurston Moore contributed liner notes to the *Collision Time Revisited* anthology. Later still, J. Mascis of *Dinosaur Jr.* and Evan Dando of the Lemonheads, would rank among the guest credits on Soundtracks' solo albums.

Swell Maps broke up on the eve of the release of their second album, *Jane from Occupied Europe*. Soundtracks and brother Sudden briefly reunited in a new project, the Jacobites; then in 1985, Soundtracks threw in his lot with Crime and the City Solution.

It was there that he truly came into his own as a musician and arranger. Having until now buried his talents beneath the squelching, scratching disciplines of Swell Maps, or the folky pastorals of the Jacobites, Crime offered him a full canvas on which to work, psychodramatic soundscapes whose lineage belied their melodicism.

He would remain with Crime for three years, until he and Rowland S. Howard (plus Howard's bassist brother Harry) quit to form a new band of their own: the immediately impressive, but infuriatingly short-lived These Immortal Souls. Two albums bracketed a five-year hiatus, with the second—1992's *I'm Never Gonna Die Again*—appearing simultaneously with Soundtracks' own solo debut, the voice-and-piano-led *Rise Above*.

Soundtracks would release two more, solo albums, *Sleeping Star* in 1994, and *Change My Life* two years later. Both unveiled fresh surprises (Soundtracks played virtually every instrument on the first); both revealed even further depths to Soundtracks' songwriting abilities. These were depths, however, which he would never come to explore.

"Music gets me through more than anything," he remarked at the time of *Change My Life*'s release. "I'm not being ironic or clever or kitschy. I truly believe that it's made a difference in my life."

He viewed *Change My Life* as his most hopeful album yet, a scorching collection which dragged Neil Young, the Beach Boys, and (perhaps inevitably) Nick Cave from Soundtracks' closetful of influences, then nailed everything down with almost unparalleled optimism, and unprecedented energy. "A lot of people think the songs are sad, because it's usually just piano and vocal," he continued. "But [this time], I want people to go away from hearing my songs with hope."

They were, several commentators mused later, brave and ironic last words. Having sought medical assistance for the bouts of depression which had long assailed him, Soundtracks—like Michael Hutchence—was prescribed Prozac, a drug that did stabilize his moods, but which also made it difficult for him to write.

He was supposedly working on an album for the Chicago-based Idiot Savant label, but the last time Geoff Travis saw him, he was working in a record shop in West London, simply trying to make ends meet. That is, until November 22, 1997, when he stopped trying.

Killed by a massive drug overdose, his body had been lying in his well-heated apartment for several days before it was discovered, just a few hours before his parents intended to drop by to see him. And it was simply a cruel coincidence that demanded that the man who, for much of his life, was happy to work in the shadows of so many talented Australians, should have his death overshadowed by another.

For Epic Soundtracks *was* overshadowed to the point where even mourners at his memorial concert weren't aware of why they had gathered together. When his brother Nikki Sudden put on the show a few weeks later, attended by fans and performed by close friends, at least two audience members walked out in dismay. "I thought it was a gig," one was overheard complaining loudly. "I didn't know it was a fucking funeral."

ON JUNE 27, 1988, Hillel Slovak, guitarist with the L.A.-based Red Hot Chili Peppers, died of a heroin overdose in his Los Angeles apartment. On June 29, somebody noticed, and by the time most people heard of his passing, his family's Jewish faith ensured that he'd already been laid to rest. In death, as in life, he slipped away far too quickly.

Slovak always stood out from the crowd. Born in Haifa, Israel, on April 13, 1962, but transplanted to America—first New York's Bronx, and later L.A.—schoolmate and Chili Peppers vocalist Anthony Kiedis remembered him simply as "a kind of funny-look-ing kid, real skinny with long hair and big lips," a near-obsessive KISS fan, and an ever-improving guitarist.

His first "band," a KISS mime act, came together at Hollywood's fabled Fairfax High School. Hillel portrayed Paul Stanley, classmate Jack Irons was Gene Simmons, and another friend, Alain Johannes, supplied the details: "They built their own KISS costumes, Jack got some frothing blood capsules which he would spit out, and they'd put on these shows in class, where they mimed to the records. They used to stay up all night doing their makeup before each show."

It was the KISS act that introduced the slightly older Johannes to the duo. "I felt really good about them," he enthused. An accomplished guitarist himself, "we started to jam together, and around the end of 1977, we put together our first group." He and Slovak played guitar, Irons played drums, and they called themselves Chain Reaction.

Existing on a wide litany of covers— KISS, of course, plus Queen and Led Zeppelin—Chain Reaction made their live debut in the school gymnasium shortly before Christmas. By the new year, they were Anthem; when they discovered

Hillel Slovak's yearbook picture

another band with that same name, they became Anthym. And when the group members graduated high school, they changed again, to What Is This, and brought in two new members, bassist Michael "Flea" Balzary, and a master of ceremonies, Anthony Kiedis on vocals. The seeds of the Red Hot Chili Peppers were sown in that group of friends. So—as that band's notoriety developed—were the seeds of Slovak's destruction. The Peppers grew out of What Is This, and for a time, the two groups existed side by side, sharing members as their schedules demanded. But they also shared lifestyles.

"Hillel got into the whole Hollywood underground scene," Johannes complained. "He was reading William Burroughs and all that stuff, and really beginning to identify with the 'underground suffering artist on drugs' thing. And of course, the Hollywood scene was very heroin-oriented—it was the accepted thing to experiment with drugs, and that kind of scene just drew Hillel right in. So we stopped hanging out together at that point."

"When Hillel and I were kids," Kiedis revealed later, "we were heavy-duty drug experimenters. We took LSD, we did cocaine, we did heroin, smoked a lot of pot, and did a lot of alcohols and different combinations of barbiturates. But it was all in good fun; we weren't slaves to the drugs." That, he acknowledged sadly, would come later. "Time passes, and you either become an addict or you don't. We did."

Hillel Slovak on stage
(Alison Braun)

Heroin became intrinsic to the pair's very existence. "It was fun," Kiedis reflected, "it was something to do, it was a relief from the pressures and boredom of life on the road."

Slovak quit What Is This in 1984, moving over to the Peppers shortly after the release of their self-titled debut album, and in time to help create what remains their most seminal contribution to the funk-rock hybrid they were now pioneering, *Freaky Styley*. But he also began elaborating on that freaky styley of his own. Occasionally he and Kiedis would clean up, only to rush headlong into the whirl-wind again. Once Kiedis suggested to Slovak that they enroll in Alcoholics Anonymous. "Why?" Hillel asked. "I'm not an alcoholic."

Many musicians justify their drug intake as a way of controlling, and inspiring, their creativity. Even Kiedis admitted, "As kids, we considered these mind-expand-ing situations [as a way to] view life in a different way." Now, however, quite the opposite was becoming true. Jack Irons became a full-time Pepper in 1986, but, as he discovered, "the group was in absolute disarray. The whole process was grinding to a halt." He did his best to keep things going, but even he knew it was a hopeless process.

"The whole band was pretty much out of control," Alain Johannes adamantly agreed. "And Jack could only do so much to stop the rot. He was the only solid cen-ter in the group, the one that would pull the whole thing together and make sure the next gig even happened. On the occasions Anthony and Hillel tried to dry out, Jack would be there for them. But he had his hands full just keeping Hillel on track. Jack kept Hillel alive for years."

Yet it was Kiedis, not Slovak, whose habits concerned the most people. "They were all afraid that I was going to die because I would just take too much, too often, for too long a period of time," Kiedis admitted later. "Hillel was much more subtle. He had everyone believing that he had it under control."

He didn't. What he did have was what Kiedis calls "cunning." No matter where the tour bus dropped the Peppers, Slovak could find a supplier.

Kiedis knew this—knew, too, that Slovak "was in as deep as me. He was just more in denial. Hillel thought he had power over the dark side." Yet even during his own moments of shocked sobriety, when he truly understood what he was doing to his body, Kiedis could never muster the strength to help Slovak comprehend what was happening to his own.

"It was real hard for me to tell him to his face how much I loved him, and how much I wanted to make music with him." The words were there: We've got to be clean. We've got the Red Hot Chili Peppers in common, we've got our friendship in common, we grew up together, we love each other. I want to spend my life with you making music. But he could never say them out loud.

The Peppers' third album, *The Uplift Mofo Party Plan*, was released in the fall of 1988, three years after its predecessor. Their first (albeit minor) hit, it would also prelude the Peppers' most intensive spate of organized giggling yet, a flurry of activity which would not only crisscross America, but would take them to Europe as well. In the weeks before the outing opened, with Kiedis himself functioning more or less drug-free, the Peppers' future appeared limitless—with just one cloud on the horizon: Slovak.

"Hillel definitely shut us out," Kiedis explained, and for a time, the Peppers considered returning the disservice, replacing him before the tour got going, so at least they could face foreign customs without fear. The band's reputation for unrestrained "partying," with all the connotations that expression bore, had preceded them around the world as well. All it would take was one weak link: one cancelled show, one well-publicized OD, God forbid, and all the hard work that had gone into taking the Peppers this far would crumble. It was time, Kiedis swore, for Slovak to "shape up or ship out."

Slovak shaped up. Ignoring the pangs of going cold turkey; ignoring, too, the temptations which seemed to present themselves in every port of call, Slovak came through the European tour unscathed. But the moment he returned to L.A., he returned to his habit.

"He was really ill," Kiedis recalled. "He was in the face of misery. But he still wasn't ready to concede that drugs were lessening his level of life and beauty." Neither did he—or anybody else for that matter—understand just how low that level was sinking.

In June 1988, the Peppers were readying themselves for their next album. A couple of songs were already ready to go; others, they knew, would come together in the studio. Producer Michael Beinhorn, who had overseen *Uplift Mofo*, was going to be back behind the controls—he knew the band, knew how they worked. Everything was going to be fine.

Certainly Slovak had few concerns for the future as he arrived home from the studio on the evening of June 27. He'd just scored, from one of his usual contacts on the other side of town. He was going to just switch on the TV, then bliss out for the rest of the night.

But the dose was stronger than he'd been expecting; stronger than his body could handle. If someone were with him, maybe it would have been okay . . . A year later, Kiedis was still struggling with that knowledge: "I could have saved him. I know CPR really well, and I've brought back a couple of friends who died from an OD." But he wasn't there; nobody was. Hillel died alone.

Alain Johannes was in England with his girlfriend at the time. What Is This had collapsed, the pair were now working together as Walk the Moon, and recording their first album at a studio in Bath. The sessions weren't going well, and the call from Jack Irons wrecked them completely. "He just told me Hillel had died" and, replacing the phone, Johannes walked to a window to look out into the rain. He'd never noticed before, but the studio overlooked a cemetery.

The Red Hot Chili Peppers would bounce back. The healing was painstakingly slow and painful, and it produced its own casualties along the way. Jack Irons quit the band, and all but turned his back on music. It would be another year before he played drums again, and another four years before he joined another band (reuniting with Johannes in the underrated Eleven).

Kiedis, too, almost abandoned the Peppers, returning from the brink only when he realized that there was nothing else he wanted to do. But "the death of Hillel completely changed our attitude. Losing your best friend at the age of twenty six is a mind- and a soul-blower. But there was definitely an inspiration which came from Hillel dying, which helped sharpen the focus of the band. Flea [bassist Michael Balzary] and I were left with each other, and we decided, 'There's something we started a long time ago that we haven't finished.'" The Red Hot Chili Peppers' next album would become their biggest yet.

As a teen, in the mid-1970s, Slovak dreamed of being KISS's lead guitarist. As an adult, in early 1980, a twenty-nine-year-old New Yorker named Peter Caravello got the chance to become their drummer. And, though he would never replace Peter Criss in the hearts of KISS's oldest fans, after a decade with the band, Caravello— or Eric Carr, as he was better known—earned his spurs in the only way the KISS Army ever awarded them, by sticking with it through thick and thin, and not letting anything deflect him from his purpose.

It was his drumming, after all, that powered KISS through the most difficult years of their career, a decadelong struggle which began with them battling to convince the world that they were not simply painted-up fiends with a nice line in flamethrowers; and ended with their very music fighting to be heard in the ever-expanding rock marketplace.

Twelve years had passed since each new KISS album was a guaranteed Top Tenner; twelve years during which the band had unleashed a misguided concept album, removed the makeup that was once their stock-in-trade, and lost lead guitarist Ace Frehley. Their last record, 1989's *Hot in the Shade*, had barely scraped the Top 30. But KISS was not about to give up, and neither was Carr. He had been through too much to get where he was.

In 1974, playing with a New York band called Creation, Carr was a witness to one of the most horrific disasters in recent New York State history. On June 30 that year, Creation was three nights—and half a set—into a new and prestigious residency at Gulliver's, a restaurant/bar at one end of a strip mall in Port Chester, on the New

Kiss. Eric Carr is second from left. (© Peter Mazel/London Features)

York-Connecticut border. The stage and dance floor were in the basement, pic-turesquely known as the Pit, three hallways and a flight of stairs removed from the main floor. When a waitress stopped Creation's set to announce there was a fire in a bowling alley on the far side of the building, few people saw any reason to worry. The flames were a long way off.

First the waitress, then the club manager, and finally Creation guitarist John Henderson repeated the warnings. Smoke was curling across the ceiling now, trav-eling through the air-conditioning ducts, and the air was growing thicker. Carr described what happened next:

"All of a sudden the lights went out, and the place just filled with thick black, choking smoke. Everybody panicked. The people who were not on the stairs, or near the stairs, could not get out because once the place filled with smoke, you couldn't see a thing."

Carr was at the foot of the stairs, with Henderson's wife, singer Sarita. "I grabbed her and pulled her, literally climbing over people, not knowing where I was going, and we got out. Me and the girl and maybe a couple of other people were the last to get out of there alive." John Henderson also got out. Inside, twenty-four others were killed by the smoke, including Creation vocalist George D. Chase, and key-board player Damon DeFeis. Just seventeen years old, he had been with the group a mere six months.

Carr, on the other hand, would remain with them for close to a decade, with the band changing its name more often than its members. Once they had been called Salt and Pepper, then came Creation, and, after the fire, Mother Earth/Father Time. They ended their days, in 1979, as Bionic Boogie, recording an album called *Disco Symphony* and playing a few gigs at Disney World.

"I used to tell people that I would either be dead or famous by the time I was thirty," Carr once said. "And in a sense, it really did happen to me." He was born on July 12, 1950. He joined KISS in February 1980. Less than five months before his thirtieth birthday, he changed his name, "and the person that I was, died. I became a different person and I became famous at the same time. So it really did come true. I died when I joined KISS."

Come the early 1990s, though, it felt as if he were dying a little bit more every day. As KISS's latest tour dragged on, every show became harder to complete. His lungs felt congested, his limbs were so tired. If he didn't know better, he'd say he was suf-fering a bout of flu. He did know better, though, so he blamed exhaustion. Only as the lethargy dragged on and on, through the end of the tour, through the Christmas holidays, into the new year of 1991, did Carr finally give in to his family's demands, and go to see his doctor.

The diagnosis was not good. The physician couldn't be sure, but Carr was displaying all the signs of pericarditis, a condition caused by inflammation and a buildup of fluid in the sac that surrounds the heart. Carr went in for further tests, and there the truth was discovered: a cancerous growth in the right atrium of his heart.

Open-heart surgery was scheduled for April 8; by April 10, Carr was back on his feet, proudly displaying his scars to visitors and making videos of anything that moved in his hospital room.

KISS originally had placed plans to record their next album on hold until Carr was fully recuperated. With his ready agreement, however, they turned a one-off track for a movie soundtrack into the first sessions for what would indeed become their next album. Eric Singer, Carr's replacement at the sessions, knew he was playing on borrowed time: "I remember during the recording, Gene [vocalist Simmons] specifically telling me, 'Look, it's only for the record, and when Eric gets better, he's coming back.' Unfortunately," he concludes, "Eric didn't get better."

In May, the heart surgery a success, Carr was informed that the cancer nevertheless had spread to his lungs, and on June 9 he began six weeks of chemotherapy. Bandmates Simmons and Stanley advanced him royalties to pay for the course of treatment, and once again, Carr came out on top. Doctors congratulated him on the speed with which he bounced back, expressed amazement at how fast his lungs were healing. By mid-August, he was in L.A., ready to get to work.

The other KISS members, however, weren't so sure. "Eric started rehearsing with us, but his chops weren't there," Simmons reflected. Although Carr would enjoy a strenuous twelve-hour percussive workout during the filming of KISS's "God Gave Rock'n'Roll to You II" video, as rehearsals progressed, so did the doubts. Eric Singer[1] could handle it; the others kept telling Carr, "Let him carry on until you're feeling better. . . ."

For Carr, the whole thing was cripplingly frustrating, all the more so since rumors were now circulating through the KISS supporters' grapevine that he either had been replaced already, or was on the verge of it. In September, still fuming over the rumors, he appeared at the MTV Music Video Awards in New York, and later people said they'd noticed just how healthy he seemed. But days later, the drummer was back in the hospital, suffering this time from a brain hemorrhage. Alone in his apartment, he just had time to call for an ambulance before he collapsed to the floor.

Once again, Carr's body responded to treatment, and within a month he was being transferred to a rehabilitation hospital . . . only to suffer a second, more serious hemorrhage in November. Yet that didn't slow him down, either. He was rushed to Bellevue Hospital in New York City for immediate treatment, yet within days, Carr was blithely baffling the doctors anew with his recuperative powers. He would be home, they hoped, by Christmas, and maybe he would have been, if a set of routine tests hadn't revealed yet another problem.

The cancer was back, and this time it was going to win. Eric Carr finally sucumbed at the age of forty-one, on November 24, 1991.

And his luck hadn't changed in the least, because even as his own friends prepared to deliver their tributes—that same day the news broke that Freddie Mercury, too, had died. When MTV reported the two passings, Mercury received a twenty-minute memorial; Eric Carr got a thirty-second postscript at the end.

Queen's Freddie Mercury was not the first known rock musician to die from AIDS, and he would not be the last. American glam rocker Jobriath, new-wave operatic Klaus Nomi, the B-52's Ricky Wilson, and the Nervous Eaters' Jeff Wilkinson, all predeceased him; former David Bowie sideman Sean Mayes and Nigerian superstar Fela Anikulapo-Kuti would be among those who followed.

But they were comparatively minor players, in the public eye at least. Mercury, like actor Rock Hudson (whose own AIDS related death finally stunned Middle America into acknowledging what until then was regarded as a minority-lifestyle illness), was a star, a superstar, and his seemingly so-sudden passing polarized the public's perception of the disease. Donations to AIDS-related charities soared; reluctant governments were pressured into increasing their own funding of research; awareness rocketed.

Mercury learned he was HIV-positive in 1989, news that would remain a closely guarded secret for the next two years. Rumor, of course, hinted around it, but even the best-intentioned speculation foundered against the wall of silence erected around the Queen camp. It was only as the end approached, with Mercury an apparent recluse inside his West London mansion, that the long silence began to sound sinister. Queen recently had completed a new album, but where were the interviews? Where were the public appearances?

On November 23, 1991, two months after his forty-fifth birthday, Mercury issued a brief statement, confirming his fans' worst fears. He was indeed suffering from

Freddie Mercury with Annie Lennox (Lan Grisbrook/Alpha/Globe Photos)

AIDS, and his only hope was that news of his illness would somehow finally unite people in the fight against the disease. Less than twenty-four hours later, his office issued another statement: that all donations in Mercury's memory be sent to the Terence Higgins Trust. Freddie Mercury was dead, but despite heartbreak, he'd gone out in breathtaking style. Which was exactly the way he had lived.

From the moment he emerged at the helm of Queen, in 1973, Mercury was clearly destined to become one of rock's great showmen. At a time when rock'n'roll was growing ever more colorful—in America, the comic-book horror of KISS; in Britain the playful tease of David Bowie and Marc Bolan—Mercury boasted a sophisticated flamboyance which cut across every musical boundary.

"Killer Queen," Queen's first American hit single in 1975, remains Mercury's statement of intent, the portrayal of a world of high sophistication, and the kind of woman who could glide effortlessly through it. Mercury sang it in the third person, but made it sound like autobiography. Neither would he outgrow the otherworldliness of Queen's earliest records, the fey ambiguity which rocketed him to stardom, so theatrically camp that his true sexuality was scarcely worth ruminating over; even the nature of his death would transcend the fiercest prejudices. Because again, he did it with such grace.

There was no long, drawn-out, public suffering; no haggard "last photograph" epitaphs. Just a final breath's farewell as he disappeared behind the curtain, and a final Queen single, "The Show Must Go On," to nail home the point. A soaring farewell, a statement of defiance in the face of the ultimate odds, Mercury wrote it at a time when the end was already close enough to touch. And the timing of its release, just a month before his final curtain call, was simply one last magnificent, flamboyant gesture.

LOOKING BACK, IN 1996, over the past six years of her life, Patti Smith sighed, "I've seen a lot death lately." In 1988, she and husband Fred "Sonic" Smith broke an eight-year musical silence to release a new album, *Dream of Life*, and Smith reflected, "I had a child, the engineer had a child, and Jimmy Iovine, one of the producers, had a child. Three children were born in the process of making *Dream of Life*. And now, when I look back at that record, Richard Sohl, my keyboard player, died and Fred died and Robert Mapplethorpe died, all of whom had key roles in the creating of that record. And so three children were born and three men died. That's the beautiful way of life."

Smith was speaking on the occasion of her own latest album, the triumphant *Gone Again*, and made no secret of the fact that "the beautiful way of life" had irredeemably colored the record. Indeed, over the past six years, she had lost her best friend, photographer Mapplethorpe, in March 1989; one of her earliest bandmates, Sohl, fifteen months later; and, over the course of just one dreadful month at the end of 1994, both her husband, former

MC5 guitarist Fred "Sonic" Smith, and her brother Todd. "I've always liked collaborating with friends," she said, "and I've lost so many of them."

Patti met the man who would become her husband on March 9, 1976, when "Sonic" Smith's latest group, Sonic's Rendezvous Band, opened for the Patti Smith Group in Detroit ("Sonic" Smith's hometown). Patti's lead guitarist, Ivan Kral, recalled, "Lenny [Kaye, rhythm guitarist] introduced Fred to Patti, I think because they were both named Smith. That's what struck Patti first, anyway."

Patti herself continued, "We just looked at each other and I was completely taken by him. I had no idea who he was, or anything about him until afterwards, when Lenny told me. Lenny introduced him and said, 'He's one of the great guitar players.' I said, 'Perhaps you'll want to play with us tonight.' And he said, 'Maybe so.' Then he left and I asked Lenny if he was really good, and Lenny said, 'The best.'

"So I was playing with him that night, and I had a lot of bravado in those days— I didn't have respect for anybody. But I totally submitted to his reign. He came on the stage and started playing, and after a while I just set my guitar down and let it feed back. I just let him take over because I felt I had met my match, that I had met the better man."

Fred Smith himself emerged out of one of the fiercest bands in American rock history. In terms of performance energy, Detroit's MC5 were the Stooges' only competition, local or otherwise. Through the late 1960s and early 1970s, both in their original incarnation as a musical mouthpiece for John Sinclair's White Panther Party, and afterward, the MC5 not only defined the sound of America's most turbulent city, they re-created it in their own image.

Honing their reputation as house band at Detroit's legendary Grande Ballroom, the group's sound was unique from the start: the Who and the Yardbirds, Chuck Berry and Motown, crammed into a pot with Sinclair's radical politics and a fascination for free jazz which had never been applied to simple rock'n'roll before.

Spread over three albums released between 1968 and 1971, allied to MC5 vocalist Rob Tyner's sassy, writhing stage act and Smith's and Wayne Kramer's guitar-as-machine-gun etiquette, the MC5 first erected the barricades of sixties youth rebellion, then armed the insurgents with white noise and slogans: "Kick out the jams, motherfuckers!"

While they led Detroit to street-fighting defiance, the rest of the country was preaching peace and love. While Tyner, tight-panted and bespangled, was kicking out the jams, Nixon's vice president, Spiro Agnew, was telling a Senate hearing that

Patti Smith with husband
Fred Sonic Smith (Globe Photos)

the MC5 were part of a communist conspiracy to corrupt the youth of America. And when they did finally settle down and start looking like they might make a go of a conventional hard-rock career, internal politics ripped the whole thing apart. If they couldn't fight the world, it seemed, they had to fight themselves.

Guitarist Wayne Kramer recalled his first meeting with the men who would shape his musical destiny—and the eventual loss of whom, almost thirty years later, would inspire his own musical rebirth after too many years in the shadows:

"I'd just moved into the neighborhood, and everyone was telling me about this juvenile delinquent who played bongos, even a little guitar—Fred Smith."

Like Kramer, Smith was already in a band. But once they became aware of one another, it was inevitable that eventually they would join forces. Around 1964, the pair linked with vocalist Tyner, drummer Dennis Thompson, and bassist Michael Davis. "We were all getting to be sixteen, seventeen, [so] we all moved away from home together. We moved to the beatnik neighborhood, [which is] where we met John Sinclair, the archetypal beatnik poet. John was a little older, a little better educated than we were, and seemed to be able to relate to everybody. We decided he should manage the MC5."

Looking back over twenty-five years, Wayne Kramer still seethed over the band's fate. "I got angry . . . that the MC5 never got recognized for its real importance in the history of rock. I'd see all these record albums released, *The Best of Sixties Rock*, and it'd be the Jefferson Airplane and the Grateful Dead, which to me were horseshit bands in the first place. These were the bands Fred and I used to heckle."

And now they had taken over.

The MC5 broke up in 1971, shortly after completing a final British tour. Manager John Sinclair was in prison on drug charges, "in the stir for breathing air" as John Lennon put it in the song he named for the revolutionary martyr; Kramer would soon join him there. Thompson and Davis became little more than a rent-a-rhythm-section unit, working with whoever asked them to. Tyner was playing around Detroit with various pickup bands he called the MC5, none of which had much to do with anything the original once had stood for. And none of them seemed to be talking to each other.

Only Fred Smith, still rejoicing in the "Sonic" nickname he lifted from an old guitar, maintained any kind of profile, touring around in a "Detroit legends" supergroup with Up bassist Gary Rasmussen and Stooges drummer Scott Asheton—Sonic's Rendezvous Band. Approvingly, *Bomp* magazine announced in 1977,

"[Sonic] may be the last of the guitar . . . barons for whom proponents of the new wave will rally to support. Sonic's gut-tearing [guitar] interludes are a refreshing alternative. He emerged recently from an Ann Arbor stage with bloodied fingers."

His union with Patti Smith, however, produced few of the musical dividends outside observers expected. Fred backed Iggy Pop on his abbreviated 1978 summer European tour, with Sonic's Rendezvous Band serving as Pop's opening act, but by summer he and Patti were virtually inseparable, musically if not physically.

"Because the Night," the Patti Smith Group's first hit single, co-written with Bruce Springsteen, featured lyrics dedicated solely to Sonic: "I was away from him and I was longing for him. It was written as a song for him and letting him know how much I wanted to be with him." Two other songs, "Dancing Barefoot" and "Frederick" on the 1979 album *Wave*, were inspired by him. And the following year, both the Rendezvous Band and Patti's own Group having been laid to rest, the couple were married at the Old Mariner's Church in Detroit. It was Patti's first marriage, Sonic's second.

They settled in St. Clair Shores, in the Detroit suburbs, leading private lives and raising a family, daughter Jesse and son Jackson. It was a quiet life that left room for only a handful of public appearances. In June 1980, for example, they appeared at a benefit for Detroit's symphony orchestra at the Masonic Temple in Detroit: Fred on sax, Patti on clarinet, improvising to the sound of a feeding-back guitar. And then they went back to the suburbs.

"Fred and I [were] working," Patti insisted. "It's a lot more difficult to work when you have a family. We were very devoted parents and that was always our first priority. But we were always working at home. It wasn't like we sat at home not doing anything. We still wrote music. I wrote about four books which in due time I'll be publishing. I was doing a lot of studying and Fred was also. When he wasn't creating music, he became a pilot. He learned all these new skills and we were interested in developing ourselves in various ways."

Nevertheless it was not until 1988 that the couple finally broke their recording silence, with an album which today remains indelibly tinged by sadness. Even as the pair recorded, Patti knew that one of her oldest friends, photographer Robert Mapplethorpe, was dying from AIDS, and that knowledge stained her music. "I knew he was going to die after a certain point, and I wept for him so much while he was still alive that I found when he died I was unable to weep.

"Even in the days before he died [on March 9, 1989], when he could hardly see or walk, he was still trying to create and it was the thing that really drove him. [But]

Robert's story was not a depressing story. What could be depressing about having a gift from God? It's sad, even tragic, that he died at a relatively young age, when he was still at the height of his powers, and still had a thousand ideas. But the whole scenario is not a depressing scenario."

She accentuated that belief across *Dream of Life*, a collaboration that Sonic insisted be released as a Patti Smith album alone, and which appeared in 1988. A hopeful album, an affirmative album, it was her first record in eight years. It would also be her last chance to work with one of her own favorite former bandmates, keyboard player Richard Sohl. He died less than two years after the album's release, on June 3, 1990.

"Richard [Sohl] was Patti's favorite," reflects Ivan Kral's wife Lynette. "When the band toured, Richard and Patti would always share a hotel room, they were always together." Theirs was not a romantic attachment, they simply genuinely adored one another's company, and when Sohl was taken ill shortly before work began on Patti's third album, *Easter*, Smith was in constant contact with him, even as she toured the world.

No one could have realized just how shortlived her 1988 reunion with him would be. "Richard passed away after we did *Dream of Life*. He played all the keyboards on *Dream of Life* with my husband, and then he passed away of heart failure. He was wonderful and I was actually quite heartbroken."

Shocked by two deaths so close together, and so close to home, the Smiths seemed somehow more visible through the early 1990s. They performed together at an AIDS benefit at Ann Arbor's Nectarine Ballroom in 1990, alongside remnants of both the Patti Smith Group and the Rendezvous Band; a year after that, Sonic alone would appear at a reunion of remaining MC5 members at a memorial for former vocalist Rob Tyner.

Tyner died following a heart attack on September 19, 1991, little more than a year after he'd finally put two decades of comparative inactivity behind him and resurfaced with a new album, *Bloodbrothers*. But Sonic's appearance at Tyner's memorial, according to Wayne Kramer, was very much an eleventh-hour decision.

"I got the call from an old friend . . . 'Wayne, Rob died this morning.' [And] it hit me, all of a sudden, that I'll never get to work it all out with Rob now. All of a sudden Rob was gone, and there was no more time for him. And the whole thing started crashing down all around me: the loss I had suffered in losing my brothers."

Tyner died without insurance, leaving no money for his family, for his children's education. "So I told people in Detroit, 'Anything I can do to help, count me in,' so people were trying to line up musicians to play with me, and nobody had even bothered to ask the rest of the band. All of a sudden it occurred to me, 'Wait a minute, I know the musicians who already know all the MC5 songs, it's outrageous that nobody has even asked Fred and Michael Davis and Dennis Thompson.' So I called 'em all up. Michael and Dennis said yes right away. Fred wasn't sure if he wanted to do it, but he finally agreed."

Kramer summed up the evening itself with his final words from the stage that night: "The worst thing that happened to the MC5 was that, in the end, we all denied each other, and unfortunately it took the death of our brother, Rob Tyner, to bring it all back together here tonight. So tonight it's my job to reclaim those possibilities, and to reclaim my brothers." He did it, too, and though the reunion never threatened to be permanent, the breach that once divided the members was healed; but still the MC5 would never play together again.

Early in 1994, news began to circulate that Sonic and Patti were planning a follow-up to *Dream of Life*. He was teaching her guitar, an instrument she'd long been torturing with little regard for finesse, and Lenny Kaye later acknowledged, "That was always one of her dreams, to learn how to play guitar. She showed me all her chords, and she plays them pretty well." The Smiths were writing new material and even discussing a title; Sonic, perhaps thinking back to the couple's past performances, suggested calling it *Gone Again*.

"We were working on material to record," Patti explained. "We wanted to record because we had things to say and we had ideas and also, you know, I have children—we have two children—and it's the way we make a living. It was time."

Time, however, was what they didn't have. Early in the first week in November 1994, Sonic was admitted to St. John Hospital in Detroit after collapsing at home. He died on November 4—Robert Mapplethorpe's birthday—from heart failure.

John Sinclair heard of Sonic's death from Wayne Kramer's wife, Marjorie. "I felt the way so many music lovers must have felt: What a sad thing to lose a man of such immense talents so prematurely, before he could be granted his just due in the annals of American popular music, and certainly before he could gain any of the rewards which should have been accorded him for his part in helping shape the music of the past twenty-five years."

It was a sentiment bassist Michael Davis was swift to endorse. "The way Fred was, was why the MC5 turned out to be such an enormous enigma; it made people look at themselves. He made us all reach deeper and give our best."

That was the message Todd Smith, Patti's brother, tried to reinforce when they met up over Thanksgiving weekend, just three weeks after Sonic's death. "He took me for a drive, and he had the soundtrack to *Natural Born Killers*. My song 'Rock n Roll Nigger' is on it, and he put it on really loud, and we drove around. I was just totally desolate, and he said: 'I'm going to get you back on your feet. You're going to go back to work. Working will help you.' He said, 'I'm going to be right there with you.' And that's the last time I saw him alive. We talked about it for a few days, and I felt that with his help I could do it."

Just days later, Todd was felled by a massive stroke.

Patti was working on a new book at the time—a collection, she said, "of poems and stories and things that pretty much surrounded a lot of people that I had lost. Like . . . Robert Mapplethorpe, Richard [Sohl], and other people that I know. And also people that I admired—I wrote a poem for [Rudolf] Nureyev and [Jean] Genet and Audrey Hepburn, just different people that I really liked that influenced me. But when I lost my husband and brother—I haven't been able to write much. I just find that I can't really write right now." Her work on the book stopped; her work on the album stopped.

Within a year, however, she was on her way back. "I'm very conscious of being a single parent and I want to make sure that I do a lot of work and get things ready for [my kids'] future. So I'm doing it partially in tribute to my husband and also because it helps me to work. It makes me feel better and also to get things ready for my children." And death itself, she said, "reminds me to try to take better care of myself, but also to appreciate every day. Sometimes I just feel ecstatic to wake up. I'm so lucky. My poor husband, he'll never wake up again. I just feel so happy to be able to see my children and to create and do work and just walk down the street and breathe the air."

She began performing again immediately after Todd's death. "It was his great wish that I perform," she said. "Right now it's good for me, a good test. I really wasn't sure that I was capable of performing again or how the people would respond. I think I won't be doing it for a long time, perhaps some months. Then I'll be ready to write again, which is what I really want to do."

And slowly, *Gone Again* began to re-form in her mind, a very different album from that which she and Sonic conceived, but a solid tribute to his influence nonetheless. "I am definitely on another plane," she continued, "but I don't know how much of that can be attributed to mysticism, or even intelligence. A lot of it's to do with grief. I think of my new songs as gifts from Fred—his last gifts to me. When he died, my abilities magnified through him. At this point in my life, I'm trying to rediscover who I might be. I'd been a wife for fifteen years, and my husband and I were very entwined; a lot of who I perceived myself to be was an extension of him. And now he's gone.

"The thing is, *Gone Again was* never supposed to be done. Fred and I had planned to do a record . . . that addressed a lot of issues, both political and spiritual. And when Fred passed away, I just wasn't really ready to embark on that record, and I really did an album that I never thought I'd be doing, which was an album with work in remembrance of him. And, it was a pretty—as you can imagine—complex experience."

Mapplethorpe, Sohl, Sonic, Todd . . . The spirits that hang over *Gone Again* remain a palpable presence, but theirs were not the only specters to touch that haunting album, released in 1996. One song, "About a Boy," eulogized the late Kurt Cobain, who commited suicide in April 1994. And a year later, in 1997, another tragic note would be added to that roll call, when Jeff Buckley, one of *Gone Again*'s most shimmering guests, slipped beneath the waters of the Mississippi River on the night of May 29.

The son of singer-songwriter Tim Buckley, Jeff was born on November 17, 1966. He grew up in California with his Panamanian mother, Mary Guibert, and his stepfather, and was eight years old before he finally met his father, spending a week with him in the spring of 1975.

It was the first time they'd met; it would be the last time as well. Just two months later, the twenty-eight-year-old Tim overdosed and died on the smack he'd just scored from a friend, Richard Keeling—after having to fight to get it in the first place. According to guitarist Lee Underwood, Keeling had neither wanted, nor intended for, Buckley to have the drug. But Buckley insisted, then grew argumentative and violent. "Finally, in frustration, Richard put a quantity of heroin on a mirror and thrust it at Tim, saying, 'Go ahead, take it all,' like a challenge." Buckley, defiantly, did so.

Jeff rarely spoke of his father, rarely mentioned his death. If he was going to make it in his own chosen career of music, he was going to do it on his own terms, not riding the coattails of the twisted romance of Tim Buckley's sordid end. But he was not so stubborn as to resist every overture. In April 1991, less than a year after he uprooted himself from his home base of L.A. Buckley made his official live debut in New York, midway through a Tim Buckley tribute.

He was fabulous. You saw him come onstage, and the first thing you thought was, This has to be some kind of a joke. The two looked the same, they held their guitars the same way, they almost spoke the same way. But when Jeff started to sing and play, you knew right away he was his own man. Different material, different delivery. The older "Buckley" had performed with a sad smile, a troubadour to whom the epithet "doomed" was accurately, if cornily, applied. His son was sunnier, brighter, more cheerful. He still bared his soul . . . but he kept a funny shirt on underneath.

For a short time, Buckley played alongside former Captain Beefheart guitarist Gary Lucas in the local band Gods and Monsters; by the end of 1991, however, he had split, and was now to be found hauling his guitar from cafes to clubs throughout New York's Greenwich Village, working the same circuit that had sustained the city's folk legends since time immemorial.

Of course, early reviewers continued to draw out the "like father, like son" comparisons, but slowly, even the most dogged voice changed its tune; as Buckley widened his repertoire, so did the critics. Over the next few years, Buckley would be aligned with everyone from Bob Dylan and Edith Piaf (whose "Je n'en connais pas la fin" he was prone to cover in concert), to Art Garfunkel and Freddie Mercury—while one reviewer even suggested imagining "Jane's Addiction playing a Ramone's song with a jazzy influence by Sting."

In 1993, Buckley released the in-concert EP, *Live at Sin-é*. A year later, his first album, *Grace*, appeared, Buckley trading in his lone guitar for a full band, and wiping the paternal slate clean for good. He also became a favored special guest around town, turning up on albums by Brenda Kahan, the Jazz Passengers, and, most impressively of all, the newly reborn Patti Smith. And within weeks of that appearance, he was back in the studio in his own right, recording with Smith's lieutenant, Lenny Kaye.

The sessions were eventually scrapped, but their spirit remained intact, even after Buckley headed down to Memphis in February 1997, to resume work. He had around thirty songs in place now, and a suitably haunting title for the album he envisaged: *My Sweetheart the Drunk*. *Grace* producer Andy Wallace was due to join him at the end of June. In the meantime, Buckley simply hung out.

"He wanted to be in a more laid-back place," his mother, Mary, reflected. "To get away from the New York scene and its distractions."

He rented a little white house on Rembert Street, close to the city zoo, then tried out new songs on the regulars at Barristers, a little club down the road. Every

Jeff Buckley 1994 (London Features)

Monday night Buckley would be there, playing his songs and chatting with the crowd, reveling in their reactions, and letting everybody know that this new album would be theirs as much as his.

Buckley's Barristers show on May 26, 1997, was an extra special one. His band, Michael Tighe and Mick Grondahl, would be flying in from New York in three days' time, for three weeks of rehearsal. The next time the club saw him, he laughed, it was gonna be "a lot louder than this."

On May 29, Buckley and a friend, Keith Foti, paused on the way to rehearsal to swim in the Mississippi River. The pair were hopelessly lost. They'd eaten at a nearby restaurant, then wandered out knowing only that the studio was somewhere in the vicinity. Neither was there anybody they could call for directions—Buckley's tour manager was on his way to the airport to meet the rest of the band. The pair finally decided that the best bet would be to waste some time near the water, then catch up with everyone when they returned from the airport.

Tim Buckley (Photofest)

gone again

It was Buckley's idea that they should step down to the river—a few yards from the monorail bridge, and just across from the Mud Island tourist hot spot—switch on the boombox and go for a swim. After all, he'd swum there before, and was perfectly aware of the pitfalls of that particular spot—the mud, rocks, and all-purpose junk that led down to the water. That was why he always kept his boots on.

Foti waited on the shore, playing DJ with the boombox, while Buckley waded out, still wearing his jeans and a T-shirt plugging the rock band Altamont, singing along with Led Zeppelin's "Whole Lotta Love." As the water reached his waist, he turned around and began backstroking out.

Dusk was fast approaching by now. So, Koti noticed, was one of the large tugboats that regularly ply the Mississippi waters. Buckley had seen it, too; as Koti turned to step out of the boat's rising wake, and lift the boombox onto drier land, he saw the singer began to swim back toward the shore. When Koti turned back, Buckley was nowhere in sight.

His first thought was that Buckley was messing around, but as time passed and the singer did not reappear, Koti began to worry. He called; no response. Briefly, he considered going into the river himself, to look for him, but quickly put that idea aside. Finally, keeping one eye on the water in case Buckley should resurface, he began to call for help.

At 9.22 P.M., Memphis police received a call from a passerby, informing them of a possible drowning. By ten, divers were on the scene. The possibility that Buckley had been dragged below the surface by the passing tugboat's undertow was becoming more and more real with every moment; so was the nightmare of having to call off the search until daylight. A helicopter equipped with a searchlight and heat-imaging equipment was ordered, and for three hours more, the police scoured the scene. They found nothing, and the following morning, Buckley was officially described as missing—presumed drowned.

It would be another week before Buckley's body was discovered, snared in branches floating downstream, by sightseeing passengers aboard the riverboat *American Queen*. Earlier rumors that he might have been drunk or stoned were swiftly dispatched by the autopsy report: He had simply drowned, one month shy of the twenty-second anniversary of his father's death.

"There is a distinct separation of sensibility between art as commerce and art as a way of life," Buckley once told author Dmitri Ehrlich. "If you buy into one too heavily, it eats up the other. If, instead of having songs happen as your life happens, you're getting a song together because you need a number of songs on a release to be sold, the juice is sucked out immediately. That approach kills it."

Such high principles, according to the people who knew him, were among the things which made Jeff Buckley "special"—not as an artist per se, but as a performer who would inspire a devotion that far surpassed his own meager recording career. He had just one full album to his name when he died, and a second in the works: Pieced together under his mother's supervision, *Sketches from My Sweetheart the Drunk* emerged in 1998 rounding up his outtakes and demos, and maybe cementing his reputation as a visionary performer with a lot more to offer than he ultimately was able to give. It was that reputation, after all, which prompted Elvis Costello to plead, "I hope that people who liked him resist the temptation to turn his life and death into some dumb romantic fantasy. He was so much better than that."

THE FIRST TIME MELVINS drummer Dale Crover saw Malfunkshun, the hottest new thing on the early-eighties Seattle scene, "there was this girl in a furry coat. She was walking up to the front of the stage, and people were trying to pick her up. I was looking at her, and she was pretty huge. Then she got onstage and started playing bass." "She" was Andrew Wood, and in the years before his sudden death, Wood was set to put Seattle back on the map like no one since Jimi Hendrix.

Malfunkshun grew up in a harsh environment, made harsher by the sheer weight of local groups forming and reforming around them. But Wood ensured that his band would rise above the rest, transforming himself into the ultimate vision of a rock'n'roll frontman, the white-faced and caped "Landrew the Love Child," allowing sheer charisma to do the rest. "We'd be onstage," recalled his bandmate and brother, Kevin, "and everybody would be looking at Andy, paying attention to every little thing he'd do, even Regan [Hagar, drummer] and I."

Hagar agreed. "We became the big flamboyant concert in a small club setting. We were really tongue-in-cheek; people found us amusing. I think people came to see Andy as much as to hear the music"—and, of course, to have things thrown at them. "Andy threw stuff for years," he continued. "But people never retaliated! He had this thing about throwing fluids on the audience. It happened at every show. It used to amaze me. I'd talk to him, and say, 'People are going to get mad,' but he'd just answer, 'no they won't,' and he was right, the audience loved it. Everyone knew he was so good-natured that he didn't mean it in a bad way."

What they didn't seem to know, and what Wood never told them, was how much he needed to be Landrew. Because when he stripped the mask away, what he found beneath wasn't pleasant. "Something dark haunted him," wrote journalist Jo-Ann Greene years later, "a darkness that eventually saw him turn to drugs."

In 1985 Andrew entered a rehab program, putting Malfunkshun on hold while he detoxed, then returning to preside over their slow but inexorable breakup. By 1987, Andrew was hanging out with members of local punk veterans Green River, Jeff Ament and Stone Gossard. Inevitably the three began jamming together; inevitably too, as their friendship deepened, their own bands began to fade from their minds.

Through the last months of 1987, under the name Lords of the Wasteland, Andrew Wood, Hagar, Gossard, and Ament began playing occasional shows between their regular commitments. Then, as those commitments fell away and other musicians moved into the picture, they began to take the Lords more seriously.

They changed the group's name: to the Dum Dum Boys (from the Iggy Pop song) for a short while, and then to Mother Love Bone. It took Wood a week to convince his colleagues that this new name was any kind of improvement, but once they believed him, they stuck with it, and in February 1988 the newly christened band entered the studio, to record their first demo.

They hoped the tape would help them get a few gigs. Instead, it introduced them to manager Kelly Curtis. A second demo, aimed at getting more gigs, instead introduced them to the first of the myriad record labels who would want a slice of Mother Love Bone.

The group ended up signing with Polygram, whose inducements included the formation of a custom label for the band's use alone, and in January 1989, Mother Love Bone began work on their debut EP, *Shine*. A tour, opening for glam-metal hopefuls Dogs D'Amour, followed—and after that, nothing. For a full six months, the group was kept on hold, while the label waited "till the time was right."

The frustration was crippling. Andrew Wood spent his time getting high, killing time by deadening the torment of waiting for things to get going again. He slowed down a little in September, when Mother Love Bone moved down to Sausalito to record, but once that was over, he picked up the pace again. By November 1989, Wood was back in rehab.

On March 15, 1990, Wood did an interview with Seattle journalist Michael Browning. The album, *Apple*, was finally imminent, the promotional wheels were turning, and as he talked through his past and the problems that once had dogged him, Wood sounded confident and carefree. Rehab had worked, he said; all he wanted now was to get on with the band. The following evening, Wood's fiancée, Xana La Fuente, came home around ten-thirty, to find Wood collapsed on their bed. He had taken a heroin overdose.

The singer was rushed to Seattle's Harborview Hospital, and immediately placed on life-support. But the damage was already done. Oxygen starvation ensured that recovery was out of the question. On March 19, the machines were turned off.

Five days later, most of the Seattle music community turned out to attend a memorial service at the Paramount Theater. A more lasting tribute appeared later in the year, with the respectfully delayed release of *Apple*. But the most heartfelt one of all appeared on the outside wall of the Vogue, one of the Seattle clubs where Wood felt most at home.

For five years, until it was obliterated by a new condo development, both Wood's name, and his band's, shone out in bright graffitied color, a magnet not only for local fans but also, as the "Seattle sound" spread around the world, for newfound admirers from farther afield.

The future success of Pearl Jam, too, would ensure Mother Love Bone's name lived on, as Stone Gossard and Jeff Ament placed the tragedy of Wood's death behind them and struck out anew. And Kevin Wood, Andrew's brother, for one, remains delighted by the testament. Mother Love Bone, he still insists, were "a good rocking band who probably would have got as big as Pearl Jam. You've got to hand it to Stone and Jeff for keeping the ball rolling"—and for helping take Seattle's name as far afield as Mother Love Bone might have done.

The release of Pearl Jam's debut album *Ten*, just weeks after fellow Seattleites Nirvana released their album *Nevermind*, remains among the defining moments in modern rock'n'roll history, rewriting the laws of hard rock for the decade—reinventing the very concept of the genre. Such moments of streamlined synchronicity, after all, are rare, even when they're intended to happen. For two wholly dissimilar groups to simultaneously erupt from the same geographical locale, is itself

Pearl Jam (Michael Ferguson/Globe Photos)

unusual; for them to do so independently is all but unheard of.

Nirvana and Pearl Jam actually were touring together as the madness unfolded, second- and third-billed, respectively, to the Red Hot Chili Peppers. But the moment *Nevermind* hit number one in America, in December 1991, it was clear that such a generous package could not survive for long. By February both bands had left the Peppers tour, to be replaced for the final burst of northwestern gigs by another Seattle outfit, the all-female Seven Year Bitch.

If the outgoing supporting bands epitomized "grunge," Seven Year Bitch were at the forefront of another movement entirely: the "riot grrrl" movement, which apparently included any busload of female musicians who knew how to turn their amps up loud.

It was not necessarily a tag the bands themselves agreed with. "Everybody's just got to lump us in some little fuckin' category, and it's a bunch of bullshit," complained Bitch vocalist Selene Vigil. But as with grunge, it served its purpose. The marketing departments seemed to like it—and besides, with songs like the avowedly feminist "Dead Men Don't Rape," Seven Year Bitch were hardly going to be lumped in with the sensitive singer-songwriter pack. When Seven Year Bitch were nominated (by Pearl Jam) as a suitable contender for the Peppers tour, it was an offer neither they nor the headliners could turn down. Nobody ever could have guessed just how morbidly relevant the pairing would become.

On June 27, exactly four years to the day after Peppers guitarist Hillel Slovak passed away, Seven Year Bitch guitarist Stefanie Sargent died in almost identical circumstances. Alone in her apartment, the official cause of her death was suffocation, but the heroin in her system told its own story.

Seven Year Bitch had just returned home from a triumphant showing at the New Music Seminar in New York. Feted by the assembled press, building a buzz around their soon-to-be-released debut album, *Sick 'Em*, Seven Year Bitch could not have been in a stronger position. Sargent's death sent the whole edifice tumbling down, and though the group rebuilt it, around the delayed release of their album and her replacement, Roisin Dunne, still she was rarely far from their thoughts.

"I think about Stefanie every single day," bassist Elizabeth Davis remarked two years later. "She was really an amazing person. Before I ever even met her, I'd seen her around Seattle. She was, like, the queen of the scene, obviously. I'd see her pouring herself beers at all the bars. I'd see her get up onstage with L7 [a female band from L.A.] and sing a song with them. She knew everybody, and I'd see her ruling on the pool table, and she was so beautiful, just gorgeous.

"I remember being kind of intimidated by her like, 'Who's that girl?' The first time I went down to the practice space to play with Selene [Vigil] and Valerie [Agnew, drummer], there she was. I was like, 'Oh, my God, it's that girl playing guitar.' She was really enigmatic. But she also had a real dual personality. I mean, she could get really excited and happy and then get really upset and freaked out, too. Everything was always hanging from a thread all the time, because that's how she was. Everything was always on the edge with her."

The delayed release of *Sick 'Em*, naturally, meant delaying work on Seven Year Bitch's next album. Finally, however, it was time, and it was a twisted irony indeed that inflicted another sudden death on the group, just as they were ready to begin work.

On July 7, 1993, Mia Zapata, vocalist with Seattle punk band the Gits, was murdered on her way home from the the Comet, a bar in Seattle's Capitol Hille. She'd spent the evening there with Seven Year Bitch.

Elizabeth Davis recalled, "We were all at this bar, hanging out together and talking about the tour we were supposed to be doing together. Then we all went home from the bar and Mia was picked up and killed."

The facts of Zapata's murder are simple; the truth about it remains unknown. Leaving the Comet, Zapata walked a couple of blocks to a nearby friend's apartment, sometime around midnight. She left two hours later, and at some point soon after, somewhere along one of the busiest late night thoroughfares in Seattle, an area fringed by clubs, bars and a college, Zapata was raped and strangled, and dumped in an alleyway in another part of town. Her body was discovered by a passing prostitute. At first the woman thought she'd simply come upon a heap of discarded clothing. It was only when she moved in closer that she realized it was a body, its limbs, she reported, arranged in the shape of a cross. Zapata's killer has never been found.

"She was one of our best friends," Davis told Vancouver, B.C.'s *Discorder* magazine. "When we first started, we played all of our shows with the Gits. [But] her death has changed all our lives irrevocably, not just because she was one of our best friends, but because she was raped and murdered. It's made us all a lot more afraid of familiar places. You know that every few minutes someone is raped, but when it happens to someone close to you, that's when you realize, 'This is a really dangerous place that I live in.'"

Rallying themselves yet again, Seven Year Bitch plowed into the new album with renewed intent. Their first release since Sargent's death, it was already scheduled to feature one tribute, the moving memorial "Rockabye." Now Zapata, too, would be eulogized, in the song "M.I.A."—and in the album's title, *Viva Zapata*.

"[Mia's death] had a big effect on the whole music community in Seattle," Davis continued. "Mia was beloved. A very talented and loved person. That's why we dedicated the record to her." It was also why vocalist Vigil could put so much passion behind the line in "M.I.A." which was directed personally toward Zapata's murderer. *"Will there be hundreds mourning for you?"* she asked. *"Who, besides your mother, will stand in sorrow at your grave?"*

Within days of Zapata's death, the Seattle community was pledging its support—both to the police investigation into the slaying, and in Home Alive, an organization fronted by Bitch drummer Valerie Agnew, to promote women's safety via self-defense, verbal boundary-setting, weapons safety, and simple common sense. Nirvana played the first of many benefit concerts. Later, the Gits themselves would regroup, as the Dancing French Liberals of '48, and then as Evil Stig ["Gits Live" spelled backward], a collaboration with Joan Jett, to finance the murder investigation. Still wholly dependent upon fund-raising and donations, Home Alive continues its work to this day.[1]

Viva Zapata was released in May 1994. Two years later, now signed to Atlantic Records, Seven Year Bitch released their third album, *Gato Negro*. Nobody died beforehand.

"With both of our records," Agnew mused when journalists raised this point, "people [were] always saying how sad and tragic it must be for us, like we're alone on some fucking island or something. When it's not just us dealing with the loss; it's our friends in San Francisco and Seattle and everywhere else that people are dealing with it, too. I don't want people to think we're just having all these horrible, horrible experiences. Because we've turned it around . . . sort of, and gotten past all that.

"I started feeling like we were the little martyrs or something. You know, like, 'Oh, poor Seven Year Bitch, so beaten down by tragedy, blah blah.' I wanted to really get away from being portrayed that way. It was like we were just sitting there whining. I do understand people were trying to be sympathetic, and they don't know us. But bad things happen to a lot of people. I'm not trying to diminish the fact that we've lost some really key friends, but it's a sad fact of life. It's not something we want to make a focal point."

Discussing his own reemergence from the legend of Nirvana, in 1997, bassist Krist Novoselic would make precisely the same point. All but silent on the subject for the three years since Kurt Cobain put a shotgun to his head and blew a hole through a multimillion-dollar-a-year phenomenon, Novoselic was finally launching his own new group, Sweet 75, and though he would address inquiries about Nirvana if he needed to, it was obvious it wasn't the first topic on his mind.

The most pertinent questions, in any case, had already been answered: by Novoselic's decision to remain bound to both the record label (Geffen) and the management company (Gold Mountain) which, sundry quickie whodunnits once insisted, had played their own major part in Cobain's demise; and by his own jealous stewardship of Nirvana's legacy.

Just two "posthumous" albums have appeared since Cobain's suicide: the soundtrack from Nirvana's appearance on MTV's *Unplugged* show; and its corollary, *From the Muddy Banks of the Wishkah*, an electric live anthology which catches the band at its disheveled best, It was all a very far cry from the "respectful pause, then unceasing deluge" which normally accompanies a superstar death. There would be no "cashing in" on this legend.

And yet for Novoselic and fellow former bandmate, drummer Dave Grohl, the short lifespan of Nirvana remains an experience that cannot be ignored, and one which they, alone of the myriad spokesman who have volunteered their opinions over the years, are uniquely placed to judge—not only for its impact upon their own lives, but also for life's impact on Cobain himself.

Seattle was always the unlikeliest place for rock'n'roll futures to be nestling, forget the mass of geoeconomic conditions that render it as potent a musical breeding ground as Liverpool—surely Seattle's closest living relative, in first-world terms, at any rate. Forget, too, its reputation as Suicide City and Heroin Central, a rain-drenched breeding ground for notorious serial killers, Disneyland for computer nerds. The vast influx of 1980s-era transplants who essentially transformed Seattle from a sleepy backwater harbor town named after a Northwest Indian chief, into a teeming metropolis with not enough parking, had nothing to do with the music—neither did Microsoft, neither did Ted Bundy. The music just happened, like it happens everywhere—a regional twist on a national creed.

The difference was, this time outsiders heard it—first through the "Buy this record" imperatives of British journalist Everett True, then through the nonstop airplay of Nirvana's "Smells Like Teen Spirit," every time you switched on the TV or radio.

It was that saturation which made stars of Nirvana; arguably it was the ensuing stardom that pushed Cobain to the brink. Not since the sixties' shock/horror heyday of the Beatles and the Rolling Stones ("Would you let your daughter marry one?") had any single pop group been subject to the intense media scrutiny Nirvana now received; not since the exclusively British obsession with the punk-rocking Johnny Rotten, had an individual musician been held up for so much examination. Crucified when he was not being smothered, adored, and explored everywhere else he turned, Cobain could hardly breathe without someone smelling his breath, and then editorializing on the subject.

In the war of self-mythologizing words waged between star and star-spotters, the gloves have been removed many times before, and both sides bear the scars. But Cobain and his wife, Hole vocalist Courtney Love, were not Roseanne and Oprah, had not spent their lives training for the starburst which now greeted them. Nirvana's first album, *Bleach*, had done little—sold a few thousand copies to a few thousand misfits—and Geffen made no secret of that fact that, before *Nevermind* took off, Nirvana should consider themselves lucky if it sold many more. That it did become so massive was due neither to promotion nor image, nor even a grassroots reputation. It was purely a matter of luck.

Nirvana

(Matt Anker/London Features)

"We came along at a time of great change, politically and socially," Novoselic reasoned. "Suddenly all the people who'd been waving yellow ribbons during the Gulf War were wondering what it was for, how things had changed because of it. And when they found they couldn't answer those questions, they got angry."

Lyrically and musically, Nirvana fueled that anger. To a media starved for newsworthy celebrities, who looked at their own kids to see what they were obsessed by, then checked out the Cobains and saw a cobra's nest of sensationalism, that was all that mattered. It swooped.

Cobain was not, as was widely murmured in the days following his death, killed through the neglect of those associates who should have protected him from the unbridled attentions of the media. Nor, though countless rumors exist to the contrary, was he killed by any of the half dozen or so suspects pitched by conspiracy theorists.[2]

But the feeding frenzy that erupted when it became clear he was not protected from the effects of his fame, be it the critical attentions of the media or the cloying adoration of his fans, certainly played its part. It would prove tragically ironic, then, that it took another high-profile death, that of Diana, Princess of Wales, for the world to truly comprehend what Nirvana (and countless—if more fortunate—others) had been saying all along.[3]

"A lot of people look at us and wonder what we're complaining about," Dave Grohl mused in July 1993. "Money, fame, groupies, the world at your feet . . . I wouldn't have any problems with that. What they don't understand, what they'll never understand unless it happens to them, is the way it changed everything overnight."

Cobain agreed, likening the experience to waking up one morning to discover that local TV has named you as an escaped Nazi child killer, but the first you know about it is when the firebombs land on the bedspread: "Of course we reacted badly." And, of course, he found it increasingly difficult to weather the storm—from the tabloid tattletale nightmare surrounding Love's pregnancy, to the incessant chatter of tape recorders and cameras whenever he left the family house; through the increasing, scandal-soaked revelations leaking from even the most tightly sealed police rooms and hospitals.

When Cobain overdosed in Rome in early March, 1994, photographers followed the ambulance to the hospital, chased the gurney to his bedside, and mounted a twenty-four-hour watch on his door, waiting for an opportunity to snap him lying there comatose. When guns were confiscated from Cobain's Madrona home later that same month, after Love had called the police, believing that he was about to commit suicide, the news was on the street before the singer had closed his front door.

And, when the first early-morning reports came in, that the body of an unidentified man had been discovered lying in an apartment they called "the greenhouse," above the Cobains' detached garage, the media were there as well, climbing the trees overlooking the property, shooting pictures through the unscreened windows, then slamming them into the papers by lunchtime. Cobain died alone, and lay undiscovered for up to two days. It was, as one writer grimly observed, the first peace and quiet he'd enjoyed in almost three years.

On that Friday morning—April 8, 1994—Gary Smith, a contracted electrician,

Kurt Cobain with wife Courtney Love and daughter Frances Bean (Archive Photos)

arrived at the Cobains' Seattle home. There was no answer at the front door, although a television was on inside, so he got to work, following wires along the garage to the upstairs room once used by the Cobains' daughter's nanny.

Looking in a window, he saw an upended potted plant—and what he initially thought was a mannequin. It was only when he saw the blood that he realized he was wrong. It was about eight-forty A.M., and Kurt Cobain was dead.

Smith called the police. It was his employer who notified the media, by phoning the local rock radio station KXRX. They initially ignored the report—hoax calls were fairly commonplace; hoaxes involving Cobain equally so. It took a second conversation, and a confirmation call to the police, to convince the station, and by nine-thirty A.M., the news was cutting into the late-rush-hour traffic.

Cobain wasn't supposed to be in Seattle at the time. A week earlier, on March 28, the singer had entered the Exodus Recovery Center in Marina Del Rey outside

Los Angeles, finally making good on his repeated promises to seek help for his drug problems. Three days later, however, he quit and flew home.

Hooking up with one of his oldest friends, musician Dylan Carlson, immediately upon his return, Cobain then had Carlson purchase a shotgun.

The next day, according to Courtney, he called Love in L.A. where she was gearing up for the release of Hole's new album, *Live Through This*.

"No matter what happens," he told her, "I want you to know you that made a really good record."

Love was taken aback. "Do you mean you want a divorce? Or are you going to kill yourself?"

"Just remember, no matter what, I love you."

Understandably alarmed, Love called Seattle police immediately, and twice again over the next few days, Seattle police visited the Cobain home in search of the singer. They never found him; neither did a private detective hired by Love; neither did the workmen who were installing new security lights around the grounds of the house.

But Cobain was there all the same. Sometime on the evening of April 5, in the apartment above the garage, a mixture of heroin and Valium coursing through his system, he scrawled a red-inked note to Courtney, planting it in a mound of soil he'd tipped out of a plant pot. Then he reached for the newly purchased shotgun, and, lying on the floor with the stock held between his sneaker-clad feet, he pulled the trigger.

"The . . . newly dead," wrote author Thomas Lynch, "are not debris nor remnant, nor are they entirely icon or essence. They are, rather, changelings"—beings caught between states, and ascending toward one or the other according to the will of the masses. Cobain became an icon, his death igniting a frenzy without parallel. Not since Lennon had such a high-profile musician died so violently; not since Kennedy had so beloved an American been taken away.

But it was peculiar, friends and fans alike noted, how Cobain was suddenly now so "beloved." Just six weeks before, the mainstream media had been demanding the authorities take the Cobains' child, Frances Bean, into care, rather than subject her to a life with such appallingly improper parents; less than a year before, the music press had been speculating about Nirvana's musical future, fueled by rumors that their next album would be an almighty mess. Now, it seemed, Kurt was a doting father, and *In Utero* was a masterpiece.

■ ■ ■

Not that there was room for such ruminations in the shell-shocked days following his death. A candlelight vigil in Cobain's hometown of Aberdeen, Washington, south of Seattle, was followed, on April 9, by a memorial at the Seattle Center, site of the 1962 World's Fair. Upward of five thousand fans gathered, in shock, in shame, and of course, curiosity. Rumors swept the crowd that members of Seattle's remaining rock aristocracy, Pearl Jam, Soundgarden, Mudhoney, might play a tribute concert; rumor, too, insisted that Courtney would appear to say a few words.

In the event, she did, arriving late in the proceedings, following a private and unannounced service at the Unity Church of Seattle. But even before then, her presence was palpable. Earlier in the day, she had recorded a tear-choked message for the fans, culminating in a virtual dialogue with her late husband, as she read his last words and punctuated them with her own.

Barely audible in parts, desperately bitter in others, she dismantled his suicide note piece by piece, speaking aloud the thoughts Cobain's words demanded by contemplated. He concluded with a quote from Neil Young's "Rust Never Sleeps": "*It's better to burn out than to fade away.*"[4] She ended by asking the crowd to tell him he was a fucker: "Okay? Just say, 'Fucker, you're a fucker.'" Then her voice softened. "And that you love him." The crowd obeyed.[5]

Hole's album was released, on schedule, a week after Cobain's body was found, but nobody had much appetite for promotion now. A projected tour was abandoned; Love herself remained sequestered in the couple's old house, surrounded by the things, and the people, her husband loved: his mother, their daughter. "Kurt wanted me to stay here," she reasoned. "Otherwise he wouldn't have done it in the greenhouse."

Hole, meanwhile, was left in limbo, grinding through the same shadowy half-life Nirvana's Novoselic and Grohl themselves had been thrown into. "A few times after it happened, Dave and I would get together to rehearse," Novoselic recalled. "And for a moment, it would be like old times, we'd be playing, and we'd be waiting for Kurt to show up, late as usual. And then we'd remember—'oh yeah, he's not going to show up is he?'"

Hole, however, didn't even have that luxury, and by May, watching as the album they'd worked so hard to complete suffocated from grief and withdrawn promotion, bassist Kristen Pfaff decided she'd had enough.

She rejoined Janitor Joe, the Minneapolis band she'd played with before joining Hole, and announced she was going back home. She was finished with Seattle; she was finished with the drug scene; she even—according to some friends—might have been finished with Hole. Flying back to Seattle to pick up her possessions, she spent her last day in town saying good-bye to friends and colleagues. Two hours later, and after two months on the wagon, she picked up some heroin and drew a bath. She was still in the tub when she died.

In a city still numbed by Cobain's suicide—grieving fans maintained a vigil in the small lakeside park next to his house well into late summer—Pfaff's death was simply too much to take, and certainly too much too soon. But that knowledge was no consolation for her stunned family, when they flew into Seattle to collect Pfaff's body. They were mortified by what they perceived as a collective lack of response and, when they met their daughter's friends, those people's reactions.

"There was no sign of the type of remorse you would look for in a person who'd lost someone they care about," Pfaff's shocked father later declared. "There was no visible sign of mourning; barely any regret. Just stony commiserations, and grim-faced acceptance of another senseless death.

"It could have been that Kristen had died," he said. "Or it could have been that somebody missed a bus."

BODY BAGS ARE BLACK for a reason. It's the color of death, of course, and the color of mourning, but more than that, black is respectful, unobtrusive enough that it doesn't scream out from an accident site, *Look at me, I'm over here*, but apparent enough that witnesses will avert their eyes, knowing instinctively what it portends. But body bags aren't always black, as Electric Hellfire Club vocalist Thomas Thorn discovered when he watched a television news report of his best friend's death in a car accident.

"I was sitting there with the news on, and they do this flash called *The Chicago Minute*: 'this happened, that happened, and a Kenosha, Wisconsin, man was killed when his car struck . . . ' I looked up, and first they showed the car for a flash, then they showed him in a body bag. And this sounds so horrible, but I looked and I said, 'Well, it *was* his favorite color.' Shane had these pants, these bright red PVC [vinyl] pants. And he had this body bag, this bright red body bag like I've never seen before. They're always black, and he got a bright red one."

Dead at twenty-six, keyboard player Shane Lassen was widely

regarded as one of the rising stars on the electro-industrial circuit his band did so much to pioneer. Mourning his death in song, on Hellfire's 1996 *Calling Dr. Luv* album (Lassen's stagename was the Reverend Dr. Luv), Thorn incorporated a Ray Manzarek sample into the memorial "Book of Lies."

"It's Ray saying, 'You never know when you're giving your last performance,' and for me that was apropos, because when Shane's playing was compared to Manzarek's by *Keyboard* magazine, that really was a high point of his career. I don't know if a musician can talk about how much his band, or his music, has influenced others, but I do know that Shane's playing really did make a difference, in that it reminded people what keyboards were capable of.

"When we first started, electronic bands seemed to think they were only allowed to make funny noises, farts and rattles and clever sound effects with their keyboards. Shane reminded them that they could play melodies again, and I think a lot of the bands that came after us, who did make 'industrial' music, or electronic music, or whatever you want to call it, learned that from him."

In a scene which, through the early 1990s, was in a perpetual state of flux, the Electric Hellfire Club arrived like a breath of fresh brimstone. Named for the libertine gentlemen's club whose activities titillated Regency England, Hellfire initially appeared to be little more than another in a long line of rock'n'roll shock monsters, touting a nice line in Satanic imagery, but lacking the convictions to back it up in private. Like Ozzy Osbourne once said of his best-known band, "the nearest [Black] Sabbath ever got to black magic was a box of chocolates"—Black Magic being a trademark English confectionery.

Hellfire, however, was different. Hellfire actually practiced what they preached.

"We're not saying we're out to turn everybody into a devil worshiper, and they should go out and sacrifice babies, but. . . ." From the outset, Thorn made no attempt to camouflage the philosophy behind Hellfire. "You're only allotted a certain amount of life. You shouldn't waste it being scared, and worrying what people are going to think. I could die tomorrow and be content, I've done everything I've wanted to do with my life."

A year after he walked out of My Life With the Thrill Kill Kult, the archindustrial disco combo he had already provoked to new heights of salacious indignity, Thorn—TKK's Buck Ryder—had every reason to feel proud of what he'd accomplished. *Burn Baby Burn*, Hellfire's debut album, was hot on the shelves, a raucous blend of traumatized techno, bad-trip psychedelia, and blistered heavy metal, wrapped up within lyrics that questioned orthodoxy in every guise they could find it. "It's an honest expression of what we're interested in and how we live our lives," Thorn continued.

"What Satanism truly is, is indulging in what you truly want to indulge in, and basically having a good time with the life you're allotted." And though you wouldn't know it to look at them, arrayed in standard goth black, with their stage props like so many gaudy trinkets around them, he was right on target when he concluded, "We are probably far more demonic than any of these evil, demonic bands"—a lesson Hellfire learned when they toured the Bible Belt with Danzig.

"The Danzig tour was just crazy, because a lot of those places in the Carolinas, people'd be going, 'Yeah, y'all rock, this is real good.' And then at the very end of the set, we'd do the song 'Age of Fire,' which has the 'God is dead, Satan lives' thing, and I'd come out in this black pope's outfit and tear up a Bible.

"Now, these people went insane, throwing beer bottles, spitting, threatening to kill us. Then after the show, some of them would come up and say, 'That's not right, you can't tear the Bible up,' and I'd be: 'What are you doing at a Danzig show, then?' And these people would go, 'Glenn Danzig's not into this devil shit'. . . So why's he's got all these inverted crosses everywhere? 'Well, he's singing like that to warn people.'"

Electric Hellfire Club formed, portentously enough, in January 1991, on the day the Gulf War got under way. Against a televised backdrop of the first-night bombing raid, Thorn, Lassen, guitarist Ronny Baleo, percussionist Richard Frost, and dancer Sabrina Satana finally combined months of talking about their own dreams of music, to create a band. A band, Lassen later smirked, "which would give Satan a better reputation. People keep saying the devil's got all the best tunes, but what does he really have?"

Thorn answered his question. "You've got to remember that at that time, there was no Marilyn Manson, so it wasn't like we were going, 'Oh well . . .' There was a void, for the people who were into the philosophy from the standpoint of the Black Metal people, but who didn't want to listen to music that sounded like a jet engine."

It was Thorn's meeting Lassen that planted Hellfire's seeds. "He was one of those ingenious individuals who somehow gets himself a fake ID card, I'd see him at any show that was within a couple of hours of Chicago, because he was somebody who had a very distinctive appearance, very tall, very thin. So I'd say, 'Hey, how's it going,' and we started talking.

"So he was just someone that I ended up seeing around, and when I really start-

"you never know when you're giving your last performance"

ed to sour on my involvement with Thrill Kill Kult and things in Chicago, I was try-ing to get out a lot and Kenosha was one of those places where I'd stop in and hang out with these guys."

The rudiments of Hellfire's act and image, too, were hashed out in those earliest days. Thorn recalled, "Shane was the total glam-rock guy, in the way that any of those bands, be it Guns N' Roses or Mötley Crüe or whatever, had their involve-ment along [Satanic] lines. And as somebody whose main band was Thrill Kill Kult, he also had some orientation toward that tongue-in-cheek blasphemy, if not the full-fledged.

"It wasn't something that he was deeply immersed in; for Shane, it was more the pop-culture end of things. For me, Satanism has been a spirituality as well as a life's philosophy, while Shane was one of those people who tend to lean toward it more as a philosophy, as opposed to a theology or a spirituality. But at the same time, he certainly believed in the premise of the band."

In fact, Lassen was even more pragmatic in many ways. Having been raised in a Catholic household, "he was the guy who would defend to his parents what we were doing, from the standpoint of the hypocrisy of most organized religions, and basi-cally what was striking blows against that whole Judeo-Christian infrastructure."

Burn Baby Burn was released in 1993; two years later, *Kiss the Goat* proved that the debut's success was no flash in the pan, and Hellfire embarked on a period of intensive gigging, often in the face of some equally intense hostility.

Few audiences were prepared for the full spectacle of the Electric Hellfire Club. Black-clad and starkly lit, with a battery of psychedelic lighting held back for use at the most frenzied moments, Thorn's "Satanic Pope" and Lassen's horned and goa-teed lankiness dominated the proceedings from every angle, all the more so follow-ing the departure of the bewitching Sabrina Satana.

With Thorn inciting the audience to its own peak of gratuitous blasphemy, and Lassen calmly smiling, while around them their fellow demons cavorted through the cacophony, Hellfire could not help but provoke a response. And if the music didn't do it, the rending of the Bible always did.

"Shane thought that was hilarious," Thorn reflected. "I think of Shane, and the image that always comes to mind is, he's smiling and laughing. It was this great thing, which I miss so much, that communication on stage, where without talking, he noticed everything. He was the best person to be in a band with, because he just loved every minute of it. He's the person who made it so much fun. Shane was always the guy who'd turn somewhere when we were driving to a gig; I'd say, 'Where are you going?' And he'd say, 'Well, we're an hour ahead of time . . . *go-carts!*' He would always make everything into one long fun trip."

Sliding down Washington State's infamous Snoqualmie Pass one snow-drenched winter's afternoon, heading for a show in Seattle, Thorn noticed that Hellfire's van didn't seem to be obeying the laws of driving physics. "So I called up to Shane, said that it felt as though the wheels weren't actually gripping onto the road. And he just turned around, laughed, and said, 'Nope, they're not.'"

On another occasion, driving back to Kenosha from a drunken night in Milwaukee, Thorn awoke in the passenger seat to find the car snaking its way down the road, at close to ninety miles an hour. "So, I said, 'Hey, are you okay?' 'Yeah, I'm fine'—'But you're kinda weaving all over the road,' and he said, 'I have been since we left Milwaukee.' And what can you say from that point? So I was, 'Yeah, oh, okay.'"

Lassen was returning home from another night out when he died. He and Thorn went into Chicago for the evening and, conforming to what had become a mutual tradition, 'One of us would get completely blasted, which was me, and the other one—Shane—just got fucked-up, because he was driving. We used to take turns, the driver was only allowed to get fucked-up.

"It sounds really stupid, but you have that youthful sense of invulnerability: 'Other people crash, other people do this and that,' but there aren't even any cars on the road at the time we're coming back, at five o'clock in the morning. So that's what we would do."

This particular night, January 22, 1996, Thorn met up with a friend, and decided to stay on in Chicago. Lassen left alone, and about half a mile from the final toll-booth before the Wisconsin border, his car piled into the back of a semitrailer. It was slowing down—Lassen wasn't.

"He may have dozed off for just a second," Thorn speculated. "That drive is lit-up, you're aware of everything, just enough to keep you going, and then you pass the Great American Amusement Park, and suddenly you're out in the country for two or three miles, with no lighting. It's dark, it's straight, and if you're going to fall asleep at the wheel, that's exactly where you'd do it."

Lassen was killed instantly.

According to his parents' wishes, Lassen was given a full Catholic burial, a decision that raised some eyebrows among Hellfire's following, but which Thorn himself agreed with. "Shane's parents talked to me about it, they really went out of their way and said, 'Look, we don't want to do anything that would make Shane unhappy, that would be against his wishes.' To which I said, 'The only thing that Shane would want right now is for you not to be miserable. So anything you have to do to not be miserable is the right thing to do.'"

Thorn admitted, however, that there was also an inkling of unease in his mind, an inkling planted by the service itself. "In Catholicism," he believed, "there is only one truly unforgivable sin, and that is blaspheming against God. Which Shane did for a living."

Christian Death vocalist Rozz Williams drew a similar conclusion toward the end of his own thirty-four-year lifetime, and, having been raised within a strict Southern Baptist family, he, too, understood the limitations of faith.

Reflecting upon the lessons of his youth, Williams once mused, "You're told there's this wonderful God, and this beautiful Heaven for you when you die. You're also told that death is a horrible thing, and you should be afraid of it and live in fear of it—which I found ridiculous. It's a contradiction to say there's this wonderful place waiting for you when you die, but you should be in fear of dying."

Rozz Williams (C.C. Leverette)

Yet contradiction was inherent to Williams' life and music, as he acknowledged in 1994, when he insisted, "I don't think anybody with any self-respect would admit to being goth." Reflecting upon his own career in the forefront of the gothic movement, of course, Rozz Williams both understood, and enjoyed, the irony of that remark. The music magazine *Alternative Press* was publishing a special issue almost entirely devoted to gothic rock, the black-shrouded, gloom-laden sound that had been self-consciously demonizing itself since the early 1980s. But Williams was feeling considerably more playful than his image traditionally let him be. "I thought my manager said a special 'God' issue. I got this all wrong."

Friends said he got it all wrong again, four years later, when his latest musical partner, Ryan Gaumer, arrived home at the West Hollywood apartment the pair shared, and discovered Williams' hanged and lifeless body waiting for him.

It was April 1, 1998, and immediately the local grapevine put its own, twisted spin on the tragedy. If Gaumer had got home earlier, Williams still would have been hanging there, but he'd be laughing as well: What better April Fool's joke, after all, could the King of Death Rock play?[1]

But there was another, even sadder possibility—that Williams finally had succumbed to the rumor mill's longstanding belief that he was suffering from AIDS, and had taken his destiny into his own hands, before sickness took it away from him. Bruce Duff, of Williams' Triple X record label, reflected, "Some people felt [Rozz] might have been afraid he was ill. But he wouldn't go to the doctor, the big dork."

At the same time, though, the last time Duff had seen the singer, a week before his death, there was little to suggest Williams was living his last days. "I was hanging out in a club with him, and he was partying and everything was fine. Most people I know were caught off guard. He didn't leave a note; I don't think there was any real warning, and you can only speculate as to why."

Rozz Williams, born Roger Painter, was sixteen when he first emerged in America's nascent gothic scene at the helm of Christian Death, but he had been imbibing the imagery for years before that. Raised in Pomona, in Southern California, in a stern Southern Baptist family, he confessed, "I have a lot of strange memories of that place. It was an unusual place to grow up in. It was much seedier than Los Angeles proper, but in a very secretive sort of way. Very bizarre people around, but you usually wouldn't know it until it was too late. Kind of like growing up in one of those out-of-the-way places you read about in the *World Weekly News*, where someone's being sacrificed every other night by some Satanic cult that the sheriff and the mayor are a part of.

"you never know when you're giving your last performance"

"Everyone with smiles on their faces, but darkness in their hearts. How dramatic, but it really was like that!" And of course, the adolescent Williams played his own part in the city's sublife; such a part that today, there are still people around who remember the time he crucified a friend to a chair, using real nails. . . . As for whether it really happened, though, Williams refused to be pinned down. "As far as rumors go, there's been so many of them, that I'm not even sure anymore which ones may have been true and which ones not."

What was certain, was that in a city where the bizarre burgeoned on the inside, Williams wore his weirdness in mile-high skywriting. "I really don't know why I ended up putting on a dress and drawing strange designs on my face," he admitted, but around the age of thirteen, "I began getting really influenced by that whole punk scene. I went through that whole thing, like the shaved head. I was always interested in what people called 'the darker side,' whatever that was, and the kind of look that you would see in the old horror films. So I let that become more of my persona."

His teenaged goal was to "get things out of my system." His upbringing ensured that "the fear-of-God thing was pretty set and I blindly followed it. But then I reached a certain age, and I just began questioning my belief system." That questioning followed him through a string of formative bands, with names like the Crawlers, No ("as opposed to Yes"), and the Asexuals; it pursued him, too, through a series of sexual and chemical encounters that would set the stage for the hedonistic lifestyle with which future observers would credit him. "If I'd really done everything people say I've done," he once smirked, "I very much doubt I'd be here now to deny it. But I did do a lot of them. . . .

In 1979, Williams set about forming Christian Death, a band whose stance was apparent from the moment they settled on a name. He initially built up on the punk premise that anyone could just put together a group and make it work, "but then it became a little more detailed after I realized that it was something serious, not just a one-off situation. I had to put a lot more into it, but I also took a lot out of myself, things that had been put there while I was growing up in my family. A sort of exorcising of demons."

The original lineup of Williams, James McGearthy on bass, Jay on guitar, and George Belanger on drums, "just kind of worked small shows around town, rehearsing in the garage." They cut a weird shape in the clubs and bars of Pomona, though. "When we first started playing out, almost never a show went by without hecklers, or something being thrown at us. 'Who's the fag in the dress?' 'Pardon me?'"

Visually a sexually surreal combination of Satanism, drugs, and cross-dressing; musically the iconoclastic offspring of vintage Bowie, and Isherwood's *Cabaret*; lyrically Christian Death was cataclysmic, a roar of inverse religious iconography slammed through the blasphemous wringer which, regardless of whether or not Williams truly believed in it, was sufficient to rouse the wrath of every right-thinking Christian in the land.

Within weeks of Christian Death's debut album, *Only Theater of Pain*, hitting the streets in 1984, Williams was overjoyed to see it discussed on television, "on a religious television program that my parents used to watch. They did a special on Satanic influences in music. They had the record on and broke it. That rather impressed me; I thought if these people knew of it and have such a strong feeling about it, I'm sure other people are doing the same."

His parents, too, were shocked. "They questioned what I was doing at various times . . . they were not too pleased with a lot of the lyrics. But when I explained to them what it was about to me, they left it at that." A couple of years later, though, Mr. and Mrs. Painter were still coming to terms with their son's peculiar identity. "I remember my mom screaming from the living room to come out of my room. I came out, and she said, 'Oh, look at this guy on TV, he dresses like you.' It was Boy George! I went, 'No, Mom, please.'"

The very nature of Christian Death was to shock; it was inevitable, then, that the group's first album also should have been their last. Nothing so brittle, so demanding, and so purposefully painful as Death could have survived any longer—not without becoming a cliché or, as Williams saw it, worse. "We were having a lot of problems, most of it to do with drugs. That was becoming more important than the music, for some of us. We went through a lot of personnel changes. People I can't even remember were there—I can't remember, because there were so many people drifting in and out. I just saw the whole structure crumbling, and I just thought that this should end."

But it didn't. New blood entered the band, a new lineup coalescing, however, not around the increasingly distanced Williams, but around a brand-new frontman, Valor, and the remains of his own band, Pompeii 99. Two albums later, and Williams was out of the picture for good. "I felt I had properly rid myself of the religious demons inside of me. And I had always been interested in surrealism and the Dada movement, so that began to surface in my thoughts. I kind of purged myself. I wanted to move into a more experimental situation and they wanted to stay in a musical format. But I was a lot more interested in sound structure. I saw no point working in a medium I was not happy with. It had a strong purpose at the time, but when interest in the band starts waning, I feel it's time to move on."

Shortly after the release of *Ashes* in 1985, then, a disillusioned Williams quit. And while the rest of the new-look Christian Death soldiered on, a state of bedraggled happenstance which survives to this very day, Williams turned his attention to Premature Ejaculation, an outfit he first worked with as a part-time project in 1981.

In an age when performance art had by necessity exploded far beyond its original confines, into an arena where only the vilest act was valid, the original Premature Ejaculation lost little time in making their mark. Williams remembered one particular show where his partner started eating—and simultaneously regurgitating—a very dead cat he had found, and explained—perhaps unnecessarily—"I've always been a great believer in provoking a reaction. I would rather make a record that is loathed by ten people, than one which is ignored by everyone; I'd rather play a show which the audience walks out of en masse, than one they just stand around and talk through."

Very few people stood or talked through a Premature Ejaculation show, and the group swiftly found itself unable to get a booking anywhere in L.A. Concentrating instead on creating taped soundscapes, it was this area Williams returned to, when he and Chuck Collison formed the ironically titled Happiest Place on Earth. Not until the early 1990s, in the heat of the "industrial revolution," would Premature Ejaculation again find a musical space in which to maneuver.

Having alienated himself from the present, Williams next discovered that he had been written out of the past as well, when he opened one of Valor's regular Christian Death newsletters and read that he was dead. "It was kind of odd," Williams reflected. "There were some shows where people didn't believe who I was. Valor told people I was dead. [Then] he printed this in one of his newsletters. Which very much angered me." Williams responded by piecing together his own Christian Death outfit, and taking the conflict on the road.

It didn't last. Whereas Valor had made Death his life, Williams' interest started waning immediately. Just months earlier, Williams and his wife, former Superheroines leader Eva O., formed a new group of their own, Shadow Project, "and that was more in the forefront at the time. The Christian Death thing was more of a reminder to get back together and work as musicians, and let people know that I wasn't dead. But Eva and I had plans to work on Shadow Project, and I didn't want to make Christian Death a full-time thing."

Purposefully, Shadow Project—named for a U.S. scientific examination of the effects an atomic explosion has on the human body—was far removed from Christian Death, "a different thing totally, musically and structurally. But it's also an extension, because anything I do musically is an extension of the emotion and the thought that made me start doing anything in the first place. What I like to do with anything I do is push it past the boundaries. I like to break a lot of new ground and try new things, that's why the second Shadow Project album is so different from the first. We're not interested in staying in a format, we don't want to be labeled as just a gothic band."

The existence of one band, of course, did not preclude the formation, or continuation, of others. Both Premature Ejaculation and Christian Death continued to raise their heads as the 1980s turned into the 1990s, alongside a wealth of projects which ranged from vague notions hatched and immediately forgotten, through full-fledged recording projects: Heltir, Daucus Karota, a clutch of spoken-word recordings, and more.

"My interest in music has a lot to do with the freedom it allows," Williams elaborated in 1994. "Both Shadow Project and Christian Death have become very limiting." That was not at all what he had intended to happen, "but because of the way most people perceive those bands, it has. I'm into reaching as many people as possible with my music, so the restrictions presented by those names alone have left me kind of cold. I've gone through a lot of personal changes recently, both mentally and spiritually, and I really want to take the time I have now to explore those changes.

"People tell me I'm an influence . . . but I don't want to take too much responsibility. Now, it's so strange, goth has become a way of life for so many people. If that's making them happy, then I guess it's a good way for them to live, but I never imagined it being where it is now. It's kind of baffling in a way. How do these people maintain it? Wake up, 'Have to put in my fangs, do my hair. . . . Got to make it down to the graveyard before it's closed.' The only time it really gets bad, is when people get stuck just in that, not just that, anything, where they can't go outside of that. Where it's so strict with so many rules. Life is about experiencing different things. Sometimes I'll be trying out new material, and people will be screaming out 'Romeo Distress,' and I think, 'Go home, play the record, and don't come, please.' God forbid I end up going on a Sound and Vision tour like David Bowie."

Of course, he didn't. Indeed, at the time of his death, Williams was working as consistently, and coherently, as he had in some years. A new Shadow Project album,

From the Heart, was just one of several new recordings he had completed in recent months, and, having spent much of the early 1990s forcing himself through a string of ever-more-desperate Christian Death reunion/revival/remix projects, simply to make some money, he had finally settled into a career niche that kept the wolves from the door on his own terms. In 1993, a one-off Christian Death reunion almost descended into riot when Williams appeared onstage in full 1974 Bowie drag: platforms, flairs, suit and tie. In 1997, he'd opened so many minds that he could release a full-fledged collection of glam-tinged cabaret, *Dream Home Heartache*, and win some of the best reviews of his life.

Recognition also was slowly filtering through from the platinum-selling excesses of a new generation of musical monsters. The likes of Ministry, Nine Inch Nails, and Marilyn Manson all apparently learned their personal truths at the altar of Rozz Williams' greatest excesses. But his death robbed the world of more than the template for the outrage of various lesser talents. Though his best (and best-known) work, with Christian Death and Shadow Project, remains intrinsic to the soul of modern "alternative" music, it also stands among the most distant musical frontiers rock has yet aspired to. And though other talents may emerge to step into his shoes, few will ever travel so far, or make the journey with such wide-eyed curiosity.

Satanism (or at least, anti-Christianity), of course, is nothing new in rock'n'roll, and nothing new to its detractors, either. Rozz Williams and the Electric Hellfire Club, however, eschewed all the stereotypes, indoctrinating American youth with a whole new perspective on an increasingly mundane stance. "Nobody comes out and says they're devil worshipers now, unless they really think they are," insisted religious journalist Julian St. Paul. "It just isn't a bluff you can pull off any longer, because what is the point? Nobody goes around pretending to be a Christian rock band!"

"Besides," he said. "The stakes are a lot higher than they used to be"—a fact of life which became painfully evident to German demonologist Gunther Dietz.

Dietz, a German heavy-metal vocalist, had a reputation for arrogance long before he sacked his lead guitarist, Kugel, just moments before he took the stage in August 1997. Already two hours late for the concert, Dietz's barely apologetic appearance left a restless crowd feeling angry and vengeful. Few onlookers, however, were prepared for what happened as the climax to the show approached.

Traditionally Dietz ended gigs by swan-diving into the audience, to be borne aloft by his salivating fans. Tonight, however, when he screamed, "Catch me," and jumped, the audience rebelled.

"Gunther punched his fist in the air and jumped," one onlooker told German journalists. "But we didn't even try to catch him. Oh no." As one, the audience stepped out of the way, and when Dietz slammed headfirst into the concrete floor, "we roared with laughter.

"He remained conscious for about a minute, and kept crying out for his mummy. Somebody pissed over him, which I thought was a bit rude. But if you ask me, he got what he deserved."

Dietz's unfortunate end received little coverage outside of Germany. Elsewhere, however, 1997 would see the tangled skein of the European metal scene make headlines all around the world with the arrest, and subsequent imprisonment, of one of Norway's best-known musicians, the outspoken Count Grishnackh. The charge was murder, and the victim was a fellow metal superstar, Oystein "Euronymous" Aarseth.

Euronymous was just fifteen when he founded Mayhem in 1983, as an immediate successor to Venom, the prolific British thrash-metal band whose Satanic stance had come to spawn its very own subgenre, Black Metal.

Across Europe, and particularly in Scandinavia, Venom's poison found a ready and willing audience, fascinated by the dark imagery, and living to its fullest extent a lifestyle which until then had been the stuff of Fundamentalist Christian nightmares alone. When Cernunnos, drummer with the Belgian Black Metal act Enthroned, hanged himself in 1997, his suicide note was unflinching in its reasoning. He died, he said, because "this Christian world" was not made for him. He wanted to return to the Kingdom Below with his own Lord. It was, wrote Julian St. Paul, "as though rock'n'roll itself was tired of having all societies' ills lain at its door, and finally conjured up a halfbreed which really was as evil as the Bible botherers said it was."

Mayhem's domestic popularity was immediate, and incredibly far-reaching. Under Euronymous's baleful glare, Mayhem secured its own record store, Helvete, several Black Metal magazines, and the Deathlike Silence record label—the first ever to devote itself exclusively to "bands that represent total evil"—a stance summed up in a press release accompanying Darkthrone's *Transilvanian Hunger* album. "We would like to state that [this album] stands beyond any criticism. If any man should attempt to criticize this LP, he should be thoroughly patronized for his obviously Jewish behavior."

Behind the scenes, too, Euronymous was all-powerful, assuming leadership of the Black Circle, a secretive, even Mafialike, coalition of Norway's leading Black

Metal groups: Mayhem and Darkthrone, Emperor, Enslaved, and Burzum, a band formed by one of Euronymous's closest friends (and an occasional Mayhem member), Varg Christian Vikernes, or Count Grishnackh. It was he who joined Euronymous in an even more secretive union, the Satanic Terrorists.

The pair lived up to the organization's name with a passion. Their involvement was cited in some thirty church burnings, including one in which a fireman was killed. They were linked to a chain of desecrations (graveyards, of course, were a favorite target), while rumor also credited them with instigating a literal reign of violent terror, a rampage which ranged from assault and vandalism to rape and murder. Long before it was proven, Emperor drummer Faust was widely suspected of having stabbed a young gay man to death in Lillehammer; the same band's guitarist, Samoth, and bassist, Tcort, would subsequently be charged with arson and attempted murder respectively.

No charges could ever be brought to bear against Euronymous and Grishnackh, however, for the simple reason that there were never any witnesses to their direct participation. The pair was far too powerful to cross, and among their disciples, far too convincing in their own self-belief.

"Human beings are worthless and stupid," Grishnackh told Britain's *Kerrang!* magazine. "They're supposed to follow a God or a leader. I support Stalin, Hitler, and Ceauşescu, and I will become the dictator of Scandinavia."

He was supremely confident. But he was also growing increasingly reckless, the total opposite of Euronymous's more devious style.

It was Grishnackh, it was said, who first publicized the truth behind the curious bonelike amulet Euronymous started wearing in 1991, shortly after the April suicide of Mayhem vocalist Pelle Dead.

The singer had blasted his own brains out with a shotgun, and it was Euronymous who discovered his body. Wasting not a second in any outward display of grief, Euronymous first photographed the corpse for a proposed future album cover, and then, morbidly parodying medieval Catholic relic hunters, he gathered up fragments of his fallen fellow's shattered skull, and had them fashioned into jewelry.

It was Grishnackh, too, who recruited many of the foot soldiers who did the Satanic Terrorists' dirtier work—teenagers, mostly—and Euronymous constantly cautioned him to be more selective. As public outrage over the Terrorists' activities grew, the police drew closer to the source, aided by the ever-more-boastful kids on its fringe. In July 1992, they got the break they needed.

That month, an eighteen-year-old girl named Maria set fire to the home of Christotter Jonsson, vocalist for the Swedish death metal act Therion. Jonsson and his family escaped unharmed. Investigators, however, swiftly discovered Maria's other calling card, a note impaled on the front door with a knife, reading, *"The Count was here, and he will come back."*

Maria was arrested, and with her, a diary loaded with references to Grishnackh. Around the same time, presumably unaware just how far advanced the police investigation was, Grishnackh himself wrote a taunting note to Jonsson.

Again he was able to escape being charged with any crime, but as Grishnackh turned the media's curiosity into a personal publicity forum, Euronymous's patience finally was exhausted. Insults were hurled, accusations were thrown. In one outburst, Grishnackh claimed Euronymous was cheating him out of thousands of dollars in royalties and T-shirt sales; in another, he accused him of aligning with the communists.

Euronymous's bandmate Mortiis remembered Euronymous telling him, "'Grishnackh is a man it's best to have on one's side.' I saw no [enmity] between the two of them. But a few weeks later, he was saying that [Grishnackh] was getting out of control . . . starting to think himself invincible, losing his grip on reality. He said something was going to happen—soon. And the best thing was to stay as far away as possible."

Early in August 1993, Mortiis received another call from Euronymous. "He now suspected the Count was up to something, for example, killing him. He wanted . . . advice, whether he should go and get the Count first, or if he should get technical evidence against him for the burning of four churches." He decided on the latter, and a couple of days later, Euronymous called again, to discuss his plans. Two days after that, he was dead.

Late on the night of August 8, Grishnackh and a carload of supporters drove the seven hours from Bergen to Oslo, arriving at Euronymous's apartment building a little after five in the morning.

They had planned their trip well in advance; back in Bergen, another friend was preparing to spend the day shopping with Grishnackh's credit card, furnishing a cast-iron alibi of signed receipts and purchases. And while he did that, Grishnackh would put an end to Euronymous forever. He nursed just one regret. "The only negative thing about killing is, when you kill someone, they can no longer suffer." He would just have to prolong Euronymous's death pains for as long as he possibly could.

"you never know when you're giving your last performance"

Entering the guitarist's building alone, Grishnackh pounded on his door until Euronymous finally answered it, still clad in his underpants, and obviously half asleep. The door opened, and Grishnackh pounced, stabbing his victim a total of twenty-five times. Most of the wounds were nonfatal; almost all were in the face. Euronymous's body was discovered lying in a vast pool of blood, on the stairs between the first and second floors of his building.

Even as he denied responsibility for the killing, Grishnackh made no secret of his glee. Less than four hours later, in a call to Lee Barrett, owner of the British-based heavy-metal label Candlelight, Grishnackh gloated, "Euronymous is dead! And I'm going to piss on his grave!" Later on, talking to the Norwegian press, he floated the rumor that Euronymous was murdered by rival Black Metal musicians, probably Swedes. Then he announced a new Burzum album.

But Grishnackh had not covered his tracks as well as he thought he had. The credit-card trick, for example, backfired miserably—in his haste to hit the road, he had left his lackey with his telephone calling card instead. Meanwhile, the identity of the murderer was an open secret within the Black Metal community itself, one which was finally blown into the open when a friend of both men gave police an accurate (if unnamed) mental image of "the kind of person who would do such a thing."

Four days later, even as Mayhem's latest album, *De Mysteriis Doom Sathanas*, soared to the top of the national chart, Grishnackh was arrested and charged with Euronymous's murder.[2]

"I'm not sure why Grishnackh did it," Mortiis puzzled. "I am not even sure if he knows it himself. He says it was self-defense, which I doubt. Why would he come armed in the middle of the night anyway? And why would Euronymous attack somebody in his trousers, half naked?

"Running around looking stupid, that would *not* be his style."

"THE THING WITH SKINNY PUPPY was, it was very 'fuck off' music. 'You're not going to like this so fuck off.' And what we were talking about was, instead of going 'fuck off, fuck off, fuck off,' try a strategy of 'Oh, excuse me, would you mind coming here, here's a nice glass of wine—and then bang! A knee in the testicles.' The end result is people completely fucked up out of existence, rather than a bunch of people who've been told they're not welcome."

When Martin Atkins, the British-born, Chicago-based master-mind behind noise terrorists Pigface was first recruited to oversee *The Process*, the latest album by Skinny Puppy, the options seemed very clear-cut. But he also knew they would never be exercised, not under the circumstances into which the band was placed. "Skinny Puppy were not the Brady Bunch. They don't need to be a happy family in a house in Malibu, and to introduce that to a very tenu-ous situation was folly of the highest degree."

Ever since their emergence in 1984, and more so since the recruitment of keyboard player Dwayne Goettel in 1986,

Vancouver, B.C.'s Skinny Puppy had not simply pioneered the industrial music scene, they had invented it; and with every passing whim reinvented it, over and over, until nothing—not the electronic hardcore convolutions of Ministry, not the angst-filled student bardery of Nine Inch Nails, not even the bands from whom Skinny Puppy took their own initial impetus—could ever sit back on its laurels again.

Other groups, in other genres, enjoyed far more commercial success than the Canadian trio, but few ever made such an impact. Yet as Skinny Puppy convened in 1994, to begin work on their ninth album, the portents were bad from the beginning.

American, Puppy's latest (and first major) label, had indeed sequestered them in a residential studio in Malibu, and Puppy keyboard player and founder cEvin Key recalled, "The very first day we were there, we set up the studio. We got up the following morning, and five miles in one direction, ten miles in the other, was the biggest cloud of smoke you've ever seen."

Malibu was ablaze with some of the fiercest brush fires in living memory. "We were ordered to evacuate; we had to load the whole studio back up. Then we had an earthquake, and I can't begin to explain just how enormous that was. At the time Dwayne and I were working on the song 'The Process,' it was four-thirty in the morning, and I was just about to press play. I pressed it and, oh my God, I thought something was feeding back. The whole place was shaking, then it seemed to lift up off the ground, it was like a ship on a rocky ocean."

The sessions never got past that sensation. Neither did Goettel.

The first time Key saw Goettel play, he knew he wanted to work with him. Key was already well aware that Puppy was on the verge of creating something, but not until he saw Goettel, onstage in Edmonton with his own band, Water, did he begin to comprehend what that something was.

"I went out and watched them," Key remembered, "and I was really amazed by [Dwayne's] abilities. I talked to him for a minute after the show, and he rambled on something to me that was very technical, which just went right above my head, and I realized that he must be a pretty technical kind of guy. So, I figured that Puppy could utilize someone that was so technical and very efficient at what they did."

At Key's insistence, Goettel headed out to Puppy's home city, Vancouver, B.C., and within twenty-four hours, they had written their first song, "Antagonism." Whatever else was to happen during the turbulent years ahead, "Dwayne not only turned out to be my best friend, but he turned out to be the best keyboard player I ever knew. He was definitely the right guy, I'm never going to miss anyone more than Dwayne."

Goettel was especially excited about the album, *The Process*. A new record company instilled the band with fresh purpose; new material was shaping up better than anything Puppy had recorded before. He had everything to look forward to—which made it all the harder for him to take when it all came crashing down. Key still looks back on the sessions and shrugs, "I've never seen anything turn into such a disaster."

Yet according to other observers, the disaster was already under way. It was just waiting for somebody to notice it. Puppy vocalist Nivek Ogre said, with regret, "We kept going, and things just got more and more intense. Dwayne started having problems with what he was doing, and some incidents started happening involving him"—little things, barely remembered flare-ups that only took on greater resonance in hindsight. But there was one event, Ogre reflected, which almost crippled Puppy on the spot.

Ogre and Dwayne sat up late one night, having "a bit of a talk about work ethics. Dwayne had incredible work ethics; I envied them. He was able to go in and work twelve hours on something, he was so diligent, he was incredible, the kind of person who could just focus in on something. I'm a different person, I have a short span of attention, so we would have arguments. He felt I wasn't putting as much into [the recording] as much as he was, and this particular night, that was our big argument."

Later that evening, Dwayne was repeating the conversation to his girlfriend. Ogre continued, "She said, 'Well why don't you go and tell him how you feel?' It was in a very sensitive moment, at a very sensitive time, when he was in a very detached area, not Dwayne at all. But I was in my room with my girlfriend, and all I heard was someone running down the hallway and then, a huge slam against my door. I opened it and there was blood all over the door, which had been knocked off its hinges—and Dwayne was not the heaviest guy. Then he ran on down the hallway.

"We chased him. No one's going to knock down my fucking door without telling me what's up. But he ran back into his room and we didn't see him for the next day. What he'd done, he'd taken barbed wire, he'd wrapped it around his arms, and then he threw himself against the door. He cut himself up really bad.

"It was a big warning sign when you look at it now, but for three days after that, we were all walking around unable to talk to each other, because when something that powerful happens, it's going to leave a huge impression. And Dwayne was so uncomfortable with himself, it was really painful to see. I was thinking, 'God, he's really going to have to deal with the pain of all this healing, and looking down every day at the scars' . . . all this shit.

"Dwayne wasn't very confrontational; I think that was the most confrontational he'd ever been in his life. It was him expressing this huge amount of emotion which had built up over however many years. . . . I think he had a lot of stuff going on inside of him that we'll never know."

"Dwayne's problems were evident," insisted Atkins. "His state of mind was evident. And all of us who were in that house share a responsibility for his death, I think. I have no time to say, 'Ooh, ah'—it's, What did you do to help at the time? Everybody's a Monday-morning, Friday-afternoon, whatever-the-fucking-phrase-is quarterback, but we were there and we all tried to help, but we shied away from making the larger intervention, and that was obviously a mistake."

The band's relationships lay in tatters, not only between the individual musicians, but with their management and record label, too. Nobody trusted anyone, and when the rent finally ran out on the Malibu house, and Goettel and Key announced they were returning to Vancouver to complete *The Process*, Ogre simply shrugged. He was staying in California. They could do what they liked, because that's what he was doing.

The final time Ogre saw Goettel, "we hugged and we made amends for everything, and the last thing I told him was, 'Whatever happens, it's not your fault. If this band breaks up it's not your fault.' Weeks later, American dropped Skinny Puppy from its roster; days after that, Ogre quit the band.

For a time, Goettel and Key continued working—on the Skinny Puppy album, and on their own latest side project, Download. Goettel, however, was gutted. Key later said the best news he heard all summer was when Goettel announced he wanted to get out of Vancouver for a while, and return to Edmonton to stay with his parents. Maybe things would calm down now; maybe they would work out all right.

And maybe they would have, if a friend hadn't mailed him some heroin from Vancouver. On August 23, 1995, Goettel was found dead in his room at his parents' house, the victim of a massive overdose.[1]

"cEvin and I had this one horrible argument after Dwayne died," Ogre revealed. "Rave called me the next day, I immediately called cEvin, and he turned it all against the label, saying that was the reason why Dwayne killed himself. But that's not Dwayne; Dwayne didn't give a rat's ass about the label. Dwayne made music and that's all he cared about, that's where his mind was at." Neither, Ogre was adamant, were Internet rumors of suicide based on any kind of reality. "It definitely was not, that's just not Dwayne.

"But looking back, everyone has their reason why all this happened, everyone has their view; and it's just sad to me, and I think this is what affected Dwayne the most, that after ten years, we couldn't work it out. Dwayne was looking for a home and we gave him a war zone."

Goettel's death, received very little mainstream media attention. But was that a reflection upon his musical status? Or a condemnation of the complacency of the anti-drug lobby?

A decade had passed since then first lady Nancy Reagan had launched her "Just Say No" campaign, aimed at deterring "young people" from getting involved in drugs; only marginally less time had elapsed since MTV had launched its Rock Against Drugs crusade, a series of public service announcements made by rock stars, aimed at striking the peer-pressure issue at its core. And the intervening years indeed saw a marked reduction in the number of teen drug offenses. Just two years into the campaigns, the National Institute on Drug Abuse was reporting that drug use among high-school seniors had declined in almost every category.

Though the battle had been won, however, the war was still to be fought. And just two months after Goettel's death, a second rock'n'roll casualty told the world how much farther the fight needed to go.

Shannon Hoon was the vocalist with Blind Melon, one of the clutch of young American bands that arose in the early 1990s, then scored a monstrous, and ultimately career-defining hit, 1992's "No Rain." Supported by an eye-catching video, tracing the tribulations of a little girl dressed as a bee, "No Rain" made the Top Ten, and Blind Melon's eponymous debut album turned triple platinum. Grammy and American Music Awards nominations followed, but Hoon himself was also attracting attention for other reasons.

He was arrested in Vancouver, B.C., for pissing on the audience, he was thrown out of the AMA ceremony for being drunk, and he spent the spring of 1994 drying out at the Betty Ford Clinic. In New Orleans, recording Blind Melon's second album, *Soup*, Hoon was nailed again, on a drunk-and-disorderly charge. When he was found to be carrying pot as well, he reacted by kicking in the windows of the squad car.

Soup was served up in September 1995, and Blind Melon immediately discovered the downside of having enjoyed such success so early in their career. There was no new "No Rain," there was no new bee girl. *Soup* was two years in the making, and spent just two months on the charts.

The man *Entertainment Weekly* had recently described as "rock's most annoying singer" was upbeat nevertheless. He'd spent much of the spring back in rehab, kicking cocaine and smack in time for the July 11 birth of his daughter, Nico. Now Hoon spoke convincingly of his future duties.

"Having a child can make you reevaluate how you need to be there. I need to start caring about myself if I'm going to be the proper father." Blind Melon confirmed their determination to keep him clean by hiring an on-the-road drug counselor to accompany Hoon throughout their fall tour.

Guitarist Roger Stevens revealed, "There [were] so many times . . . in the middle of the night, I'm grabbing Shannon by the ears and telling him, 'You're going to kill yourself, and you're going to ruin everyone's life around you.' There's a lot of people that you would just write off in that situation. But he was so amazing, and he made up for it in so many other ways, that you wanted to stay with him." By mid-October, Hoon was behaving so well that the drug counselor was finally sent home; he'd had nothing to do all tour long.

Early in the morning of October 20, following a show in Houston, Blind Melon returned to New Orleans for the first time since *Soup* was completed, and parked

Blind Melon from l.: Shannon Hoon, Christopher Thron, Roger Stevens, Brad Smith, Glen Graham
(Showtime Archives, Toronto)

outside the evening's venue, Tipitina's. Hoon got off the bus with everyone else, then returned on his own. Five hours later, the band's sound engineer, Lyle Eaves, tried to awaken him. He couldn't. Hoon was pronounced dead, from a cocaine over-dose, at 1:20 that afternoon.

Afterwards it was speculated that Hoon was not physically or emotionally ready to resume touring, a charge his friends were swift to dispel. Suggestions that he had never really given up drugs, too, were vanquished. "He wanted to go on tour, and he felt like he was ready," Roger Stevens said. "This was not a pressure situation. He had been generally healthy for a long time—he was in rehab that summer, and he was staying clean on the road." In fact, Stevens believed that Hoon was actually healthier than ever "when he was out playing and singing every night, and getting his emotions out onstage."

But the questions did not end there, and neither did the suggested answers. And the following month, the most intensive-ever industrywide campaign was launched, in a bid to break what was fast shaping up to be a burgening cycle of rock-'n'roll deaths. The difference was, it wasn't the impressionable kids, the so-called MTV generation, that was the target this time. It was the industry itself.

The Substance Abuse Initiative was launched specifically to wage war on drug abuse at all levels of the music business. The brainchild of Michael Melvoin and Michael Greene, past and present presidents of the National Academy of Recording Arts and Sciences (NARAS), and placed under the banner of the farther-reaching MusiCares organization, the SAI's maiden meeting was staged in December, and swiftly established its principles.

A 1-800 help line was set up. The organization's first social worker was employed, and the committee drafted the guidelines under which financial aid could be given to applicants. They were generous, far-reaching, and essentially unimpeachable. There was just one flaw. All supplicants needed to have enjoyed full-time employment in the music industry for a minimum of five years—which meant that a support system established to assist the likes of Will Shatter,[2] Hillel Slovak, Andrew Wood, Kurt Cobain, Stefanie Sargent, Kristen Pfaff, and Shannon Hoon, would not actually have been available to any of them. Not one had met that initial requirement.

Nevertheless it was a start, and it didn't arrive a moment too soon. In April 1996, the California grunge group Stone Temple Pilots announced that they were can-celing a planned American tour while vocalist Scott Weiland went into drug rehab. He would come out the other side. So would Depeche Mode's Dave Gahan, who was raced to the hospital on Memorial Weekend, after ingesting a massive overdose of cocaine and heroin.

But such triumphs were offset by yet another tragedy. The same week as Gahan's misadventure, on May 25, 1996, Brad Nowell, the twenty-eight-year-old vocalist with the up-and-coming L.A. ska-punk combo Sublime, was discovered dead from a heroin overdose in his San Francisco motel room.

Riding high on the chart with their "What I Got" radio smash, an acoustic beach jam extolling the virtues of getting high; awaiting the imminent release of their much-anticipated third album, *Sublime*; with Nowell himself newly married—Sublime not only put years of struggle behind them, they had apparently overcome Nowell's own nightmare as well.

"Brad had been struggling with heroin for about three years," Sublime manager Jon Phillips confessed; and bassist Eric Wilson continued, "if you tried [to talk to him about it], he'd get mad. He thought he was invincible. When someone would die, other artists, he'd just go, 'Okay, they're stupid, they shot too much, they didn't know what they were doing." Nowell, on the other hand, was completely in control. Or so he thought.

One evening in late May, Nowell announced that he was kicking the habit. Talking with Sublime's drummer, Floyd Gaugh, he declared, "My next hit will be

Sublime
(Courtesy of MCA)

my last." Later on, *Time* magazine would comment on that same proud promise, pointing out that "addicts always say that [and] it's usually a lie. Unfortunately . . . this time it proved true."

It was still early in the morning of May 25 when Nowell woke up and decided to take a walk with his dalmatian, Louie. He tried to convince Wilson to join him on the beach: "It's a beautiful day out there!" But the bassist ignored him, pretending to still be asleep. Nowell went out alone. A few hours later, Gaugh wandered into Nowell's room and found the singer dead. He had taken that last hit—and overdosed.

The *Fort Worth Star-Telegram* ruminated upon these latest incidents with Blind Melon's manager, Chris Jones, himself now taking a leading role in the NARAS campaign. His words proved appallingly prescient. "[These events] put an exclamation point on what we've been talking about. Unfortunately, we're going to lose more people."

Nobody, however, could ever have guessed just how close to the SAI home the next victim would be. Just a month later, Jonathan Melvoin, the son of SAI founder Michael Melvoin, and the newest member of Chicago supergroup Smashing Pumpkins (on keyboards), was found dead in his hotel room by bandmate, drummer Jimmy Chamberlain. He and Melvoin had shot up together the previous evening, and even before the autopsy results were published, there was no doubt what killed the keyboard player.

Jonathan Melvoin joined the Smashing Pumpkins in December 1995, just as the band's newly released fourth album, *Melon Collie and the Infinite Sadness*, went crashing into the American charts at number one. A video, "Bullet with Butterfly Wings," became a seemingly permanent fixture on MTV, at home and abroad. American, British, European, and Far Eastern tours, scheduled to keep the Pumpkins on the road for the next eighteen months, sold out in record time. The Pumpkins were on top of the world, and Melvoin possessed the credentials to keep them there.

A former pupil at Julliard, both Melvoin and his sisters, Susannah and Wendy, were members of (The Artist Formerly Known as) Prince's extended family through the mid-1980s. Wendy was singer and guitarist with Prince's band the Revolution (and later, the spin-off duo Wendy and Lisa). Jonathan and Susannah were members of the Prince-produced Family, and played on Prince's 1985 album, *Around the World in a Day*.

From the sublime to the ridiculous—departing the Paisley Park setup, Melvoin moved to L.A., and in 1991 became the drummer for comic punk rockers, the

Dickies. "That was his energy gig," sister Wendy told *Rolling Stone*. "That was him saying, 'I need to get out and play 164 beats per minute for about two and a half hours onstage.'"

Bad Religion's Bobby Schayer was Melvoin's personal roadie through much of this period. "The day I tried out for Bad Religion, he tried out for the Dickies the same day. What happened was, I said, 'Whatever band we get in, we'll roadie for each other,' so I ended up being his roadie!" According to Schayer, too, "The rest of the Dickies knew him as Mr. Perfect. He always ate well, never ate fried food, drank bottled water. He was very conscious about that, and he was a very serious musician."

Melvoin quit the Dickies, and L.A., in 1993. "One of the reasons," Bobby Schayer recalled, "was to get away from the drugs. He never did drugs, he was always a straight guy." Melvoin returned to Chicago briefly, to tour with the industrial balladeer Chris Connolly, and then moved with his wife Laura to North Conway, in his childhood home state of New Hampshire. It was Connolly who would introduce Melvoin to the Pumpkins.

Sequestered away in North Conway, Melvoin would earn an emergency medical technician's license. For Smashing Pumpkins, knowing that their own drummer, Jimmy Chamberlain, was fighting a serious drug problem, Melvoin's nonmusical qualifications doubtless sounded as impressive as his playing abilities. What they didn't know was that he, too, was not averse to using.

"Jonathan dabbled, as almost everybody else in our life did," reasoned sister Wendy. "[But] we've all been around people who do drugs. We've all been around people who have problems with it. We've all seen people go through programs. And my brother just didn't have, in our minds—in any sense—any of those classic symptoms."

In Bangkok, in February 1996, Jimmy Chamberlain overdosed outside a hotel while hanging with Melvoin. Three months later, in Madrid on May 3, both Chamberlain and Melvoin ODed. They were rushed to a hospital and revived with adrenaline—"real *Pulp Fiction* stuff," grimaced Pumpkins singer Billy Corgan. Only this wasn't a Tarantino film. Horrified to see how low Chamberlain was sinking, and loudly blaming Melvoin for his plight, the Pumpkins fired the newcomer. But they reinstated him for the rest of the tour, because he swore he would clean up, and Chamberlain followed suit.

"I spoke to [Jonathan] personally," Corgan said later, "and he assured me up and down that there would be none of that going on on this tour, that playing with us was a completely great opportunity and he would do absolutely nothing to fuck that up. And except for these forays off the deep end, there was no evidence that he was ill intentioned."

Wendy Melvoin summed up her own take on her brother's position. "Everything was going great for him. He was having a fabulous life. He just had a brand-new baby [Jakob Arthur was born on March 26]. He never had any problems with his friends or family." And talk of a burgeoning drug habit was news to her. "The only thing I can speculate is that somehow, some way, Jonathan developed this incredible jones with Jimmy on this tour. At the same time, we never heard of any of these episodes that had happened to Jonathan on the road. No one knew any of this."

If they had, something might have been done about it.

The tour was already shrouded in tragedy. In March, Chamberlain's father passed away; in Ireland, teenage fan Bernadette O'Brien died after being trampled at the Pumpkins' Dublin show. If the drug incidents were "hushed up," one could hardly blame the band for doing so. They never could have predicted the consequences of their silence.

On July 11, Smashing Pumpkins were in New York City. The first of three sold-out nights at Madison Square Garden was less than twenty-four hours away, and Chamberlain and Melvoin were relaxing in their room at the Regency Hotel on Park Avenue. They'd been drinking, they'd scored, they were content.

At eleven-thirty P.M., the pair shared a fix, a heroin strain nicknamed Redrum, then happily nodded out. When Chamberlain awoke, it was to discover Melvoin's lifeless form lying on the floor beside him. Frantically the drummer tried to revive his friend; when he failed, he telephoned his tour manager, Tim Lougee. He, too, was helpless. Finally the police were summoned. At four-fifteen A.M., Jonathan Melvoin was pronounced dead.

Over at the Four Seasons hotel, Corgan got the news about forty-five minutes later, when he was awakened by a call from Lougee. His message was blunt and to the point: "Jimmy's ODed. Jonathan's dead. Cops are here."

The other Pumpkins—Corgan, James Iha, and D'Arcy Wretzky—joined Chamberlain at the Nineteenth Precinct police station, but were soon released. Chamberlain wasn't so fortunate; he was held, charged with heroin possession, and handed a court date for August 13. The Madison Square shows were canceled on the spot; instead, the stunned Pumpkins headed home to Chicago.

The Pumpkins' immediate concern was for the future. "You just refuse to accept that somebody is really dead," Corgan told *Rolling Stone* later. "It's like they're on permanent vacation." All that needed to be done, then, was to break in a replace-

**Jonathan Melvoin of the
Smashing Pumpkins being
removed from the Regency
Hotel in New York**
(Henry McGee/Globe Photos)

ment keyboard player, and away they could go. The Madison Square shows were blown, but others still remained on the schedule.

"The initial wave of thought was, 'Okay, Jimmy's got a court date, Jimmy's going into rehab," Corgan continued. "Four weeks and we'll be back on tour. You just want everything to go back to the way it was. It wasn't until forty-eight hours later, that the bomb hit. The real weight of it was Jonathan's life, Jimmy's life. It was completely devastating."

On July 15, Chamberlain checked himself into drug rehab. Two days later, the three remaining Pumpkins announced his dismissal from the band. Melvoin's death, Corgan said as he looked back over Chamberlain's own drug-strewn path, wasn't the so-called "final straw. It was the final brick."

But the tragedy continued to haunt them. More than a year later, in October 1997, reports began circulating that the Pumpkins would be paying $10,001 to Melvoin's widow. Immediately afterward, it was revealed that Laura Melvoin had filed a lawsuit against Smashing Pumpkins on behalf of her son, Jakob, claiming that the other band members contributed to Melvoin's death by failing to make sure he stayed off drugs. Her complaint included the allegation that the band should have known that her husband was shooting up and, as a result, were "in whole or in part responsible" for the death.

The next day, the Pumpkins themselves refuted the settlement story, claiming that they had already made a "substantially larger contribution" to Melvoin's family and that "the particular figures are a private and confidential matter between the band and the Melvoins and no other information will be provided."

Perhaps the saddest memorial of all, however, was spawned by the statement issued by Melvoin's sisters, a week after his death. Melvoin himself "was not a drug abuser," and his death remained "a tragedy and a travesty, a freak accident. We are consoled in our grief only by the hope that the circumstances surrounding Jonathan's death will inspire at least one person to reconsider before challenging the vagaries of fate."

But according to New York City police, far from scaring people off, Melvoin's death simply encouraged more to try the drug that had killed him. Officials told the *New York Times* that street users theorize that if a famous rock musician chose to use a certain "brand" of heroin, it must have a quality "high."

It was just that sometimes, that quality was just a little bit too good.

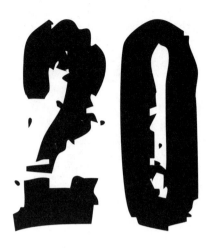

ON AUGUST 9, 1997, musicians and fans across the city of Hull, England, gathered together to remember one of their hometown's favorite sons, with a concert in the park and the dedication of a bandstand. It was a low-key affair, but still, performances by folkie Michael Chapman, local veterans the Rats, punk heroes Glen Matlock and Mick Jones, glam idol Steve Harley, and rockers Ian Hunter and Def Leppard's Joe Elliott, spoke volumes for the man they had come to honor, and for the sheer weight of talent he inspired.

Musically Mick Ronson was the direct descendent of the flash guitar gods of the 1960s; stylistically, the forebear of the bright young things who emerged in the early 1980s. Gene Loves Jezebel's James Stevenson spoke for an entire generation of British guitarists when he admitted, "Without Mick Ronson, I wouldn't be playing today. Or at least, I wouldn't be playing like I do."

Ronson's own idol was Jeff Beck, but the one time the two shared a stage, at David Bowie's 1973 "farewell" concert, Ronson claimed he didn't have the chance to be overwhelmed. "I was too

Mick Ronson

(J.Stevens/Globe Photos)

busy looking at his flares. Even by our standards, those trousers were excessive."

"Our standards," of course, were those set by the Spiders from Mars, David Bowie's backing band from 1970 to 1973, when Ronson's guitar was the defining factor which lent both style and substance to Ziggy Stardust's funny little songs about spacemen.

"We weren't famous, but our clothes were," Bowie deadpanned in 1997, but both by dress and design, the Spiders followed immediately behind Marc Bolan in dragging rock'n'roll out of an increasingly introspective rut. Their blaze of satin and spandex which not only dignified early-seventies fashion, it catapulted it into the twenty-first century—assuming the twenty-first century is peopled by alligators, Starmen, and flamboyant bisexuals.

In 1986, Ronson recalled his introduction to this bizarre lifestyle. Working as a landscape gardener in his northern English hometown of Hull, and playing in a local band, the Rats, one of their past drummers, John Cambridge, tracked him down while he was marking the lines on a rugby pitch. "He told me David Bowie was looking for a guitarist, and asked if I wanted to come down. So I put away the line-marker, and went to London."

Ronson met Bowie on February 3, 1970, when the singer played London's Marquee Club. Forty-eight hours later, he was onstage beside him, recording a live broadcast for the BBC. "And after that, I kind of moved in permanently."

The spangled uniforms (but never uniformity) of Ziggy Stardust and the Spiders from Mars materialized slowly. Through the darkness of 1971, when nothing Bowie did seemed to work, it was only the singer's continued insistence that clothes might, eventually, maketh the man, that overcame Ronson's distaste for the whole thing.

"I was into something there that the band [wasn't]," Bowie later said, reflecting on his unwilling group's first, disastrous appearance in costume, and Ronson agreed. "When we were first talking about it, I had a few different ideas, but I think I was caught at an off-time." His pregnant fiancée, Denise, accompanied him to London, but homesickness swiftly drove her home. Now she was nursing the couple's newly born son, Nicholas, and Ronson admitted, "I had a lot on my mind, then . . . . But once [the clothes] were made, it was fine."

With bassist Trevor Bolder and drummer Mick "Woody" Woodmansey completing the lineup, the Ronson-Bowie partnership would complete five albums together: 1970's *Man Who Sold the World* and 1973's *Pin Ups* bookending the eternal classics of *Hunky Dory, The Rise and Fall of Ziggy Stardust and the Spiders from Mars*, and *Aladdin Sane*.

"The success was very overnight," Ronson reflected, foreshadowing comments Kurt Cobain would echo precisely two decades later. "It was like waking up one morning and finding that we were suddenly superstars, with no preparation for it at all." Where Cobain, however, eventually would allow that lack of preparation to grind him into the dust, Bowie and the Spiders adapted immediately. "Suddenly we could have anything we wanted," Ronson marveled. "If you needed a car you could hire one. If you needed a guitar, go get one. I always remember the dinners. Coming from Yorkshire, we never went out for dinner. I remember saving up for a month or something, and going out to Bernies' Steak House for a steak, and that only happened once every three months. You didn't have a drink with it, just the steak. That, to me, was dinner. And when we first started going out to some of those places in London, with these huge giant shrimps and spare ribs, I couldn't believe it! It was fantastic!"

It was that ability to continually marvel at things others might have soon learned to take for granted, which remains one of Ronson's friends' favorite memories of him. Mick Rossi, a thirteen-year-old Manchester lad who Ronson befriended at the height of Bowie's fame, and who went on to his own success with the punk rockers Slaughter and the Dogs, insisted you would never have known "who" he was if you met him. But Ronson himself admitted, he could also be "pretty stubborn at times." Especially when it came to music.

Bowie told journalist Ben Fisher, "His two role models were Jeff Beck and Free [and he] would never look at anything that wasn't already in his sphere of reference. I just gave up trying to get him to come out and see other bands, or listen to interesting music. You'd mention anything new, and his pet phrase was, 'Don't need to.' If Mick had been a bit more open to [things], we may have lasted as a partnership a bit longer."

As it was, they parted company shortly after Bowie "retired" from live performance in July 1973. By the end of the year, Ronson was recording his own album, *Slaughter on Tenth Avenue*, and doing his best to live up to manager Tony DeFries' dream of launching him as British rock's next superstar.

"There were a lot of changes going on around that time," Ronson pondered. "David had all these little projects that I wasn't involved in, [which] weren't my cup of tea. So Tony DeFries said to me, 'Okay, we can make you a big star, get you a deal with RCA,' all that. So I said, 'wonderful,' and went off to make my own record. And really, David and I just drifted. It was never, 'I'm not going to work with you again,' it just happened quite naturally. We all sort of wandered away from each other, and I started work on my album."

Neither *Slaughter on Tenth Avenue,* nor the following year's *Play Don't Worry,* projected Ronson back into the stratosphere his break with Bowie had removed him from; nor, though it promised so much, did a union with Mott the Hoople, one of the many acts he and Bowie rescued from various stages of oblivion during their time together.

Mott were on the verge of breaking up when Bowie "discovered" them in 1972; he relaunched them with their own version of his anthem, "All the Young Dudes," and two years on, with Mott again teetering on the edge, Ronson came on board in a bid to bring back the good times. It didn't work. One final single, the effervescent "Saturday Gigs," tolled Mott's demise, before vocalist Ian Hunter, with Ronson at his side, set out to chart their own career together.

Hunter-Ronson would ultimately, if somewhat sporadically, survive for the remainder of Ronson's life.

So did the guitarist's habit of lending both his instrumental and production talents to almost anyone who asked for them. Jeanette Landray, vocalist with Kiss That, whose 1986 debut album Ronson produced, remembered, "We were playing at the Embassy Club and Mick was there. Lol [Hammond, guitarist] went up to say hello and asked if he'd be interested in producing us. Mick came down to see us rehearse, liked it and it went on from there."

Bobby Neuwirth, charged with putting together the musicians who would become Bob Dylan's superlative Rolling Thunder Revue in 1975, encountered the same easygoing attitude. One night at the Other End club in Greenwich Village, "Mick came in with Ian Hunter, so I said, 'Ronson, you play guitar a bit; come up and play with some American guys.'" Ronson agreed, and would spend the next year dressed down as far as he used to dress up, accompanying Dylan across the U.S. The irony was, as Ronson later grinned, "I didn't even like Dylan's stuff that much before I played with him. But Hunter was so jealous that it didn't really matter!"

Returning to New York in May 1976, and London one year later, Ronson continued reinforcing his reputation as a superstar sideman. The band Sparks, David Cassidy, and Roger McGuinn in America; Dead Fingers Talk, the Rich Kids, and Slaughter and the Dogs in England—all recorded with Ronson. In the 1980s, Ellen Foley, John Cougar Mellencamp, and a pre-Hollywood Daryl Hannah could be added to the list, with McGuinn speaking for them all when he said of his own *Cardiff Rose* album, "I think Mick got $5,000 for [producing] it. He mostly did it just for fun, a few extra bucks. Most producers get $50,000, $100,000 for that kind of job."

"Mick was just incredible to work with," exclaimed Sandy Dillon, the New York singer-songwriter who worked with Ronson during 1985-86. "We'd be in the studio with a song, and I'd be going, 'Mick! What do I do?' and he'd just say, 'You do your bit, I'll do mine.' He'd tell me just to sing the song, no instruments at all, then built it up around me."

Bowie confirmed Dillon's impressions. "He provided this strong, earthy, simply-focused idea of what a song was all about. And I would flutter around on the edges and decorate."

The news, in 1991, that he was suffering from inoperable liver cancer, did not slow the guitarist down. Ronson initially visited his doctor to complain of chronic back pain, but the diagnosis was not a complete surprise. He was never an intemperate drinker, as his wife, Suzi, acknowledged. "Mick did have a tiny problem with drinking. He drank a lot and gambled a lot—'I'm a rock star and this is what I do,' that kind of thing."

And he would keep on doing it, as far as he could. Producing Morrissey's 1992 album, *Your Arsenal*, at a residential studio near Bath, Ronson arranged to have the gamblers' newspaper, *The Sporting Life*, delivered every morning. "Then every morning at breakfast," guitarist Boz Boorer laughed, "we'd sit there and work out our little bets, then me and Mick would get into his mum's car, which he was using, and go down to the bookies." But it was a far cry from the Rolling Thunder Revue, where Ronson lost so heavily at cards that he actually owed Dylan money when they came off tour. Boorer estimates their combined bets amounted to "no more than two pounds a day."

When Morrissey first announced his determination to work with Ronson, many people were shocked. For all his experience, the guitarist was not exactly a "big name" studio maven; nor had his past productions exactly set the charts afire. But Morrissey was adamant. According to Boorer, "We were talking about producers and Mick's name came up, so Morrissey got in touch. He went to see him in the hospital the first time, came back and said he was a bit ill, and didn't think he'd be able to do it. And then the next thing, he was doing it. We were rehearsing in this pokey little place in Child's Hill, and Morrissey just walked in one night with Mick. We went up to the pub afterwards, talked about a few things, then got started."

Neither would Ronson's illness impact on the sessions. "I think he was on pretty strong medicine, and if he drank any alcohol he used to go bright red in the evenings," Boorer reflected. "But the only time he seemed really ill was after he played with Bowie and Hunter at the Freddie Mercury tribute concert. I drove back to the studio with him, and he'd been drinking champagne all afternoon, which I don't think he'd done for a long time. And the next day, he was very ill."

There was one event, however, which did pinpoint the immense strain the normally mild-mannered Ronson was under. Boorer recalled, "Because he had cancer, Mick had to be very careful what he ate, and pure fruit juices that were freshly made were very good for him. So he bought this juicemaker that would crush anything and chuck all the peel out the side, and in the top there was this plunger thing that crushed the fruit, and without that, it was useless.

"Someone used it one morning, then Mick came down looking for it, and he couldn't find the top, the plunger thing. His face went bright red, he was trying to work out what happened to it: 'When you use things you should clean them and put them back.' And he just went completely loony about it. Completely mad, and that really was the only time we ever saw him get mad over anything. Anything at all."

Even as the Morrissey sessions rolled on, Ronson started planning his next move. He began work on the long-awaited follow-up to *Play Don't Worry*, recruiting a circle of friends and admirers to help out in the studio: Chrissie Hynde, Ian Hunter, John Mellencamp, and Def Leppard's Joe Elliott included. And he reunited with Bowie.

One day, a box of tapes arrived at the studio from Bowie, for Ronson to play through. Dylan's "Like a Rolling Stone," the Psychedelic Furs' "Pretty in Pink," and a new song called "Lucille" (complete with Little Richard sample!) were all included, together with a version of the old Cream hit, "I Feel Free." The pair would eventually agree on just two of the four, but still Bowie admitted, "I'm thankful we spent some considerable time together." But he added that the sessions were difficult. "He was ebbing by that time; his power was depleted, and it was a tough session in that way, because he was very tired. It was really very poignant."

On April 20, 1992, Ronson made that last-ever public performance, at the Freddie Mercury tribute concert, joining Bowie, Hunter, Elliott, and Queen's Roger Taylor and Brian May for a roaring and moving performance of "All the Young Dudes." In 1972, when Mott took that song near to the top of the charts, it was a challenge, a call to arms, the clarion call for the emergent glam-rock revolution, pitying the old back at home with their Beatles and their Stones, championing the young as they moved to center stage.

Twenty years on, it retained that old audacity, which is how the song itself has survived through so many generations of subsequent covers. But the young dudes themselves were now in their forties, and an anthem became a requiem, too. When Ronson's third solo album, *Heaven and Hull*, was finally released, sadly but posthumously, there could not have been a more fitting, or more affecting, conclusion than a reprise of that same performance.

His overindulgence on the champagne notwithstanding, Ronson looked well that afternoon. But even his close friends were convinced it was only a matter of time before the end. In one three-month period that summer, the cancer would double in size; he was in constant pain, and constantly medicated. "His nostrils always flare when he's pissed off," Ian Hunter once observed, but now, Ronson seemed too tired even for that. One night in early October, while Ronson sat sleeping in an armchair, Hunter looked across, and "I saw death in Mick's face."

Then suddenly, little more than a month later, it all turned around. Writing in the private diary he would later turn over to *Q* magazine, Hunter observed, "It's stopped, or even diminished slightly." It seemed, he said, "like a miracle is taking place," through a combination of the love of his family, the skill of his faith healers, and the constant barrage of goodwill from the "literally hundreds of others whose spirits rise and fall weekly with 'Ronson's dilemma.' He's tickled pink."

A week later, the cancer was back. And five months after that, on April 29, 1993, it killed him.

Remembering the man who had fired so many dreams two decades before, Bowie's ex-wife Angie smiled, "I always think of Mick with such pleasure. Those soaring solos, and that wonderful, manic guitar. He was brilliant, and David learned so much from him. He learned a lot from David as well, of course, which is what made their work together so special."

But it was Joe Elliott, who had worked so hard to bring Ronson's final album to fruition, who delivered the most telling statement, one which applied not only to Ronson, but to all of rock'n'roll's tragic casualties.

Just two years before Ronson's death, on January 8, 1991, Elliott had buried another friend, Def Leppard's own Steve Clark. Like Ronson, he was a stunning guitarist; like Ronson, alcohol played a significant part in his downfall. But Elliott wasn't preaching—he was simply wondering why.

"If there's a God up there," he asked, "why does he do this?" And then he answered his own question. "It can only be because he's trying to put together the ultimate band."

gallery of death credits

Jim Morrison grave site (Kevin Cummins / London Features)
Tupac Shakur (Globe Photos)
Janis Joplin (© SMP / Globe Photos)
Elvis Presley (MPTV Archive)
Stevie Ray Vaughan (Showtime Archives, Toronto)
Bob Marley (Archive Photos)
Jim Morrison mug shot (Shooting Star)
Jimi Hendrix (Showtime Archives, Toronto)
Otis Redding (Showtime Archives, Toronto)
Jerry Garcia (Archive Photos)
John Lennon (Showtime Archives, Toronto)

gallery of death

january

1   **Alexis Korner** (Blues Incorporated): 1984
      Presley Wayne (C&W young performer of 1996): 1998

2   **Larry Williams:** 1980
      Randy California (Spirit): 1997

3   **Henk Dorl** (singer "Go to it Holland Go to it"): 1993

4   **Cyril Davies** (All Stars): 1964
      Mal Evans (Beatles roadie): 1976
      Phil Lynott (Thin Lizzy):1986

5   **Charles Mingus** (jazz bassist): 1979
      Sonny Bono (Sonny & Cher): 1998

6   **Dizzy Gillespie:** 1993

7   **Kenny Pickett** (Creation): 1997

8   **Steve Clark** (Def Leppard): 1991

9   **Bill Hill** (Inkspots): 1981

10   **Howlin' Wolf:** 1976

11   **John Godrick** (bluesman): 1991

12 Jackie Wilson: 1984

13 Donnie Hathaway: 1979

14 Dee Murray (Elton John Band): 1992

15 Harry Nilsson: 1994
Junior Wells (bluesman): 1998

16 Paul Beaver (Beaver and Krause): 1975

17 Billy Stewart (R&B singer): 1970
Tommy Tucker (Louisiana Red): 1982

18 Sean McDonnell (Surgery): 1996

19 Carl Perkins: 1998

20 Alan Freed (DJ): 1965

21 Colonel Tom Parker (Elvis manager): 1997

22 Shane Lassen (Electric Hellfire Club): 1996
Wally Whyton (The Vipers): 1997

23 Terry Kath (Chicago): 1978
Allen Collins (Lynyrd Skynyrd): 1990
Richard Berry (songwriter "Louie Louie"): 1997
Billy MacKenzie (Associates): 1997

24 James Sheppard (Shep & the Limelights): 1970

25 Albert Grossman (Dylan manager):1986

26 S. P. Leary (Muddy Waters)

27 Mahalia Jackson (gospel singer): 1972

28 Billy Fury: 1982

29 Willie Dixon (blues singer): 1992

30 Lightning Hopkins: 1982

31 Edwin H. Armstrong (inventor of FM radio): 1954

february

1 Dick James (music publisher): 1986
Vincent Crane (Atomic Rooster): 1989

2 Sid Vicious (Sex Pistols): 1979

3 Big Bopper: 1959
Buddy Holly: 1959
Ritchie Valens: 1959
(above three killed in aircrash)
Joe Meek: 1967

4 Alex Harvey (SAHB): 1982
Karen Carpenter (Carpenters): 1983
Paul Gardiner (Tubeway Army): 1984
Trevor Lucas (Fairport Convention): 1989

5 Tim Kelly (Slaughter): 1998
Nick Webb (Acoustic Alchemy):1998
Carl Wilson (Beach Boys): 1998

6 Jesse Belvin (writer of Earth Angel): 1960
Falco: 1998

7 David Savoy Jr. (manager of Husker Du): 1987

8 Max Yasgur (owner of Woodstock): 1973
Del Shannon: 1990

9 Bill Haley (The Comets): 1981
Brian Connolly (The Sweet): 1997

10 Dave Alexander (Stooges): 1975
Tony Secunda (manager, the Move, T. Rex): 1995

11 Billy Rogers (Crusaders): 1987

12 Ton Brandsteder (CEO Sony Netherland BV): 1992

13   Chiemi Eri (Delta Rhythm Boys): 1982

14   **Mike Bloomfield:** 1981

15   Little Walter (blues harpist): 1968

16   Brownie McGhee (blues guitarist): 1996

17   Zenon De Fleur (Count Bishops): 1979

18   Denny Cordell (producer): 1995

19   Bon Scott (AC/DC): 1980

20   Bob Stinson (Replacements): 1995

21   Jacob Miller (Inner Circle): 1980
      Murray the K (disc jockey): 1982

22   Florence Ballard (Supremes): 1976
      Andy Warhol: 1987

23   Melvin Franklin (Temptations): 1995
      Tony Williams (Lifetime): 1997

24   Johnnie Ray (singer): 1990

25   Troy Caldwell (Marshall Tucker Band): 1993

26   Cornell Gunther (Coasters): 1990

27   Ben Raleigh (songwriter): 1997

28   **Bobby Bloom:** 1974
      David Byron (Uriah Heep): 1985

29   Wes Farrell (songwriter): 1996

march

1   Odie Payne (Elmore James): 1989

2   Serge Gainsbourg (singer):1991

3   **Mamonas Assassinas:** 1996

4   Mike Patto (Patto/Boxer): 1979
      Richard Manual (The Band): 1986

5   **Patsy Cline:** 1963
      Cowboy Copas (Patsy Cline): 1963

Hawkshaw Hawkins (Patsy Cline): 1963

Randy Hughes (manager of Patsy Cline): 1963

(above four killed in aircrash)

Mike Jeffrey (manager): 1973

Vivian Stanshall (Bonzo Dog Band): 1995

6   **Delroy Wilson:** 1995

7   Jack Anglin (country singer): 1963

8   Ron "Pigpen" McKernan (Grateful Dead): 1973
      Bobby Chouinard (Billy Squier band): 1997
      Ingo Schwichtenberg (Helloween): 1997

9   Notorious B.I.G. (rapper): 1997

10   **Andy Gibb:** 1988

11   Stacy Guess (Squirrel Nut Zippers): 1998
      Claude Francois (French singer): 1977
      Richard Brooks (director Blackboard Jungle): 1992

12   Charlie "Bird" Parker (jazz saxophonist): 1955

13   Judge Dread (ska performer): 1998
      Bill Gazzarri: 1991

14   Linda Jones (soul singer): 1972

15   Budd [Lawrence] Freeman (jazz saxophonist): 1991

16   **Tammi Terrill:** 1970
      Joseph Lee Pope (the Tams): 1996

17   Ric Grech (Family/Blind Faith): 1990

that?!! be the day that i die: a calendar of rock'n'roll casualties

18 James McCartney (father of Paul McCartney): 1976

19 Harry Womack (co-writer "Its All Over Now"): 1974
Paul Kossoff (Free): 1976
Gary Thain (Uriah Heep): 1976
Tony Stratton Smith (Charisma records founder): 1987
Andrew Wood (Mother Love Bone): 1990

20 Randy Rhoads (Quiet Riot): 1982

21 Leo Fender (inventor Fender guitar): 1991

22 Dan Hartman: 1994

23 Zoot Simms: 1985

24 Harold Melvin (Bluenotes): 1997
Kenny Moore (Tina Turner/Labelle): 1997

25 Alonzo King (Motown songwriter): 1996

26 Harold McNair (Airforce): 1971
Easy E (rapper): 1995
Duster Bennett: 1976
Jon Jon Poulos (Buckinghams): 1980

27 Dwayne Wilson (Earl Bostic): 1978

28 Dorothy Fields (singer): 1974

29 Richard O'Brien (actor Rocky Horror Show): 1983

30 Kenneth W. Clinton Sr. (Ink Spots): 1997

31 O'Kelly Isley (Isley Bros): 1986
Selena: 1995
Jeffrey Lee Pierce (Gun Club): 1996

april

1 Marvin Gaye: 1984
Rozz Williams (Christian Death): 1998

2 Buddy Rich: 1987

3 Booba Barnes (jazzman): 1996
Rob Pilatus (Milli Vanilli): 1998

4 Danny Rapp (Danny & The Juniors): 1983

5 Kurt Cobain (Nirvana): 1994
Cozy Powell (Black Sabbath): 1998
Monica Danneman (Hendrix associate): 1996
Allen Ginsberg: 1997

6 Bob Hite (Canned Heat): 1981
Tammy Wynette: 1998

7 Phil Ochs: 1976
Lee Brilleaux (Dr. Feelgood): 1995
Wendy O. Williams (Plasmatics): 1998

8 Paul Clayton: 1966
Laura Nyro: 1997

9 Mae Boren Axton (writer "Heartbreak Hotel"): 1997

10 Chuck Willis: 1958
Stuart Sutcliffe (Beatles): 1962
Ronnie Quinton (Deep Purple roadie): 1975

11 Edward Freche (Neville Bros): 1995

12 Abbie Hoffman: 1989

13 Margo Henderson (blues vocalist): 1979

14 Pete Farndon (Pretenders): 1983

15 Cleo Brown: 1995

16 Charley West (producer): 1976

17 **Eddie Cochran:** 1960
Vinnie Taylor (Sha Na Na): 1974
Felix Pappalardi (Mountain): 1983
Carlton Barrett (Wailers): 1987
Linda McCartney (Wings): 1998
18 **Martin Hannett** (Joy Div producer): 1981
19 **Bernard Edwards** (Chic): 1996
Cernunnos (Enthroned): 1997
El Duce (Mentors): 1997
20 **Steve Marriott** (Small Faces): 1990
21 **Sandy Denny** (Fairport Convention): 1978
22 **Earl "Fatha" Hines** (jazz pianist): 1983
23 **Pete Ham** (Badfinger): 1975
Johnny Thunders (New York Dolls): 1991
Carl Albert (Vicious Rumours): 1995
24 **Otis Spann:** 1970
25 **Dexter Gordon** (jazz tenor saxophonist): 1990
Yutaka Ozaki (Japanese rock artist): 1992
26 **Count Basie:** 1984
27 **Phil King** (Blue Oyster Cult): 1972
28 **Tommy Caldwell** (Marshall Tucker Band): 1980
29 **J. B. Lenoir** (bluesman): 1967
30 **Richard Farina:** 1966
Frankie Lymon (Teenagers): 1968
Lester Bangs (rock critic): 1982
Muddy Waters: 1983
Mick Ronson (David Bowie): 1993

may

1 **Spike Jones** (jazzman): 1965
2 **Dolores Dickens** (Red Caps): 1972
3 **Les Harvey** (Stone The Crows): 1972
Helmut Koellen (Triumvirat): 1977
4 **Paul Butterfield** (Butterfield Blues Band): 1987
5 **Rev Gary Davis:** 1972
6 **Clarence Paul** (Motown producer): 1995
7 **Sonny Rodgers:** 1990
8 **Graham Bond:** 1974
9 **Eddie Jefferson:** 1979
10 **Kenneth Walker** (Platters): 1976
11 **Lester Flatt** (Flatt & Scruggs): 1979
Bob Marley: 1981
12 **Jimmy Fernandez** (God Machine): 1994
13 **Chett Baker:** 1988
Rhett Forrester (Riot): 1996
14 **Keith Relf** (Yardbirds): 1976
Matthew Fletcher (Heavenly): 1996
15 **Barbara Lee** (Chiffons): 1992
16 **James Honeyman-Scott** (Pretenders): 1982
17 **Johnny "Guitar" Watson:** 1996
18 **Ian Curtis** (Joy Division): 1980
Kevin Gilbert (songwriter) 1996
19 **Coleman Hawkins** (jazz musician): 1969
20 **Gilda Radner** (comedienne): 1989
21 **Blue Mitchell** (John Mayall): 1979
22 **T. J. Fowler** (producer): 1982
23 **Tim Taylor** (Brainiac): 1997

that'll be the day that i die: a calendar of rock'n'roll casualties

24 **Elmore James** (blues guitarist): 1963
Gene Clark (Byrds): 1991
25 **Eric Gale** (Stuff): 1994
Brad Nowell (Sublime): 1996
26 **William Powell** (O'Jays): 1977
27 **Willie Woods** (Jr Walker): 1997
28 **Dr. Ross** (bluesman): 1993
29 **John Cipollina** (Quicksilver): 1989
Ollie Hallsall (Patto): 1992
Derek Leckenby (Hermans Hermits): 1994
Jeff Buckley: 1997
30 **George Chase** (Creation): 1974
Damon deFeis (Creation): 1974
(above two died in club fire)
30 **Carl Radle** (Derek and the Dominos): 1980

june

1 **Martin Lamble** (Fairport Convention): 1969
Jeannie "the Taylor" Franklyn (fashion designer): 1969
(above two died in highway crash)
David Ruffin (Temptations): 1991
2 **Doc Cheatham** (jazz musician): 1997
3 **Richard Sohl** (Patti Smith Group): 1990
4 **Stiv Bators** (Dead Boys): 1990
Ronnie Lane (Small Faces): 1997
5 **Conway Twitty** (country singer): 1993
6 **Claudette Orbison** (wife of Roy): 1966

7 **Meade Lux Lewis** (boogie woogie pianist): 1964
8 **Yogi Horton** (Luther Vandross): 1987
9 **Arthur Alexander** (singer/songwriter): 1993
10 **Earl Grant** (pianist): 1970
11 **Lovelace Watkins:** 1995
12 **James F. "Jimmy" Dorsey** (orchestra leader): 1957
13 **Wendy Bagwell** (The Sunliters): 1996
Clyde McPhatter (Drifters): 1971
14 **Pete DeFreitas** (Echo & Bunnymen): 1989
Rory Gallagher: 1995
15 **Ella Fitzgerald:** 1996
16 **Kristen Pfaff** (Hole): 1994
John Christian Wolters (Dr. Hook): 1997
17 **Dewey Balfa** (bayou fiddler): 1992
18 **Evelyn Mitchell:** 1992
19 **Thurman Green** (Natalie Cole): 1997
Bobby Helms: 1997
20 **Ira Louvin** (Louvin Brothers): 1965
Lawrence Payton (4 Tops): 1997
21 **Reg Calvert** (Fortunes manager): 1966
Jim Ellison (Material Issue): 1996
22 **Peter Laughner** (Pere Ubu): 1977
Arthur Ross (Motown songwriter): 1996
23 **Elton Britt** (country singer): 1972
24 **Tony LeMans** (singer/songwriter): 1992

25 Boudleaux Bryant (song writer for Everly Bros): 1987
26 Mick Wayne (Pink Fairies): 1994
27 Hillel Slovak (Red Hot Chili Peppers): 1988
Stefanie Sargent (7 Year Bitch): 1992
28 Chuck Wagon (Dickies): 1981
G. G. Allin: 1993
29 Tim Buckley: 1975
Lowell George (Little Feat): 1979
30 Wong Ka Kui (Beyond)

july

1 Rushton Moreve (Steppenwolf): 1981
Philip "Snakefinger" Lithman (Residents): 1987
Brent Mydland (Grateful Dead): 1990
2 Clara Lewis Bow (Ella Fitzgerald): 1962
Tony DeVit (club DJ): 1998
3 Brian Jones (Rolling Stones): 1969
Jim Morrison (Doors): 1971
Phyllis Hyman: 1995
4 Don McPherson (Main Ingredient): 1971
5 Harry James (band leader): 1983
6 Louis Armstrong: 1971
7 Mia Zapata (Gits): 1993
8 Louise Dean (Shiva): 1995
9 Anthony Bee (New Edition manager): 1989
10 John Hammond: 1987

Gerome Ragal (author of *Hair*): 1991
11 Delmore Schwarz (poet): 1966
12 Minnie Ripperton: 1979
Chris Wood (Traffic): 1983
Sean Mayes (David Bowie): 1995
Jonathan Melvoin (Smashing Pumpkins): 1996
Howard Pickup (the Adverts): 1997
Jimmy Driftwood: 1998
13 Charlie Rich: 1995
14 Clarence White (Byrds): 1973
Malcolm Owen (Ruts): 1980
15 Rick Garberson (Bizarros): 1979
16 Harry Chapin: 1981
John Pazanno (Styx): 1996
17 John Coltrane (jazz saxophoniost): 1967
Don Rich (The Buckeroos): 1974
Chas Chandler (Animals): 1996
18 Bobby Fuller (Bobby Fuller 4): 1966
Nico: 1988
19 Lefty Frizzell: 1975
20 Jud Phillips (Sun Studios): 1992
21 Joe Turner: 1990
22 Charles Aitken (Motown choreographer): 1989
23 Keith Godchaux (Grateful Dead): 1980
Rob Collins (Charlatans): 1996
24 Bobby Ramirez (Edgar Winter's White Trash): 1972
25 Dr. Feelgood: 1985
26 Mary Wells: 1992
Dave "Chico" Ryan (Sha Na Na): 1998
27 Lightning Slim (bluesman): 1974
28 Marguerite Ganser Dorste (Shangri-Las): 1996

that'll be the day that i die: a calendar of rock'n'roll casualties

Jason Thirsk (Pennywise): 1996

29 Cass Elliot (Mamas and Papas): 1974

30 Don Myrick (Earth Wind & Fire): 1993

31 Jim Reeves: 1964
Miami Showband (three members killed in terrorist attack): 1976

august

1 Johnny Burnette: 1964

2 Brian Cole (Association): 1972

3 Fela Anikulapo-Kuti: 1997

4 Ralph Cooper (founder of Amateur Night at the Apollo): 1992

5 Pete Meadon (Who manager): 1978
George Scott III (8 Eyed Spy): 1980
Jeff Porcaro (Toto): 1992

6 Memphis Minnie: 1973

7 Esther Phillips: 1984
Ossie Clarke (60s fashion designer): 1996

8 Steve Perron (Chillen): 1973

9 Jerry Garcia (Grateful Dead): 1995

10 Freddie Slack (T-Bone Walker): 1965

11 Mel Taylor (Ventures): 1996

12 Bill Chase (Chase): 1974
Walter Clark (Chase): 1974

12 John Emma (Chase): 1974
Wally York (Chase): 1974
(above four killed in aircrash)
Luther Allison (bluesman): 1997

13 King Curtis: 1971

Biggie Tempo (Bhundu Boys): 1995

14 Roy Buchanan: 1988
Robert Calvert (Hawkwind): 1988

15 Norman Petty: 1984

16 Elvis Presley: 1977
Nusrat Fatel Ali Khan: 1997

17 Paul Williams (Temptations): 1973

18 Marshall Jones (Ike Turner Band): 1984

19 Dorsey Burnette: 1979

20 Steve Goodman: 1984

21 George Jackson (U.S. political prisoner): 1971

22 Huey Newton: 1989

23 Dwayne Goettel (Skinny Puppy): 1995
Eleanor Guest (G. Knight & The Pips): 1997

24 Tete Montoliu (jazz pianist): 1997

25 Stan Kenton (orchestra leader): 1979
Arnie Treffers (Long Tall Ernie): 1995

26 Ronnie White (Miracles): 1995

27 Brian Epstein (Beatles manager): 1967
Stevie Ray Vaughan: 1990

28 Bernie Baum (songwriter): 1993

29 Lee Marvin (actor): 1987

30 Thomas Allen (War): 1988
Sterling Morrison (Velvet Underground): 1995

31 Diana, Princess of Wales: 1997

september

1 Joseph Hutchinson (Emotions): 1985

2 **Bennie Payne** (Cab Calloway): 1986
3 **Al Wilson** (Canned Heat) 1970
4 **Billy Williams:** 1992
5 **Charley Charles** (Ian Dury and the Blockheads): 1990
6 **Nicky Hopkins** (session musician): 1994
7 **Keith Moon** (The Who): 1978
Derek Taylor (Beatles publicist): 1997
8 **Alex North** (songwriter): 1991
9 **Bill Munroe** (bluegrass guitarist): 1996
10 **Herman Sherman:** 1984
11 **Peter Tosh** (Wailers): 1987
Ray Barbieri (Warzone): 1997
12 **Stig Anderson** (Abba co-writer): 1997
13 **Tupac Shakur:** 1996
14 **Julie Bovasso** (actress *Saturday Night Fever*): 1991
15 **Willie Bobo** (jazz drummer): 1983
16 **Marc Bolan** (T. Rex): 1977
Doug Palompo (Flying Medallions): 1995
17 **Rob Tyner** (MC5): 1991
18 **Jimi Hendrix:** 1970
Jimmy Witherspoon (bluesman): 1997
19 **Gram Parsons** (Byrds): 1973
Rich Mullins (Christian rock singer): 1997
20 **Jim Croce**: 1973
Maury Muehleisen (Jim Croce Band): 1973
(above two killed in aircrash)

Steve Goodman: 1984
Nic Traina (Link 80): 1997
21 **John "Jaco" Pastorius** (Weather Report): 1987
22 **Tom Fogerty** (Creedence Clearwater Rev): 1990
23 **Robbie McIntosh** (Average White Band): 1974
24 **Gregory McCoy** (Mass Production): 1984
25 **John Bonham** (Led Zeppelin): 1980
26 **Tino Rossi** (French singer): 1983
27 **Cliff Burton** (Metallica): 1986
28 **Jimmy McCulloch** (Wings): 1979
Miles Davis (jazz trumpeter): 1991
29 **Clarence Hall** (Fats Domino): 1969
30 **James Dean:** 1955

october

1 **Harry Ray** (Moments): 1992
2 **Hazel Scott** (singer/pianist): 1981
3 **Woody Guthrie:** 1967
4 **Janis Joplin:** 1970
Danny Gatton (session musician): 1994
5 **Ted Daffan** ("Born To Lose" songwriter): 1996
6 **Solomon Grant** (Blind Boys): 1981
7 **Ed Blackwell** (jazz drummer): 1992
8 **Jonas Bruce** (Afro Celt Sound System): 1997
9 **Jacques Brel:** 1978
10 **Al Jackson** (Booker T & the MGs): 1976
11 **Tex Williams** (country singer): 1985

that?ll be the day that i die: a calendar of rock'n'roll casualties

that'll be the day that i die: a calendar of rock'n'roll casualties

12 Nancy Spungen (girlfriend of Sid Vicious): 1978
Mel Street (country singer): 1978
John Denver: 1997
Gene Vincent: 1971
13 Ricky Wilson (B-52's): 1985
14 Frankie Kennedy (Altan): 1994
15 Melvin Franklin (Planet Patrol): 1996
16 Art Blakey (Jazz Messengers): 1990
Tennessee Ernie Ford (singer): 1991
17 Criss Oliva (Savatage): 1993
Nick Acland (Lush): 1996
18 Lee Allen (Fats Domino): 1994
19 Alan Murphy (Level 42): 1989
Glenn Buxton (Alice Cooper): 1997
20 Steven Gaines (Lynyrd Skynyrd): 1977
Cassie Gaines (Lynyrd Skynyrd): 1977
Ronnie Van Zant (Lynyrd Skynyrd): 1977

(above three killed in aircrash)
Henry Vestine (Canned Heat): 1997
21 Jo Ann Kelly (British blues singer): 1990
Shannon Hoon (Blind Melon): 1995
22 Jimmy Miller (producer): 1994
23 David Box: 1964
Bill Daniels (David Box Band): 1964
Buddy Groves (David Box Band): 1964

(above three killed in aircrash)
Merle Watson (country star): 1985
24 Sahib Shihab (blues musician): 1989
25 Ronnie Smith (Crickets): 1962
Gary Holton (Heavy Metal Kids): 1985

26 Tommy Dorsey: 1956
Alma Cogan: 1966
27 Steve Peregrine Took (Tyrannosaurus Rex): 1980
28 Baby Huey (Babysitters): 1970
29 Michael Holliday: 1963
Duane Allman (Allman Brothers): 1971
Wells Kelly (Orleans): 1984
30 Bill Josey (discovered Johnny Winter): 1976
31 Lloyd Lambert (Guitar Slim): 1995

november

1 John Rostill (The Shadows): 1973
Jose Santana (musician father of Carlos): 1997
2 Freddie Simon (Louis Jordan): 1973
3 Eddie "Lockjaw" Davis (jazz saxophonist): 1986
4 Art Tatum (jazz pianist/composer): 1956
5 Miss Christine (G.T.O.'s): 1972
Bobby Nunn (Coasters): 1986
6 Bill Murcia (New York Dolls): 1972
7 Johnny Kidd (The Pirates): 1966
Tracey Pew (Birthday Party): 1986
8 Keith "Red" Mitchell (jazz bassist): 1992
Dick Montana (Beat Farmers): 1995
9 Troyce Key (blues musician): 1992
10 Berry Oakley (Allman Brothers): 1972
Tommy Tedesco (Partridge Family): 1997

11 **Ingvar Johansson** (Sonny Rollins): 1997

12 **Rainer Ptacek** (Robert Plant): 1997

13 **Ronnie Bond** (Troggs): 1992
Bill Doggett: 1996

14 **George Adams** (Changes One): 1992
Keith Hudson: 1984

15 **Harold Burnside** (Stax arranger): 1986

16 **Dino Valenti** (Quicksilver): 1995

17 **John Glascock** (Jethro Tull): 1979

18 **Danny Whitten** (Crazy Horse): 1972
Tom Evans (Badfinger): 1983

19 **Alan Hull** (Lindisfarne): 1995

20 **Earl Phillips** (Howlin' Wolf): 1990

21 **Matthew Ashman** (Bow Wow Wow): 1995
Peter Grant (manager): 1995

22 **Michael Hutchence** (INXS): 1997
Epic Soundtracks (Swell Maps): 1997

23 **Ray Acuff** (country singer): 1992
Tommy Boyce (Monkees): 1995
Freddie Mercury (Queen): 1991

24 **Eric Carr** (KISS): 1991

25 **Nick Drake:** 1974
Bill Graham (concert promotor): 1991
Steve Gilpin (Mi-Sex): 1992

26 **Scatman Crowthers:** 1986

27 **Lotte Lenya** (singer/actress): 1981

28 **Alexander Lightfoot:** 1971

29 **Ray Smith** (Heads Hands & Feet): 1979

30 **Tiny Tim:** 1996

december

1 **Ray Gillen** (Black Sabbath): 1993
Stephane Grappelli (jazz violinist): 1997
William Smith (Pointer Sisters): 1997

2 **Michael Clarke** (Byrds): 1993

3 **Michael Hedges** (guitarist): 1997

4 **Patsy Collis** (Deep Purple roadie): 1975
Tommy Bolin (Deep Purple): 1976
Frank Zappa (Mothers of Invention): 1993

5 **Douglas Hopkins** (Gin Blossoms): 1993

6 **Michael Dempsey** (Adverts manager): 1981
Roy Orbison: 1988

7 **Darby Crash** (The Germs): 1980

8 **John Lennon** (Beatles): 1980
Nicholas Dingley (Hanoi Rocks): 1984

9 **Will Shatter** (Flipper): 1987
Patti Donahue (Waitresses): 1996

10 **Ronnie Caldwell** (Bar-Kays): 1967
Carl Cunningham (Bar-Kays): 1967
Phalin Jones (Bar-Kays): 1967
Jimmy King (Bar-Kays): 1967
Otis Redding: 1967
(above five killed in aircrash)
Faron Young: 1996

11 **Sam Cooke:** 1964

12 **Ian Stewart** (Rolling Stones): 1985

13 **Pigmeat Markham** ("Here Comes The Judge" hitmaker): 1981 that'll be the day that i die: a calendar of rock'n'roll casualties

14 **Patti Santos** (It's A Beautiful Day): 1989

15 **Kurt Winter** (Guess Who): 1997

16 **Nicolette Larson:** 1997

17 **Irving Caesar** (songwriter): 1996

18 **Jimmy Nolan** (James Brown): 1983

19 **Curtis Peagler** (Ray Charles): 1992

20 **Bobby Darin:** 1973

21 **Paul Avron Jeffreys** (Cockney Rebel): 1988

22 **Dennes Boon** (Minutemen): 1985
Albert King: 1992

23 **Johnny Coles** (jazz trumpeter): 1997

24 **Johnny Ace:** 1954

25 **Johnny Heartsman** (blues musician): 1996

26 **Buddy Ace:** 1994

27 **Chris Bell** (Big Star): 1978

28 **Freddie King:** 1976
Dennis Wilson (Beach Boys): 1983

29 **Tim Hardin:** 1980

30 **Bert Berns** (songwriter): 1967

31 **Dave Iannicca** (Destructor): 1987
Rick Nelson: 1985
Floyd Cramer (pianist): 1997

notes

CHAPTER ONE

1. Ritchie Valens would be the first of three artists to be raised by
    L.A. based manager Bob Keene, and then slain by circumstance.
    On December 11, 1964, soul giant Sam Cooke, whose first hits
    were released through Keene's own label, was murdered by an
    L.A. motel owner; two years later, on July 18, 1966, the body of
    rocker Bobby Fuller was discovered lying in his new Corvette
    outside the 1776 Sycamore apartment where he lived with his
    mother, "stretched out under the steering wheel," Keene report-
    ed, "stiff as a board, soaked in gasoline." He had also been
    severely beaten, and the official verdict of suicide has never
    been accepted by Fuller's friends and associates.
2. Grammy award winning songwriter Ben Raleigh, co-author of
    "Tell Laura I Love Her," died on February 26, 1997. Preparing
    breakfast that morning, his robe caught on fire, engulfing the 83
    year old in flames. His wife, who lived in a nearby apartment,
    discovered his still burning body on the kitchen floor.
3. Neither would this run of bizarre coincidences end here. The

first song murdered Beatle John Lennon ever recorded was Holly's "That'll Be The Day"; the last song Ricky Nelson performed before he perished in a fire on board his chartered aircraft was "Rave On." And in 1990, on the 41st anniversary of Holly's death, Del Shannon played his last ever concert, fronting the Crickets. Five days later, suffering heavily from depression, popping Prozac in a doomed attempt to lighten his mood, he took a rifle and ended his own life. It can also be noted that the first week of February remains the optimum time for rock-'n'roll deaths.

4. On May 8, 1974, Graham Bond, who grew increasingly estranged from his musical career as his occult interests developed, purchased a ticket for the underground railway at Finsbury Park station, in north London, made his way down to the northbound Piccadilly Line platform, and threw himself in front of an oncoming train. It took two days for the authorities to identify his mangled body. The coroner returned a verdict of suicide while the balance of his mind was disturbed; friends later revealed that Bond performed an exorcism the day before his death.

CHAPTER TWO

1. A childhood attack of rheumatic fever left Billy Fury, the sexiest of all Britain's early rock'n'rollers, with a pandora's box of harmful complaints, from kidney stones to a serious heart problem, leading ultimately to his retirement in 1967. Few people expected him to live till 30 (even his latest record deal was scheduled to end that year). He hung on another decade, and in 1981 agreed to stage a comeback, commencing with a television show called *Unforgettable*. Filming was set for January 28, 1982, and all through that week, Fury threw himself into rehearsals. "I'm becoming a cabbage," he told his manager. "I might as well go out in a blaze of glory." He died, from heart failure, the morning that filming was scheduled to start.

2. In 1982, three years before the heart attack which ended his own life, Hawkwind vocalist Robert Calvert released *Hype*, an album and attendant novel detailing the most chilling conclusion yet to this particular notion: the creation and manipulation of a rock star, with the express intention of having him killed, so that his backers might then start milking the legend.

3. When "Shakin' All Over" went to #1 in 1960, Johnny Kidd became the first British rock'n'roller to reach number one without having first to change his style. By 1966, however, he was reduced to releasing revamped versions of that great-

est hit, and playing increasingly desultory one night stands, simply to keep in touch. Returning home from one such show, in Bury on October 7, the van carrying Kidd and the Pirates was struck by a skidding lorry, just outside Radcliffe. Bassist Nick Simper was injured; Kidd was killed.

4. Jim Morrison would die in Paris, France, on July 3, 1971. The extraordinary conditions under which he was buried included a closed casket, prompting lingering debate over whether or not he really died; friends and conspiracy theorists alike insist he was just as likely to have staged his death in the hope of starting a new life in anonymity.

5. Alice Cooper guitarist Glen Buxton died on October 19, 1997, from complications arising from pneumonia. Cooper himself remembered him a few days later. "I think I laughed more with him than anyone else. Wherever he is now, I'm sure that there's a guitar, a cigarette and a switchblade nearby."

6. Sha Na Na vocalist Vinnie Taylor would die from a drug overdose just four years after that sensational performance.

7. Bob Grace, Bowie's music publisher, remembered, "Micky was a very young, very pretty boy, a male prostitute who David knew. I was on the verge of taking him to Peter Gormley, with a view to Peter managing him, but nothing ever came of that. And I saw David around the time of *Let's Dance* [1983] and he told me Micky had been murdered rather horribly, hacked to death, by one of his clients. The police never found the killer."

CHAPTER THREE

1. Carl Perkins passed away on January 19, 1998.

CHAPTER FOUR

1. Alan "Rory Storm" Caldwell's Hurricanes were one of the handful of better established bands who turned down the August 1961, Hamburg engagement which the Beatles finally won, and at the time, they were the better band. A marked lack of ambition, however, coupled with Storm's refusal to learn new material, swiftly saw them fall behind. Hitless, they broke up in 1967, following the onstage collapse, and death, of bassist Ty Brian, from complications arising from a recent appendectomy. Storm went on to work as a DJ in Benidorm, Spain, but plagued by insomnia and a mysterious chest condition, he sank into virtual retirement. He died on September 28, 1972, after downing a massive overdose of sleeping pills.

2. Decca's Dick Rowe wasn't the first record company A&R man to turn away the Beatles, on New Year's Day, 1962; and he wouldn't be the last. Joe Meek enjoyed several meetings with Brian Epstein before finally rejecting the foursome; even EMI, the Beatles' eventual home, sent them packing. But Rowe would be the one who everyone remembered; the one who clocked the four young rockers from Liverpool, and told them they weren't for him. "Nobody cares about guitar groups any more." That would become his claim to fame; that would become his epitaph. Rowe died, from complications arising from diabetes, on June 6, 1986, shortly before he completed work on his autobiography. It was titled, *The Man Who Turned Down The Beatles*.

3. Paul McCartney never died, but throughout late 1969, most of America believed he had, and turned to the Beatles' own records for proof. Upward of 100 "clues" were found scattered throughout the band's music and album covers, all conclusively proving that McCartney perished in a car wreck in the early hours of November 9, 1996—coincidentally, around the same time that many Americans were mourning the supposed death, in a similar crash, of Mick Jagger! Not until *Life* magazine hunted McCartney down at his Scottish home was the rumor finally quashed, but it would be another 11 years before anybody realized they might have been burying the wrong Beatle. Amongst the pictorial evidence is a still from the *Magical Mystery Tour* movie, depicting John Lennon standing alongside a poster reading "M.D. & C is the way to go." The full name of Lennon's killer was Mark David Chapman.

4. "Jimmy went in a lion and came out a lamb," said Keith Richard of producer Jimmy Miller's five year (1968-73) stint as the Stones' producer of choice. Burned out on music, and battling drugs, he remained a shadowy figure through the next two decades, although work with Johnny Thunders, Primal Scream and the Dripping Lips proved he still possessed an ear for excellence. Aged 52, he died of kidney failure in 1994.

CHAPTER FIVE

1. On September 7, 1978, almost exactly one month after the Who's first manager, Pete Meadon, died from a barbituate OD at his parents' north London home (August 5), drummer Keith Moon was also found dead in bed, with 32 Heminevrin tablets in his stomach, a massive overdose of a drug ironically prescribed to treat heroin withdrawal symptoms.

2. After twelve years as the percussive powerhouse behind Led Zeppelin, John Bonham joined his bandmates at guitarist Jimmy Page's Windsor mansion, to begin rehearsals for the band's next American tour. As usual, he spent September 24, 1980, downing copious quantities of vodka; as usual, after such a marathon, he had to be helped up to bed at the end of it. He was found dead the following morning, having choked on his own vomit while he slept.

3. The "sixth" Rolling Stone, pianist Ian Stewart, passed away on December 12, 1985, in his Harley Street doctor's waiting room, after suffering from severe chest pains. The cause of death was a massive heart attack.

CHAPTER SIX

1. The circle continues: violinist Ric Grech, one of the musicians who helped Fairport out in the period following the crash by guesting on a BBC radio session with them, would also perish from the effects of a cerebral hemorrhage, suffering fatal liver and kidney failure on March 17, 1990.

2. Originally written for actress Marilyn Monroe, in which form Denny recorded it, "Candle In The Wind" has subsequently been rededicated to A.I.D.S. victim Ryan White (1990) and Diana, Princess of Wales (1997).

3. Chicago's Terry Kath died from a self-inflicted gunshot wound on January 23, 1978.

4. Drake was amongst the support acts at one of the biggest shows of the year, Fairport Convention's much-heralded return to the stage following Martin Lamble's death.

CHAPTER SEVEN

1. Following Jones' death in 1969, Nico wrote and recorded the song "Janitor Of Lunacy" in his memory. She described him as "my little brother," but complained "he took too many drugs. I had to stop him sometimes from destroying everything, including himself."

2. Sterling Morrison was diagnosed with non-Hodgkin's lymphoma in 1994, shortly after the Velvet Underground reunion tour. All three of his surviving bandmates were at his side during his last weeks, and Lou Reed recalled asking Morrison if he had a guitar he could play. Morrison nodded; he did. But he'd just watched seven layers of skin peel away from his body, and it was too painful to even try. Days later, on August 30, 1995, what Reed subsequently called "the warrior heart of the Velvet Underground" stopped beating.

3. Bunnymen drummer Pete deFreitas was killed in a motorcycle accident in Rugley, England, on June 14, 1989.

4. Alexander was replaced in the line-up by one of the Stooges' roadies, Zeke Zettner, recalled by Cheatham as "probably one of the sweetest guys I ever met in my life. He was, almost like a character in a novel, this innocent from east Detroit, working class neighborhood, big good-looking guy, liked everybody. Everyone loved him as well, they couldn't help it. Girls were crazy about him. Damn heroin did him in . . . and his brother Miles too." He quit the band in 1971 and joined the U.S. Army because he'd heard that heroin was cheaper in Vietnam. Zettner died, still a junkie, in 1975.

CHAPTER EIGHT

1. Shortly before vocalist Brian Connolly left the Sweet in 1979, he was warned that cirrhosis of the liver left him with just months left to live. In fact, he would continue performing well into the 1990s, overcoming not only a string of mid-1980s heart attacks (including 14 in one day), but also pneumonia, and a nervous disorder which in turn led to serious spinal problems. Interviewed on British T.V. in 1995, a pale reflection of the rock God he once had been, he simply shuddered. "I guess my metabolism just wasn't as hardy as I thought it was." He died from renal failure two years later.

2. In 1980, Currie and his girlfriend emigrated to Portugal, and it was there that Currie lost his life, killed when his car spun off the road just outside the village of Val Da Paira.

3. Just two months after he guested on Marc Bolan's last ever television broadcast, Bowie would make a similarly ill-starred appearance on Bing Crosby's 1977 Christmas special. Like Bolan, the old crooner passed away within days of filming a duet with Bowie.

4. Guitarist on Bowie's *Space Oddity/Man Of Words, Man Of Music* album in 1969, and subsequently a member of the Pink Fairies, Mick Wayne was working as a session musician, in 1994, when he was given the opportunity to record a solo album. He flew to the U.S. for the recording, and it was there that he died, when the friends' house where he was staying caught fire on the night of June 26, 1994.

CHAPTER NINE

1. The former manager of both the Animals and Jimi Hendrix, Mike Jeffrey was on

business in France when the light aircraft in which he was travelling exploded, on March 5, 1973. His body was never recovered, and the cause of the explosion remains uncertain.

2. Original Cockney Rebel bassist Paul Avron Jeffreys and his wife Rachel would be amongst the victims of the December 21, 1988, destruction of Pan Am Flight 103, over Lockerbie, Scotland.

3. *Breaking Glass* was the first movie to be made by Allied Stars, a new movie company operated by the Egyptian playboy Dodi Fayed. The would-be mogul would die in the same Paris car accident that killed Diana, Princess of Wales, on August 31, 1997.

4. On the night of February 20, 1980, Scott and a musician friend, Alistair Kinnear, attended a Classix Nouveaux gig at London's Music Machine. Downing double whiskeys all night, Scott fell asleep in the car on the way home, and as he had so many times before, Kinnear wrapped a blanket round him, then went indoors to bed. He awoke the following evening, to find Scott still slumped in the passenger seat. The doctors later told him that Scott had been dead for hours. Disproving initial reports that Scott was killed by alcohol poisoning, an autopsy eventually revealed that the singer shifted in his sleep, vomited and choked to death.

CHAPTER TEN

1. A former heavyweight wrestler turned rock entrepreneur, famed for his violent protectiveness, Grant retired from management following the death of Zeppelin drummer John Bonham, sinking into a rumored twilight of coke and smack. He re-emerged in the late 1980s, cleaned up and reminding one old associate of a genial uncle, "a pussycat." Grant died on November 21, 1995.

2. Harvey was the first of three high profile British musicians to be electrocuted and killed by their guitars over the next three years. Shadows guitarist John Rostill was found dead in his home studio on November 1, 1973; Yardbirds vocalist Keith Relf was killed in a smiliar fashion on May 14, 1976. In addition, Uriah Heep bassist Gary Thain received a near fatal shock onstage in Dallas in 1974. Thain would die from an overdose two years later.

3. The greatest songwriting team in early rock'n'roll history was finally sundered by death. Lou Reed's 1992 album *Magic And Lies* was dedicated in part to Pomus.

4. Brel would dedicate "JoJo," a cut on his final album, to Pasquier.

CHAPTER ELEVEN

1. Dempsey died on December 6, 1981. Overbalancing on a chair while changing a lightbulb in his west London home, his body was found at the foot of four flights of stairs.

2. Two further Dolls would die in the early 1990s; guitarist Johnny Thunders, once voted (by England's *NME*) second only to Keith Richard as "the rock star most likely to OD," defied both probability and expectations, when he succumbed to leukemia on April 23, 1991; drummer Jerry Nolan followed, eight months later, killed by a stroke while being treated for meningitis.

3. Journalist Bangs overdosed and died on April 30, 1982.

4. Stacey overdosed and died a year after Bators' death.

CHAPTER TWELVE

1. A career-long addict, Thin Lizzy frontman Lynott overdosed and fell into a coma on Christmas Day, 1985. Ten days later, on January 4, 1986, he died from liver, heart and kidney failure.

2. Vicious' mother, Ann Beverly, died at her Swadlincote, Derbyshire, home in 1997 from a drug overdose, The 63-year-old's death was ruled a suicide, after police discovered cut-up credit cards lying near her body.

CHAPTER THIRTEEN

1. Tubeway Army co-founder and bassist Paul Gardiner was found dead, from a heroin overdose, on a park bench on February 4, 1984, four years after his drug use provoked his break-up with Army leader Gary Numan.

2. Producer Hannett died of heart failure, exacerbated by years of drug use, on April 18, 1991.

CHAPTER FOURTEEN

1. On May 18, 1996, the same practice killed songwriter Kevin Gilbert, author of Sheryl Crow's "All I Wanna Do." Apparently, his naked corpse was discovered with sexual obscenities scrawled upon it in lipstick. Two years earlier, a member of Britain's ruling Conservative Party, politician Stephen Milligan, was discovered hanged in his apartment, partially clothed with an amyl-soaked mandarin orange in his mouth, and a plastic bag on his head.

2. Students of the arcane note that Geldof himself predicted his love rival's death,

some 15 years earlier, with the hanging death described in the Boomtown Rats hit "Diamond Smiles."

CHAPTER FIFTEEN

1. Following his time with KISS, Singer joined metal legends Black Sabbath in time for 1986's abortive *Eternal Idol* album sessions, with vocalist Ray Gillen. The tapes were scrapped when Gillen was sacked from the group; the singer, the forgotten man of Sabbath history, went on to form his own band, Badlands, but died of cancer on December 1, 1993.
2. The semi-fictional cock-rocking demi-Gods have, of course, lost an inordinate amount of drummers over the years, normally in hideously mysterious circumstances.
3. John had played another memorial just one month earlier. On March 15, he headlined two shows at the Grand Ole Opry, to benefit the family of former bandmate Dee Murray, killed by a stroke on January 14, following treatment for malignant melanoma.

CHAPTER SEVENTEEN

1. Home Alive can be reached by phone at (U.S.) 206-521-9176 or by post at 1202 East Pike Street, Seattle 98122 U.S.A.
2. On April 19, 1997, Eldon "El Duce" Hoke was killed after falling beneath a railroad train in Riverside, CA. Vocalist with the Mentors, a long running L.A. punk band, El Duce had found tabloid fame almost exactly a year before, when he told *The Globe* that Courtney Love offered him $50,000 to kill Kurt Cobain, in December, 1993. His statement set a new web of Cobain conspiracy theories rolling; his sudden, "mysterious," death gave them even greater impetus, all the more so following the 1998 release of Nick Broomfield's *Kurt And Courtney* "documentary," in which El Duce's claim would take center stage.
3. Diana died in a Paris car crash on August 31, 1997. At the time of the accident, her car was being pursued by a posse of paparazzi photographers.
4. Less than four months before Cobain's suicide note misappropriated another of Young's lyrics, five prison guards in Boise, ID, had been moved to other duties after piping Neil Young's "The Needle And The Damage Done" onto death row, following the execution, by lethal injection, of murderer Keith Wells.
5. According to authors Ian Halperin and Max Wallace, upwards of 60 teenagers

would commit suicide in the four years following Cobain's death, each unable to continue living in a world where their idol himself could not survive. If their data is accurate, the morbid fall-out to Cobain's demise easily exceeds the much-publicized rash of youth suicides which shook Japan following the deaths of singer Yutaka Ozaki, who collapsed and died of an edema of the lungs, on April 25, 1992, and guitarist Hideto "Hide" Matsumoto, who hanged himself, on May 5, 1998.

CHAPTER EIGHTEEN

1. With eerie synchronicity, Williams' suicide was followed, on April 3, by that of Milli Vanilli's Rob Pilatus; two days later, former Jeff Beck Group/Rainbow drummer Cozy Powell perished in a road accident; April 6 saw the death of country star Tammy Wynette; April 7 brought the shotgun suicide of Plasmatics founder Wendy O'Williams amongst whose last hits, ironically, had been a cover of Wynette's "Stand By Your Man"; and on April 17, Wings keyboardist Linda McCartney died of cancer.

2. Grishnackh would receive the maximum penalty allowed under Norwegian law, 21 years imprisonment, and confidently expects to be back in business by the time he is 40.

CHAPTER NINETEEN

1. Ironically, early reports on the tragedy insisted it was Ogre who was dead, adding his name to the lengthening litany of other artists whose demises have been prematurely mourned. In 1997, the *Tulsa World* newspaper was forced to run a story denying that Zac Hanson, of the teenaged Hanson singing group, had been killed in a European bus accident. "It was cool," the boy said afterwards. "It was like, wow! I'm dead! Yeah, right!"

2. Shatter, lead vocalist and bassist for Flipper, died of a heroin overdose on December 9, 1987, at the age of 31.

sources/further reading

INDIVIDUAL REFERENCES

DAVE ALEXANDER (STOOGES)
"Whatever Turns You On" by Cliff Jones and Paul Trynka
(*Mojo* 4/96)

BIG BOPPER (see Buddy Holly)

MARC BOLAN
20th Century Boy by Mark Paytress (Sidgwick & Jackson, 1992)
The Marc Bolan Story by George Tremlett (Futura, 1975)

DAVID BOX (see Buddy Holly)

JACQUES BREL
Jacques Brel: The Biography by Alan Clayson (Castle, 1996)
"Jacques Brel" by Amy Hanson (*Goldmine* 12/19/97)

ERIC CARR (KISS)
Black Diamond by Dale Sherman (CGP, 1997)

KURT COBAIN
Come as You Are by Michael Azerrad (Doubleday, 1994)

Never Fade Away: The Kurt Cobain Story by Dave Thompson (St. Martin's Press, 1994)

EDDIE COCHRAN

"Eyewitness" by Johnny Black (*O*, 6/94)

IAN CURTIS

"Torn Apart" by Dave Simpson (*Uncut*, 12/97)

Touching From A Distance by Deborah Curtis (Faber & Faber, 1995)

PELLE DEAD

"Bloody Hell! Norwegian Black Metal" by Phil Sutcliffe (*O*, 4/94)

Lords of Chaos by Michael Moynihan and Dirk Soderlind (Feral House, 1998)

SANDY DENNY

Meet On The Ledge by Patrick Humphries (Eel Pie, 1982)

"The Angel of Avalon" by Jim Irvin (Mojo, 6/98)

NICK DRAKE

Nick Drake: The Biography by Patrick Humphries (Bloomsbury, 1997)

EURONYMOUS (see Pelle Dead)

DWAYNE GOETTEL

"Skinny Puppy" by Jo-Ann Greene (*Goldmine*, 9/27/96)

ALEX HARVEY

"Alex Harvey" by Dave Thompson (*Goldmine*, 6/7/96)

BUDDY HOLLY

A Biography by Ellis Amburn (St Martin's Press, 1995)

The Day The Music Died by Larry Lehmer (Schirmer Books, 1997)

JOBRIATH

Children Of The Revolution by Dave Thompson (self-published 1988)

BRIAN JONES

Death Of A Rolling Stone by Mandy Aftel (Delilah, 1982)

Stone Alone by Bill Wyman (Viking, 1990)

Symphony For The Devil by Philip Norman (Simon & Schuster, 1984)

Who Killed Christopher Robin? by Terry Rawlings (Boxtree, 1994)

MARTIN LAMBLE (see Sandy Denny)

RONNIE LANE

Happy Boys Happy by Uli Twelker and Roland Schmitt (Sanctuary Publishing, 1997)

The Young Mods Forgotten Story by Paolo Hewitt (Acid Jazz, 1995)

PETER LAUGHNER

"Peter Laughner" by Lester Bangs (*New York Rocker*, 9-10/77)

TREVOR LUCAS (see Sandy Denny)

STEVE MARRIOTT (see Ronnie Lane)

JOE MEEK

The Legendary Joe Meek by John Repsch (Woodford House, 1989)

FREDDIE MERCURY

Queen: These Are The Best Days Of Our Lives by Stephen Rider (Castle, 1993)

The Show Must Go On by Rick Sky (Citadel, 1994)

NICO

Nico: The End by James Young (Overlook Press, 1993)

Nico: The Life And Lies Of An Icon by Nicholas Witts (Virgin, 1993)

TRACEY PEW

Bad Seed: The Biography Of Nick Cave by Ian Johnston (Little Brown & Co, 1995)

The Birthday Party & Other Epic Adventures by Robert Brokenmouth (Omnibus, 1996)

KRISTEN PFAFF

Courtney Love: Queen Of Noise by Melissa Rossi (Simon & Schuster, 1996)

HOWARD PICKUP

"TV Smith and the Adverts" by Dave Thompson (*Goldmine*, 9/12/77)

RAMASES

"Footnote Archives" by Dave Thompson (*Goldmine*, 2/14/97)

10cc by George Tremlett (Futura, 1976)

MICK RONSON

Alias David Bowie by Peter and Leni Gillman (Henry Holt, 1986)

"But Boy Could He Play Guitar" by Ben Fisher (*Mojo*, 10/97)

Moonage Daydream by Dave Thompson (Plexus Books, 1987)

HILLEL SLOVAK

Red Hot Chili Peppers by Dave Thompson (St. Martin's Press, 1993)

RONNIE SMITH (see Buddy Holly)

STUART SUTCLIFFE

Paul McCartney: Many Years From Now by Barry Miles (Henry Holt, 1997)

Shout by Philip Norman (Hamish Hamilton, 1981)

JOHNNY THEAKSTONE

Alvin Stardust by George Tremlett (Futura, 1976)

STEVE PEREGRINE TOOK

Space Daze by Dave Thompson (Cleopatra, 1994)

(see Marc Bolan)

RITCHIE VALENS

The First Latino Rocker by Beverly Mendheim (Bilingual Press, 1987)

(see Buddy Holly)

GENE VINCENT

"Hell's Angel" by Mick Farren (*Mojo*, 3/96)

The Day The World Turned Blue by Britt Hagarty (Talonbooks, 1983)

WALLY WHYTON

liner notes to CD box *The Vipers: 10,000 Years Ago* (Bear Family) by Paul
  Pelletier (1996)

ANDREW WOOD

"Pearl Jam" by Jo-Ann Greene (*Goldmine* 8/20/93)

MIA ZAPATA

"Death on a Dead End Street" by Alex Tizon (*Seattle Times*, 8/23/98)

GENERAL DEATH REFERENCES

No-One Waved Goodbye ed. by Robert Somma (Charisma, 1972)

Rock'n'Roll Heaven by Nikki Corvette (St Martin's Press, 1997)

Three Steps To Heaven by Roma Wheaton (Warner Books, 1993)

GENERAL REFERENCES

A Wop Bop A Loo Bop A Lop Bam Boom: The Golden Age Of Rock by Nik Cohn
  (Da Capo, 1997)

Beat Merchants by Alan Clayson (Blandford, 1995)

Black Leather Jacket by Mick Farren (Plexus, 1985)

Collectors Guide To Heavy Metal by Martin Popoff (CGP, 1997)

Days in The Life: Voices From The English Underground 1961-71 by Jonathon
  Green (Heinneman, 1988)

Electric Muse: The Story Of Folk Into Rock by Laing/Dallas/Denselow/Shelton
  (Methuen, 1975)

Encyclopedia Of Rock Stars by Rees/Crampton (DK, 1996)

From The Velvets To The Voidoids by Clinton Heylin (Penguin, 1993)

Halfway To Paradise by Spencer Leigh & John Firminger (Finbarr Int, 1996)

Make The Music Go Bang ed. by Don Snowden (St. Martin's Press, 1997)

Rock Family Trees by Pete Frame (Omnibus, 1993)

Rock'n'Pop Day By Day by Frank Laufenberg (Sterling, 1992)

Rock'n'Roll Babylon by Gary Herman (Plexus, 1994)

Rolling Stone Interviews vols 1/2 (Warner Books, 1972/73)

Starmakers And Svengalis by Johnny Rogan (Futura, 1988)

The Beatles And Some Other Guys by Pete Frame (Omnibus, 1997)

The Road To Rock: A ZigZag Book Of Interviews (Charisma, 1974)

This Ain't No Disco: The Story Of CBGB by Roman Cozak (Faber & Faber, 1988)

Trouser Press Guide To 90s Rock by Ira Robbins (Simon & Schuster, 1997)

Waiting For The Sun by Barney Hoskins (Viking, 1996)

index

index